ANGLING
IN
NORWAY

Edited by
ERLING WELLE-STRAND

Published by

 NORTRABOOKS

(Norwegian Tourist Board)
Oslo, Norway

Published by
NORTRABOOKS

Norwegian Tourist Board

The editor would like to express his gratitude
to Mr. P. H. Tombleson of the National
Anglers' Council for his kind reading of the
manusctript and helpful suggestions offered
to make the book more useful to foreign
readers.
The author is also indebted to the officers of
the Directorate for Hunting and Fishing
which have helped him greatly by their va-
luable co-operation. The consultants of the
Directorate in the various parts of Norway
have by their knowledge of local conditions
contributed to the reliability of the present
guide book.
This new edition is a thouroughly revised
edidition of the book that appeared in 1971.

Printed in Norway 1981
byEngers Boktrykkeri A/S, Otta
ISBN 82-90103-24-7

CONTENTS:

FINNMARK

TROMS

Tromsø

NARVIK

NORDLAND

NORD-TRØNDELAG

Trondheim

SØR-TRØNDELAG

MØRE & ROMSDAL

HEDMARK

SOGN & FJORDANE

OPPLAND

HORDALAND

BUSKERUD

Bergen

AKERSHUS
Oslo

TELEMARK

ØSTFOLD

VESTFOLD

Stavanger

ROGALAND

AUST AGDER

VEST AGDER

KRISTIANSAND

INTRODUCTION

ANGLING IN Norway falls into three parts: Salmon and Sea Trout Fishing — Trout and other freshwater Species — Sea Fishing.

The «Salmon and Sea Trout» part is an enlarged revision of the chapters compiled and written by Mr. Peter Prag for the 1962-edition of «Angling in Norway».In 1978 this part of the book was completely revised by Mr. Julius Ytterborg.

«Trout and other freshwaters Species», makes up two thirds of the present book. The basic material for this part of the book are reports on angling conditions by local experts. A main source of information have been SPORTSFISKERENS LEKSIKON (Angler's Dictoary), Gyldendal, Oslo 1968 and replies to a questionnaire sent out by «Norwegian Tourist Board», in the years 1965—70.

Norwegian Tourist Offices have supplied the information contained in the «Sea Fishing» section.

In all sections information is arranged by counties, wherefore a map showing the counties is found on the opposite page. There is also a large-scale reference map in a pocket at the back of the book. This is referred to constantly in the text. For instance: *Lågen river, Larvik, Oslo fjord (D 12—13)* means

that the Lågen river falls within the squares D 12 and D 13 on the reference map.

This book should also be used in conjunction with «Hotels in Norway». The latest edition of the list is available from the offices of the Norwegian Tourist Board abroad and tourist offices all over Norway. As fishing often takes place in little frequented areas, by no means all centres referred to in the text are found in the list. In that case «not listed» is added in brackets after the place name. With respect to mountain lodges run by mountain touring clubs, and accessible only on foot, only a few of these are listed in «Hotels in Norway». On the other hand they do not accept advance bookings, everybody who arrives is accommodated, therefore we have not referred to the hotel list in these cases.

Anglers will need detailed maps of the respective areas. Survey maps are referred to under each salmon river and angling area. If a map is referred to as 1734 II (Kvænangen) it is in 1 : 50 000. If only the name is given, for instance «Hallingskarvet», the scale is 1 : 100 000. These maps can be ordered from Edward Stanford Limited 12—14 Long Acre, London WC 2 or bought from a bookseller upon arrival in Norway. An index of Norwegian maps is sent by Edward Stanford Limited on request.

NATIONAL FISHING LICENCE

An act of March 6, 1964, relating to salmon fishing and fishing in inland watercourses lays down that any person wishing to fish for salmon, sea trout, migratory char or freshwater fish must purchase a national fishing licence. Children under the age of 16 yeas are exempt from payment. The national fishing

licence can be obtained by means of special post giro forms available at any post office. ,The licence is valid for a calendar year, and at present costs 30 kroner (1980).

Purchase of a national fishing is compulsory for any fishing, but does not of itself entitle the holder to fish in any particular area.

SALMON AND SEA TROUT FISHING

With its many unpolluted rivers and its long coastline facing the Atlantic Ocean, Norway provides a natural homing ground for the salmon in its annual migration, when it leaves the banks every spring to seek a spawning ground in fresh running water. Here it came to life, and here it will ensure that new life is brought forth.

But sulphurous rainfall has caused damage, especially in the South Coast waters, but compared with the pollution met with in other countries Norwegian rivers are clear and fine. Pollution is not the big threat. Fishing at sea constitutes a graver problem, resulting not only in less salmon reaching the spawning rivers, but also in a high percentage of fish damaged by nets. Another threat is presented by extensive hydro-electrical developments, which has reduced the wather level in many rivers and disturbed the ecological processes in other waters. Yet reports from the latest seasons have been optimistic. In most rivers fishing has improved and big salmon returned. Plenty of 40-punders have been bagged, and also in typical small-salmon rivers bigger fish has been caught. Bigger salmon was expected with the extension of the closed period for netting in the fjords, but there are reasons to believe that feeding conditions in the ocean have improved. The restrictions placed on drift netting at sea have also played a part and so has probably the increased output from Norwegian «salmon farms», which has decreased the profits of drifts netters.

The Land of the Hundred Salmon Rivers

Norway possesses more than a hundred big rivers which carry sizeable stocks of salmon during the summer season. In some of these waters the salmon makes his way a considerable distance up the river into the very heart of the country. The salmon rivers are to be found spread all along the extensive coast, with the main emphasis on Norway's most northerly county, Finnmark, where there are 26 excellent salmon rivers. The following list of salmon rivers, running from north to south, gives an idea of the facilities Norway can offer.

Anglers have fished for salmon in Norwegian rivers in the last 150 years. In the last century Norway became a favourite country among British sportsmen, and for generations they rented the best rivers for most of the season. In our days fishing is enjoyed by more people. Still there are many British anglers in Norway, but there are probably just as many from the Continent and quite a few from other Scandinavian countries.

The greatest change, however, is that most Norwegian rivers have been opened for less expensive sport, and to-day Norwegians form the great majority of salmon anglers. This process of democratization has also led to the extension of fishing cards to rivers that before were held under lease and expensive contracts. For some rivers this has been a good thing, for others the effect has been negative. Anyhow, salmon fishing is now enjoyed by many more Norwegians than a generation ago.

Nevertheless one must say salmon fishing is good in Norway. This is mainly due to the excellent cultivation that goes on in most good rivers, in spite of the fact that the greatest rewards of this work is reaped at sea.

Salmon fishing in Norway is in a period of trial concerning both forms of renting and partition of fishing in the rivers. The best rivers can still be expensive, but generally speaking the introduction of tickets has granted the opportunity for a large number to experience one of the greatest thrills of angling.

There are more than one hundred rivers in Norway with considerable stocks of salmon during the summer months. In some of these rivers salmon run far inland before it is stopped by a waterfall or a dam. An even greater number of rivers have a comparatively low water level, and they rise and fall quickly in periods of rain and drought. These spate rivers may be very good for short periods, but it is difficult to know when to secure fishing if booking in advance is necessary. This is where the more reliable rivers, with strict limits on fishing cards, enjoy an advantage.

The rivers

You will find the salmon rivers all along the coast from the Swedish border in Østfold to the Russian border in Finnmark. As mentioned above, the South Coast rivers are more or less to be disregarded. To-day therefore, without reservation, one can say that the best and most numerous rivers are found from the Fjord Country and northwards to the county of Finnmark. Finnmark is probably the best «salmon county», but Møre and Romsdal is also very promising with a great number of small rivers that have been well cared for. Here is a list «salmon counties», starting with Finnmark in the north.

In addition to the rivers in this list there is a great number of very small rivers, which hold a small quantity of salmon, or where salmon run in spate periods. In Northern Norway there is also a considerable number of rivers where red char run.

Finnmark	32	salmon rivers
Troms	15	»
Nordland	19	»
Nord and Sør- Trønde-		
lag	35	»
Møre and Romsdal ..	62	»
Sogn and Fjordane ..	25	»
Hordaland	21	»
Rogaland	14	»
Telemark, Buskerud,		
Vestfold, Akershus,		
Oslo and Østfold	11	»
Total	234	salmon rivers

When to fish

The season varies with local conditions. Officially it opens on June 1 with exceptions for some early rivers. The season ends on Sept. 1, but in a few rivers fishing is extended past this date. In the late rivers Sept. can be a good month with a fair run of salmon. We shall deal with these exceptions under the respective rivers.

Usually fishing is most reliable from approx. June 20 to the end of Aug., but there will always by variations caused by weather, temperatures, latitudes, types of rivers , sources, etc. Generally speaking one may say that after winters with heavy snowfall, and late springs, salmon tend to run later. Early melting and/or warmer weather correspondingly result in early runs. It is almost a truism that heavy fish arrive first. In some rivers fly fishing only is allowed after a certain date, and in other rivers only flies and worms, whereas prawns and spinners are forbidden, or allowed only in the early season.

Size

The largest salmon ever caught with rod and line in Norway tipped the scales at just over 81 lbs. The fish was taken in the Tana river nearly 50 years ago. However, salmon weighing 60 lbs, or more, have often been landed. On July 10 1981, for instance, a 66-pounder was killed in the Tana. In some of the best rivers, there are not many of them, salmon will average 22 lbs. A more common average is 15 lbs., but no rules without exceptions, in such rivers 45-pounders are caught almost every year. Upon the whole, every summer salmon weighing 45 to 55 lbs. are landed. This high average are among the factors that make Norwegain rivers so popular in sporting circles all over the world.

Prices

It is difficult to find a common denominator. As mentioned above, fishing cards have been introduced in many rivers, and with a few exceptions that means reasonably priced, or downright inexpensive, fishing. When it comes to leasing exclusive fishing, the story is a different one. In some of the rivers, where leases from time to time are available but otherwise are taken by private interests for long periods, daily fishing per rod may be well above kr. 1 000 per day. These are the prices one must be prepared to pay in the best season for many beats in the Lærdal and Bolstad (Vosso) rivers and other waters. The Alta river is still expensive, in spite of an advanced «democratization process», mostly because fishing involves paying for a boat and a boatman. But there are still a number of rivers where it is possible to rent good and exclusive fishing for kr. 400 — 600 per rod per day. Other rivers are closed to general leasing, such as the Årøy and Stryn rivers and the Malangsfoss pool in the Målselv river, to mentinon a few of the best known. It is still a common practice for big corporations, shipping firms, banks and insurance companies to take long-term leases in good rivers and only allow their business connections to fish here. As for fishing permits, both daily, weekly, monthly and seasonal tickets exist. In most cases these tickets are issued by angling clubs, or associations of river owners, and the river is usually divided into zones where only a limited number of rods is admitted. In popular rivers the day may be subdivided into periods, of which there may be 3 or 4, and tickets are sold to each period to admit more fishermen. Prices for day tickets may vary from kr. 25 to kr. 200 in accordance with the reputation of the river and the time of the season. In exceptional cases tickets may be more expensive. In rivers where cards have been inexpensive, and admittance unlimited, overfishing and a decline in total catch, have been registered. The tendency, therefore, is towards card fishing at reasonable prices and a limited sale of tickets in accordance with the estimated yield of the rivers.

Because of a constantly rising price level we always give approximate prices, and in some case we have used the term «reasonable» instead of an exact price. By reasonable we mean rivers that can be fished for kr. 75, or less, per day.

Under most rivers mentioned in this section of the book we refer to an address where particulars on leases, prices, etc. are available. In addition there are some hotels which have their own beats, or can arrange fishing for their guests in leased rivers. Hotels may also be able to arrange contacts between subleasers and leaser. In any case, it is important that you secure fishing and accommodation well in advance. Never travel on the off-chance that things can be arranged when you arrive on the spot.

Tackle
It is quite right when heavier tackle is advised for Norway's rivers than for rivers in other European countries. The current is often strong and the pools, where you may have to hold big fish, often small. It is annoying, to say the least, to loose a big'un because something snaps. In order to maneuver big salmon in turbulent water your rod must have some built-in strength. But, of course, even in Norway there are great differences. In small and «easy» salmon rivers it is good sport, and quite justifiable, to fish with a onehanded grip and with a lead of approx. 0.40 even if you, by chance, should hook a big fish. In that case you must rely on time and patience.
If the current is strong, and the pools small, one should not use less than 0.45 when fly-fishing and a 0.50 to 0.60 line when using spoons. Salmon are not particularly shy and will hardly be frightened by a strong lead or line. On the other hand, using a thick line may affect the way your fly goes, and there are limits to what is considered «sporty» fishing. One-handed fly rods in «easy» rivers may well be 9—10 ft. (splitcane, glass-fibre or carbon-fibre), two-handed rods are usually from approx. 11 to approx. 14 ft.of the same materials, but in some rivers you may profit by using even longer rods. If fishing with a spoon, short one-handed rods, of the type used when landing pike, should be avoided. In case the vegetation along the river is hopeless, and a one-handed rod is not available, a 9 ft. two-handed may prove useful, but it should be solid. Personally we prefer multiplicator reels to bobbin (haspel) equipment in Norwegian salmon waters.
When it comes to the most important part of your equipment, the flies or spoons, it is no great help to advocate certain patterns. Conditions will vary infinitely with weather, temperature, current, vegetation along the banks, the river-bed, time of the season and so on. If you have a selection of well-known patterns such as Silver Doctor, Silver Grey, Thunder and Lightning, Jock Scott, Dusty Miller and Blue Charm you may always get your salmon. If you should meet milky, «greenish» glacier water in snow-melting periods, a more orange-coloured fly may do the trick. A good rule is big flies, up to 7/0 in a high and cold river in the early season, and decreasing sizes as the water gets lower and warmer later in the season. Some of the finest sport can be enjoyed with light equipment and flies of approx. 6/0 in Aug., when salmon are more shy and water level low.
The most common spoons are different types of Devon spinners or a Norwegian «skjesluk« (spoon). In strong currents the spoon should be flatter, but still able to sink. In slower-flowing water a fast-spinning, «crocodile-shaped» spoon will usually prove more effective. In big rivers, especially early in the season, one should try big spoons. A good sharp gaff and a pair of waders should complete your equipment, except in the small and «easy» rivers where, istead of a gaff, a long-handle and deep bag-net with a wide opening should be used. Remember, it is obligatory to disinfect equipment which have been used outside Norway.

Welcome to Norway
Norway has invested considerable sums of money in its tourist industry. The country is prepared to receive an increasing number of visitors. Not only is salmon and sea trout fishing well organised, but billetting is adequate almost everywhere, ranging from first-class hotels to inexpensive chalets and camping sites. As a rule hotels get fewer in the far north, but on the other hand good and inexpensive rivers are more numerous.
In this section of our book salmon and sea trout rivers are grouped by districts, preferably by counties. Under each river information is given about access, fishing possibilities, season, centres with accommodation, and also where further details concerning the river may be acquired and fishing permits bought.

THE OSLO FJORD

In addition to the Sandvikselv and Lågen rivers mentioned below, there are two salmon waters on the east side of the Oslo fjord, the Glomma and the Berbyelv rivers, and five more salmon rivers on the west side of the fjord: The Åroselv river 25 miles south of Oslo, the Drammenselv river which flows into the sea at Drammen 25 miles from Oslo, the Sandeelv river 37 miles south of Oslo, and the Skienselv and Herreelv rivers both flowing into the Skiens fjord approx. 110 miles from Oslo.

SANDVIKSELV river, Sandvika, Oslofjord *(D 12)*. It lies 12 miles west of Oslo. The main road to Hønefoss runs parallel with the river, 9 to 11 miles from Oslo. Map: 1814 I(Asker).
The stream is fairly fast, but there are several smooth pools. Fishing is very dependent upon the water level. The best fishing is enjoyed after heavy rain in Aug., which of course attracts a great number of anglers. Bank casting is everywhere possible, and waders are recommended. From time to time there is some pollution, but the culprits have been found and are now strictly observed. Altogether the possibilities are good in this well-kept river, which is divided into zones. The season extends from July 14 to Sept. 25. A

salmon ladder is built at Frantzefoss, 2 km from the fjord. By counting the fish running up-stream during recent seasons, it is estimated that between 1 200 and 3 800 sea trout ascend annually, and from 20 to 200 salmon.
Centre: Oslo.
Fishing permit: Available at Bærum Sport, Sandvika, approx. kr. 80 per. season.

LÅGEN, *river, Larvik, Oslo fjord (D 12—13)*. Distance by road from Oslo, 81 miles. Maps: 1813 III (Sandefjord), 1813 IV (Holmestrand) and 1713 I (Siljan),
Although Lågen, is one of the largest salmon rivers in Norway, and in some years even has topped the statistics, most of the salmon is netted by professional fishermen, so in spite of its length possibilities for sportsmen are limited. River Lågen holds salmon over a stretch of 70 km to Vittingfoss falls. The water is fairly wide and slow-flowing. Anglers are afforded the best sport in a number of rapids and waterfalls along its course. Open season from June 1 to Oct. 14. The fishing is best in June in the lower reaches, but best in July in the upper reaches.
Centres: Larvik.
Information and fishing permits: Information on leases, as well as a map of beats, available from the Larvik Tourist Office, 3250 Larvik.

TELEMARK AND AGDER

We are sorry to report that to-day there is no reason to give detailed information on salmon fishing in the counties of Telemark, Aust-Agder and Vest-Agder. For quite some time pollution have affected these waters to which, in recent years sulphurous downfall brought in from the Continent and Britain must be added. Not all rivers are completely destroyed, and efforts are made to re-stock the rivers through cultivation. The quality of fishing, however, is by ho means so good that we would recommend you to spend an angling holiday in this region. In the lower parts of some rivers sea trout fishing may still be passable.

ROGALAND

In addition to the rivers described below the following Rogaland rivers should be mentioned:
The Ognaelv and Håelva rivers, both small rivers flowing into the North Sea south of Stavanger, and the Ullaelv river which flows into the Jøsenfjord north-east of Stavanger.

FIGGJO *river, near Stavanger (B 13)*. The Figgjo is a small but pretty salmon river which flows into the ocean at Sele. It is reached by various roads from Stavanger, a distance of 12 to 20 miles. Map: 1212 IV (Stavanger.)
The salmon water is about 20 km long between the sea and Ålgård. It is only about 15 m wide and the current is smooth and slow. The river bed consists of sand and mud in the lower reaches, rocks and pebbles in the upper reaches, with greatly varied water level, dependent on rain. Mainly bank casting, but a boat is used in certain places. Waders are useful. Fly or spoon. The open season extends from March to Sept. 20. The salmon season depends on the amount of water, but is usually best from mid-July onwards. The sea trout season is best in August/September (autumn flood).
Information and fishing permits: Information is available from Stavanger Tourist Office, box 356, 4001 Stavanger. The Rogaland Hunting and Angling Ass. offers non-members reasonable and expensive beats on the river. Tickets are available from Arne Hidle Sport and G. Steens Sport, both in Stavanger, or from Kon Hetland Sport and Are Waage Sport in Sandnes. In Orstad tickets are sold by Arstein Orstad for approx. kr. 45 per day.

SANDSELV/SULDALSLÅGEN *Sauda fjord. (B 13)*. The best river in the Stavanger region. Travel by fjord steamer from Stavanger to Sand in 1¼ hours or 60 miles by road including 2 ferries. The main road between Sand and lake Suldal runs parallel with the river. Map: Sand.
River Sand which is also known as Suldalslågen, holds salmon over a stretch of 8 km. It flows mainly through arable lands in a smooth stream, but there are also some rapids. The water level is fairly constant, as river Sand drains the large Suldal lake. However, when floods, do occur, there is practically no fishing. The open season extends from June 1. to Oct. 15. At the start of the season fishing is limited to the mouth of the river and the Fosshølen pool and not open to visitors, who may only fish after Aug. 1. The salmon is rather on the heavy side — from 12 to 50 pounds, but the fishing method is mainly by spoon or prawn, pratically no fly fishing. Boat fishing at the mouth, in Fosshølen and some other places, elsewhere casting from the banks. On the SAS beat both from banks and boats.
Centre: Sand.
Information and fishing permits: SAS Royal Atlantic Hotel, 4000 Stavanger offers angling to visitors. The Stavanger Tourist Office issues day tickets to some beats in Aug.

STORELV *og* NORDELV, *Sauda, Rogaland (B 13)*. These two rivers have joint confluence into the Sauda fjord at the industrial sentre of Sauda, which is reached by steamer from Stavanger in 4 hours, or from Haugesund by bus in 4 hours, Maps: Sand and Fjæra.

Storelv holds salmon over a stretch of 8 km to Juvastøl waterfall. The river is fairly broad and smooth except at Kastfoss, which is a narrow rapid about 2 km from the fjord.

Nordelv holds salmon over a stretch of only 1 km to Høllandsfoss. This waterfall is spanned by a road bridge, from which it is often possible to watch up to 20 salmon in the pool below. The open season extends from June 1 to Sept. 30.

Centres: Saudasjøen and Sauda.
Fishing permits: Tickets at reasonable prices to both rivers from Sauda Sport.

TENGSELV river, Eigersund. (C 14). It flows into the sea at Eigersund. The road distance from Stavanger to lake Svela is 32 miles, Bjerkreim bridge 36 miles and Tengs bridge 52 miles. Maps: 1211 I (Eigersund) and 1212 II (Bjerkreim).

River Tengs suffered badly through extensive netting until 1954, when most netting rights were acquired for a period of 30 years, and the fishing improved, lately it seems to have deteriorated. Also it is difficult to acquire the best beats, as they are leased for the whole season, at any rate between Spinnevikhølen pool and the estuary. A few salmon ladders have been built in the river, where the season lasts from June 1 to Sept. 30.

The upper part is called the Bjerkreim river. In the lower part, or Tengselva, fishing is best in the first half of June, above the Fotlandfoss waterfall in Aug. and Sept. Grilse usually start the run in the middle of June. In warm and dry periods, with low water, fish will move in and out of the estuary without running up the river and will not take to flies willingly. The best sea trout season is in Aug. and Sept. Fishing is carried on both from the banks and boats.

Centre: Egersund.

Information and fishing permits: Rogaland Fishing and Hunting Ass. has acquired certain rights, especially in Bjerkreim, where day tickets are sold for approx. kr. 35 by Joakim Risnes, 4387 Bjerkreim, Vikeså Forbrukslag (Co-op), Tønnes Vikeså, 4389 Vikeså and Wilhelm A. Gjerdrem, 4387 Bjerkreim. Further down the river tickets are available from Bernt Hestnes, 4239 Tengesdal. Information available from Stavanger Tourist Office, box 356, 4001 Stavanger. Tickets to the river is also available from sports shops in Stavanger and Sandnes.

VIKEDALSELV river, Vikedal. Rogaland (B 13) has yielded fair results in the last years. Vikedal is reached by boat from Stav-

anger in 3 hours, the distance from Haugesund by car is 40 miles. The salmon water is approx. 7 km, from the fjord to the Låkafoss waterfall. Map: Vikedal.

Centre: Vikedal.

Information: Haugesund og Omegn Jeger og Fiskeforening (Hunting and Fishing Ass.), 5500 Haugesund.

Fishing permits: Haugesund og Omegn Jeger- og Fiskeforening. Haugesund; Berge Grimås, Vikedal; Kjøpmann Krogedal, Vikedal, at reasonable prices.

HORDALAND

In addition to the rivers described below two more waters should be mentioned, the Lonevågselv river and the Frøysetelv river. The Lonevågselv is found on the Osterøy Island, and the Frøysetelv in the Masfjorden area, both north of Bergen.

GRANVINELV river, Hardanger fjord (B 12). A short river which may be handy for those who are in the area. Travel by train via Voss from Oslo to Granvin in 8 hours, Bergen 3 hours, or by bus from Bergen in 5 hours, Road distances from Oslo to Granvin via Geilo 237 miles, from Bergen 80 miles. Map: Voss.

The salmon water between the fjord and lake Granvin is only a mile long. It is a small spate river, in spite of the lake. Large numbers of sea trout run up within a few hours only on isolated occasions when the river rises. The fish are then hauled out by the basketful by the locals, mostly with worms. There may be an occasional salmon, and also brown trout in the river beyond the lake. Open season: June 1 — Aug. 31. The best sea trout fishing is in July and August.

Centre: Granvin.

Information and fishing permits: The fishing is free to residents of Meland Hotel Granvin. Fishing permits for non-residents may be obtained at the camping sites, approx. kr. 35.

OPO river, Odda, Hardanger fjord (B 12). Here is a short salmon river which is well cared for. Travel from Oslo by train to Bø in 8 hours and by bus to Odda in 2 hours and by bus to Odda in 6 hours. From Bergen by bus to Kvanndal, ferry to Kinsarvik and bus to Odda in one day. Road distance from Oslo to Odda via Haukeli 251 miles, from Bergen 101 miles. Map: Folgefonni.

The Opo salmon water covers a distance of 13 km, from the fjord to Låtefoss waterfall. The river is 3 km long between the fjord and lake Sandvin, which is 4 km long. The distance between the lake and Låtefoss is 6 km. There is a 250 m long salmon ladder at

Mannsåker below the lake outlet. The salmon water is about 25 to 30 m wide with fairly swift current, particularly during June. The river bed is rocky with glacier-fed water. There is bank casting everywhere, but a boat is used at Osen at the outlet into the fjord. Waders are recommended. The usual bait is spoon, prawn or fly. There is no netting in the river itself but quite a lot in the fjord. The best salmon season is in July, with the best sea trout season in August. There is fishing for 16 rods between the fjord and the lake. The average salmon weighs about 20 pounds, sea trout about 3 pounds.

Centres: Odda and Seljestad.

Information and fishing permits: Apart from one single stretch — the Island Beat, which is fished by the landowners — the whole river between the fjord and lake Sandvin is leased to the local angling club, Odda Jakt- og Fiskelag. It is not easy to get permission to fish this part of the river. The best way is probably to try through Odda Tourist Office, 5750 Odda.

Fishing permits for lake Sandvin for sale in Odda sports shops, approx. kr. 20. per day, and so are fishing permits for the Hjøllo river, approx kr. 150 per week.

OSELV river, near Bergen (B 12). A popular salmon and sea trout water at the small village of Os, which is reached by bus from Bergen in an hour. Map: Fana.

It is a typical spate river, and the fishing is very much influenced by the water level. Open season: April 1 to Sept. 25. There is salmon of 8 to 20 pounds with an occasional record fish of 30 to 40 pounds. Sea trout will average 1 to 3 pounds, perhaps now and then a giant of 10 pounds.

Centre: Os.

Fishing permits: Between the fjord and Lundefoss, the owners have joined into an elveigarlag, and fishing cards are available from Peder Tvedt, Os, The beat between Lundefoss and Tøsdalsvatn is taken by Bergen Sportsfiskere, tickets available at approx. kr. 20 per day. The stretch between Tøsdalsvatn and Sandal comprises several lakes. The fishing is not particularly good, but tickets are available from some farmers at approx. kr. 10 pr. day.

VOSSO river, Bolstad fjord, Hordaland (B 12). Here is one of the most remarkable salmon rivers in the whole of Norway. Vosso — or at least the lower part, the Bolstad river — is said to hold heavier salmon than any other river in Norway, perhaps in the whole world as far as Atlantic salmon is concerned. In 1977 the average weight of salmon caught in the Bolstad river was 27 lbs. The Bergen railway runs parallel with the river between the fjord and Voss. The rail journey from Bergen to Voss takes 1 1/2 hours, from Oslo 7 hours, and then 6 miles by taxi or bus to Bulken. Express trains do not stop at Bulken, but there are local trains between Bergen and Voss, which stop at Bolstadøyri, Evanger and Bulken. The road distance from Bergen to Bulken is 112 miles, from Oslo via Geilo 264 miles. Maps: Voss and Bergsdalen.

River Vosso runs through beautiful country and is a good salmon river with many pools. The upper part is not so rewarding as it was some generations ago. There is greatly varied water; the river alternates between narrow and wide, smooth and swift, shallow and deep. Boat fishing and bank casting with flies, spoons and prawns.

June, July and August are best for salmon. The sea trout run commences about mid-July, but August is best. When water runs low in the upper reaches, there are usually few salmon about, but sea trout are fairly plentiful. Brown trout abound.

Between Bolstad fjord and lake Evanger, the river is 4 km long and is here often called the Bolstad river. This is by far the best and most expensive stretch of the river. Lake Evanger is 7 km long and is joined by a tributary called Teigdal river. Between lake Evanger and lake Seim the Vosso is 7 km long and is here often called the Evanger river. The current is swift with several rapids and fine pools.

Also between lake Seimsvatn and lake Vangsvatn there are several well-known pools. At the outlet from lake Vangsvatn sea trout fishing is good.

Lake Vang is 9 km long with Bulken at its western end and Voss at its eastern end. Beyond the lake, river Vosso holds salmon up to Palmafoss waterfall.

Centres: Bulken, Evanger and Bolstadøyri.

Information and fishing permits: Flyspesialisten Travel Agency, Oslo (ask for Mr. Egil Larsen) offers fishing in the Bolstad river and other parts of the Vosso from approx. kr. 800 to kr. 1 500 per day (inclusive terms). Boat and boatman, which is recommended in the Bolstad river, is not included.

ETNEELV river, Hardanger fjord. Travel by bus from Haugesund in 2 hours. 37 miles by car from Haugesund, 226 from Oslo. Maps: Skånevik and Vikedal.

This river has acquired a good reputation in recent years. The salmon water extends from the fjord to above lake Stordalsvatn. Between the fjord and the Håfoss waterfall, a distance of approx. 7 km, the water is divided into 3 zones (lower, middle and upper) each with approx. 7 beats for 1—4 roads. In most of the beats only 2 rods are allowed. The open season lasts from May 1 to Sept. 15, the salmon season is best from May 20 to the middle of July. After that the sea trout starts running. The biggest salmon caught with sporting tackle was 25 kg (55 pounds), the largest sea trout weighed 7,5 kg. (15,5 pounds).

Centres: Etne and Skånevik.

Fishing permits and information: Etne Fiskesport, Box 124, Haugesund. Beats from kr. 50 to 500 per day. The most expensive beats are in the lower and middle zones. Skånevik Fjord Hotel offers fishing at approx. kr. 900 per week.

EIO river, Hardanger fjord, (B 12). This river is blessed by some of the finest scenery in Fjord Country, including the Måbødal valley with the stupendous, 600 ft high, Vøringfoss waterfall. The best salmon water is the stretch between the fjord and lake Eidfjord. The more turbulent river above the lake is referred to as Bjoreia. The open season lasts from June 1 to Sept. 5. Access by bus and ferry from Bergen in 7 hours, or by train and bus from Oslo in 10 hours. Distance by road from Bergen 98 miles, from Oslo 205 miles. Map: 1415 IV (Eidfjord).

Centres: Eidfjord and Øvre Eidfjord.

Fishing permits: Eidfjord and Øvre Eidfjord.

Fishing permits: The zone between the lake and the fjord is taken by Bergen Sportfiskere. Fishing permits approx. kr. 200 per day. Fishing permits to Bjoreia (above the lake) are sold by Øvre Eidfjord Gjestgiveri at approx. kr. 20 per day.

SOGN AND FJORDANE

In addition to the rivers described below the following waters are said to offer fair sport: The Ervikelv river on the Stad peninsula, the Flekkeelv river which enters the Dalsfjord, and the Osenelv river which flows into the Høydalsfjord. All these rivers belong to the Sunnfjord — Nordfjord area.

SOGNEFJORD AREA

*ÅRØYELV river (B 11).*The Årøy is easily one of the five best salmon rivers in the whole world. Road distances from Oslo via Otta 311 miles, or via Laerdal 227 miles, from Bergen via Gudvangen 143 miles. Map: Sogndal River Årøy is particularly famous because the average weight of the salmon is one of the highest in Norway. 50-pounders or even heavier fish are killed every summer. Sixty pounders are landed often. It probably represents one of the heaviest types of rivers that the salmon angler is called upon to face. So fierce is that stream that boat fishing or wading is quite out of question. It is said that «one Årøy salmon takes more killing than 6 Wye springers or 2 Shannon fish». It is a most sporting river — because the odds are on the fish!

The river is very short, from the fjord to lake Hafslo, but salmon are caught only between the fjord and Helvedesfoss (Hell's Fall), which cannot be bypassed even by the strongest salmon. The lowest water is only 220 yards long. Then follows a stretch of 500 yards of almost continuous rapids, where fishing is more or less impossible. The best salmon water lies above the rapids, covering a distance of 600 yards only, up to the waterfall. The river is fairly deep, but only 25 to 45 yards wide. There are a few narrow pools. The best ones are Slo and Makkauren in the upper beat. There is fishing for 2 rods. The heaviest tackle is required. Also ample reserves of line and other accessories. The open season lasts from June 1 to Sept. 30.

Centre: Sogndal.

Information and fishing permits: Needless to say this is an expensive salmon water. The river has been leased — until 1985 — to a Frenchman, Mr. M. Bimberg.

AURLANDSELV river, Aurland, (B 12). The Aurland is particularly known for its fine run of sea trout. Travel by rail from Bergen to Flåm in 3 1/2 hours, from Oslo in 7 hours and then by bus to Aurland in 15 minutes. Aurland can be reached by car and ferry from Bergen, the distance is 134 miles. The distance from Oslo is 192 miles. Maps: Flåmsdalen and Aurlandsdalen.

The salmon and sea trout river is only 6 km long, from the fjord to lake Vassbygd. The stream is generally smooth with occasional rapids between a series of fine pools. Only bank casting. Waders are recommended. Hydro-electrical power stations and damming in the mountains have affected the river. It rises and falls irrespective of rain and snow melting, which has undoubtedly damaged the fishing.

Together with the Lærdal river the Aurland river is the best sea trout water in Norway. Before the power stations were brought into use, in the early 70-ies, it was far from uncommon with 5/0 or 6/0 flies to land 16 to 18 lbs. sea trout and the average weight in July, which was the best season, was 5 1/2 pound. To-day conditions are uncertain. In good years 15-lbs. (average weight) salmon run up the river.

The Aurland is one of the few rivers in Norway where it pays to fish with dry flies. After the sea trout run has started in the beginning of July only flies should be used, with the exception of a few deep and quiet salmon beats. In Aug. sea trout are more numerous, but size is below the July average. Leasing has become quite complicated lately. The best beats are on long-term leases (several years), but the beats along the highway have often been subdivided and enquiries should be made to the Aurland Tourist Office to find out if beats for one day or more are available. The middle part of the river, opposite the highroad, are often available from the farmers Torstein Tokvam and/or Olav Tokvann. The Aurland river is fairly expensive with prices varying with the extension of the beats. Prices may be as high as kr. 400 to 500 a day for the best fishing.

Centre: Aurland and farms along the river.

Information: Aurland Tourist Office, 5745 Aurland.

DALEELV river, Høyanger, (B 12). A smallish river at the industrial centre of Høyanger, reached by fjord steamer from Bergen to Larvik in 2 1/2 hours and bus to Høyanger 1 hours. Map: Kyrkjebø.

The salmon water is only 6 km long, up to Laksefoss waterfall. It is a typical spate river — regulated by the aluminium company — with swift current which calls for strong tackle. Bank casting only with fly, Devon spoon or prawn. Waders are not requred. There is no netting in the river but plenty in the fjord. The salmon season is best from mid-June to mid-August. The sea trout season is best in July and August.

Centre: Høyanger.

Information and fishing permits: The fishery belongs to the local angling club, Høyanger Jeger- og Fiskeforening, and tickets are sold by Ola Ormberg A/S and Høyanger Samvirkelag (Co-operative store).

FLÅMSELV river, Flåm (B 12). Travel by train from Oslo to Flåm in 7 hours, from Bergen in 3 1/2 hours. Flåm can be reached by car via Aurland (see above), only 5 miles separate the two villages, and there is a motoring road along the river. Map: Flåmsdalen.

The Flåm is rather narrow, with a rocky and boulder-strewn bed. The salmon water is only 4 km long, from the fjord to the hydro-electric plant at the Gilja pool. It is a fairly smooth river, as it only drops about 200 ft from Gilja to the fjord. The water is crystal-clear, except early in the season when it may be muddy for a short spell. There is bank casting everywhere and no boat fishing. Waders may be useful. Fly, prawn and spoon. There is no netting in the river. The best salmon seasons is from June 25 to Aug. 5. The run of sea trout commences in mid-July and is best from July 20 to Aug. 31, when the river is closed. An average salmon will run to about 18 pounds, sea trout 4 to 5 pounds. There is fishing for 2 salmon rods and 2 trout rods.

Centre: Flåm.

Information and fishing permits: Information and leasing through the Fretheim Hotel, 5743 Flåm. Approx. kr. 200 per day and rod. Aurland Jakt- og Fiskeforening (local hunting and angling ass.) has taken parts of the river and often sub-lets.

FORTUNSELV river, Skjolden, (B 11). Travel from Bergen by fjord steamer to Leikanger 4 1/2 hours and bus to Fortun in 4 hours. From Oslo by train to Otta in 4 hours and bus to Fortun in 5 1/2 hours. Road distance from Bergen via Gudvangen 174 miles. Oslo via Otta 280 miles. Map: Årdal (M 515).

River Fortun drains a number of mountain lakes and glaciers in the ranges between Jotunheimen and the Jostedal glacier, reaching the fjord at Skjolden, near river Mørkrid. The river is regulated by Årdal and Sunndal aluminium company which allows a steady flow of water during the angling season. The salmon water is about 15 km long, between the fjord and Øyabotten (also called Kleppasva). It is from 25 to 45 yards wide with varied current, from swift to placid. It is often flooded during the latter half of June. The river-bed consist of rock, gravel and sand. Bank casting everywhere and no boat fishing. Waders are useful. Spoon, prawn and fly. Much netting in the fjord and in lake Eidsvatn, but no nets in the river. There is fishing for about 30 rods and the river is often crowded.

The open season extends from June 1 to Sept 30 and is best between Mid-Summer Day and end of July. The sea trout run commences in early August and is best during the last half of August. An average salmon will scale about 15 pounds, sea trout 2 to 5 pounds.

Centre: Skjolden.

Information and fishing permits: Skjolden Turisthotell, 5833 Skjolden. Day tickets approx. kr. 20 to kr. 75.

LÆRDALSELV, Laerdal. (B 11—12). Travel by fjord steamer from Bergen to Revsnes in 5 1/2 hours and bus to Lærdal in 15 mins. From Oslo by rail to Fagernes or Gol and then by bus to Lærdal in altogether 10 hours. Road distance from Bergen via Voss 135 miles, from Oslo 200 miles via Gol or 217 miles via Fagernes. Map: Lærdal.

River Lærdal is 80 km long and holds salmon and sea trout for 38 km between the fjord and the Hegg waterfall. A few years ago salmon was halted by the Sjurhaug waterfall 22 km from the fjord, but the construction of 5 tunnels and salmon ladders has extended the salmon water. In 1982 the river above Sjurhaug will be opened to anglers. All fishing takes place from the banks or from specially constructed platforms. No boats are required.

The main road follows the river and every pool is easily reached by motor car.

The Lærdal is a very atrractive river. Fishing is well organised and there is a good and fairly stable run of salmon and big sea trout. Relatively easy to fish, with many fine pools and exciting sea trout fishing with dry flies. Its international reputation for generations has brought prices to high levels, and it is far from easy to acquire good fishing because most beats are leased for several years.

The open season extends until Sept. 14 in the upper reaches between Seltun and Hegg. June is good from the fjord to Voll. July is the best season from the fjord to Bjørkum. Between Seltun and Sjurhaug, the best season is from the last week of July. In early June, the average weight is 20 to 25 pounds, whereas the July and August fish run to about 16 to 18 pounds. 40-pounders are caught every year and 50-pounders are not unknown. Early in the season the fly kills well, but prawn is best in August, with the spoon and minnow doing well in high water.

The Lærdal is probably the best sea trout river in Norway, at least in normal summers. Sea trout may be had from mid-July in increasing quantity until the close of the season. Dry fly fishing is a very popular sport. The best fishing is from the river mouth and up to Mo beat, below the Honjum rapids. The best time is after 10 am and preferably when the sun is on the water. There is no evening rise of sea trout in the Laerdal, and the fish do not seem interested in the dry fly at dusk. The sea trout lie at the side of the main stream in depths of 1 to 8 ft. The Lærdal sea trout are wary fish, similar to chalkstream trout or carp. Sea trout of 12 to 15 pounds are fairly common, but 5-pounders are average fish.

Centre: Lærdal.

Information and fishing permits: All beats are privately owned and many are hired on long-term leases, but certain beats are available occasionally for shorter or longer periods. Please contact the chairman of the river owners' association, Mr. Per Hjerman, 5890 Lærdal. You can also make enquiries to Mr. R. S. Brooks, Sunray Lodge, 5890 Lærdal, or write or telephone Mr. Haakon Christensen, Kr. Aug. g. 19, Oslo 1, tel. (02) 20 22 41.

MØRKRIDSELV *river, Skjolden, Sogne fjord (B 11).* A short salmon water which reaches the fjord at Skjolden. Travel from Bergen by fjord steamer to Leikanger in 4 1/2 hours and bus to Skjolden in 3 1/2 hours. Road distance from Bergen via Gudvangen 170 miles, from Oslo via Otta 284 miles. Map: 1418 II (Mørkrisdalen).

River Mørkrid is fed by glaciers and flows through the Mørkridsdal valley. It reaches the sea at Skjolden, close to river Fortun. The salmon water is only 8 km long, between the fjord and Giljahølen. It is from 25 to 40 yards wide, with currents varying from swift to placid. The water is far from clear — particularly during periods of flood in June. There is bank casting everywhere and no boat fishing. Waders are required. Spoon, prawn and fly. There is fishing for about 20 rods.

The open season extends from June 1 to Sept. 30 with the best salmon period in July and August, the best sea trout period during the first half of September, although the first run usually occurs in mid-August. There is salmon of about 15 pounds and sea trout of 2 pounds.

Centre: Skjolden.

Fishing permits: Most beats are owned and fished by the local farmers. Some beats, however, are available on daily terms. Enquiries to Einar Bolstad, 5833 Skjolden or Skjolden Turisthotel.

NÆRØYDALSELV *river, Gudvangen (B 12).* Draining several mountain lakes, river Nærøy tumbles down the terrific Stalheim gorge — almost parallel with the famous hair-pin bend road — until it touches the highest point of the Nærøy valley, practically at the foot of the precipice below Stalheim Hotel, and joins the fjord at Gudvangen. Travel by rail from Bergen to Voss in 1 1/2 hours or from Oslo in 7 hours and then by bus from Voss to Stalheim in 1 1/2 hours or to Gudvangen in 2 hours. The river runs almost alongside the main road with frequent bus services. The road distance from Bergen to Gudvangen is 127 miles, from Oslo via Laerdal 211 miles or via Geilo and Kvanndal 459 miles. Map: Flåmsdalen.

The salmon water covers a distance of 7 miles, from the narrow Nærøy fjord at Gudvangen and up to the Stalheim gorge. The stream is fairly fast, narrow and shallow with a boulder-strewn bed. The ice-worn boulders are nearly whitewashed, reflecting daylight through crystal-clear water. Every movement and sign of life can be seen clearly from the banks. Consequently the fish tend to be rather shy. The fishing is best when the water runs high, but the river often suffers through droughts. It is a good casting river.

Centres: Stalheim and Gudvangen.

Information and fishing permits: The Nærøy is owned by several farmers. Information about fishing possibilities from Stalheim Hotel. Tickets available from Gudvangen camping.

VIKJA *river, Vik i Sogn (B 12).* This is a rather small river near Vik village. Travel by express boat from Bergen in 4 1/2 hours, or by train and bus via Voss in 3 hours. By train from Oslo to Voss and bus to Vik in 8

Norway has a least 240 salmon rivers. Some of them are among the best in the world, and millionaires compete for the privilege of hiring beats, while others are available to ordinary mortals at more democratic rates. Our photo shows a one-day-bag from the Lærdal, one of Norway's star rivers.

Photo: Johan Berge

The Tana with its network of tributaries forms the most extensive salmon river in the whole of Norway. If all tributaries are included, its total length is over 500 miles. The Tana contains heavier fish than any other river in the world. Reports of 60-pounders and 50-pounders killed in this river are numerous. The record was set in 1929 with an 81-pounder.

Photo: Svendsen.

In the Rauma river prices for day tickets vary from approx. kr. 25 to kr. 400. The heaviest fish arrive already in May, and the record is almost 70 lbs. Every year 45-pounders are killed.

Fish do not rise to the bait all day and a brew of coffee on the river bank belongs to the joys of the angler. Scenery is also there to be admired; witness this photo from Sogndal in the Sognefjord area.

hours. Road distance from Bergen 145 miles, from Oslo 246 miles and 2 ferries. Map: Vik. The salmon and sea trout water is only 4 km. The rest of the river runs in a tunnel built for the power station. Part of the river is private, but the east bank is at the disposal of the local angling ass., Vik Sportsfiskarlag, which sells tickets. There is a motoring road along the river. Casting from the banks with spoons, prawns and worms. Salmon up to 35 lbs. have been caught lately, 15—17-pounders are frequently killed. Also some grilse and sea trout. Vikja is a late river, fishing is best in Aug. and Sept., depending upon the water level.

Centre: Vik.

Information and fishing permits: Tickets available from Johs. Hove A/S and Vik Tourist Information.

THE SUNN FJORD AND NORD FJORD AREA

EIDSELV river, Nordfjordeid, Nord fjord (B 11). A sinuous river between Nordfjordeid and lake Hornindal. Travel by steamer from Bergen to Nordfjordeid in 12 hours. From Olden or Loen by bus in 2 1/2 hours. Road distance from Bergen via Sandane 169 miles. Map: 1218 I (Nordfjordeid).

River Eids drains lake Hornindal, Europe's deepest lake, maximum depth 1,593 ft. The lake lies at an altitude of 150 ft and the salmon water is 4 1/2 miles long and very sinuous with smooth currents. Boats are not required, but waders are essential. Mainly fly fishing. Dry fly for sea trout. Fishing starts on May 15. The best season from end of June until the end of August. There are 32 good pools for bank casting of which 29 can be fished from both banks and 3 from one bank only. A salmon ladder, completed 1967, allows salmon to enter lake Hornindalsvatn.

Centre: Nordfjordeid.

Fishing permits: Eid Sportsfiskere (Angling Ass.) rents most of the river and day tickets are sold through Myklebust Sports Shop, 6770 Nordfjordeid.

GAULA river, Bygstad, Sunn fjord (B 12). It orginates on the western fringe of the Jostedal glacier, but on its way it forms two large lakes of 10 and 15 miles which tend to act as natural reservoirs. The river flows into Dals fjord at Bygstad, and is also called the Bygdstad river. Travel by fjord steamer from Bergen to Rysjedalsvika in 2 1/2 hours and by bus to Bygstad or Osen in about 1 1/2 hours. Road distance from Bergen via Vadheim 92 miles. Map: Vevring.

The Gaula holds salmon over a stretch of about 12 km, from the fjord to Foss waterfall. It is a fairly broad river with varied currents — from swift to placid. Most pools are best fished from a boat. There is a boat in the main pools. Bank casting or wading is also feasible in some places. Waders are recommended when the water flows low. During the thaw and after heavy rain, the river is apt to run high (until the latter half of June). Fly fishing is the usual method, although a spoon and sometimes a prawn may be used with advantage.

The Gaula can be divided into two main sections. In the first place a stretch of 500 yards below the first waterfall, where most of the salmon is caught. This water has been leased. The upper, and by far the longest section, offers many good beats, and there is a chance of acquiring fishing here by contacting the farmers along the river. In the upper section fishing is best between July 1 and Sept. At the end of the season some sea trout enter the river. Angling in the Gaula is improving, and results have been good in recent years. The season starts on May 1.

Four salmon ladders are built in the Gaula, bypassing the waterfalls at Osen, Rekevik, Alvær and Sande. The Osen salmon ladder was constructed in 1873 and was the first of its kind built in Norway. The river is very well looked after.

Centres: Bygstad and Førde.

Information and fishing permits: It is safe to assume that river owners will demand at least kr. 100 per day and rod. Possible contacts are Gustav Søgnen, Ludvig Søgnen or Odd Sande, all 6830 Sande i Sunnfjord.

GLOPPENELV river, Sandane, Nord fjora (B 11). The river, which is also called Storelva or Breimselva, drains lake Breim and enters the Gloppen fjord at Sandane. Travel by steamer to Sandane from Bergen direct in 17 hours, or by steamer to Rysjedalsvika in 2 1/2 hours and bus from there in 4 hours. The road distance from Bergen via Vadheim is 152 miles, from Oslo via Lærdal 322 miles. Map: 1218 I (Nordfjordeid) and 1318 IV (Hornindal).

The river used to hold salmon and sea trout between the fjord and Eidsfossen waterfall, a stretch of 3 km. In 1970, however, the world's largest salmon ladder with 72 pools was completed at Eidsfossen. This 110 ft high ladder has made it possible for salmon to enter lake Breimsvatn, 5 km from the fjord. An average salmon will scale about 13 pounds. The open season extends from June 1. to Sept. 30. The best salmon season is June—July. Sea trout run in Aug.—Sept.

Centre: Sandane.

Information and fishing permits: All information about the river from Mr. Terje Bratt, Bank of Nova Scotia, Karl Johans g. 17, Oslo 2, tel. (02) 33 17 43.

JØLSTRA river, Førde, Sunn fjord (B 11).
This river which is also known as the Førde, drains the large Jølster lake which is glacier-fed. Travel by steamer from Bergen to Rysjedalsvika in 2 1/2 hours and by bus to Førde in 2 hours. Road distance from Bergen via Vadheim 113 miles, Oslo via Lærdal and Balestrand 298 miles.

The salmon water is 18 km long, from Førde fjord to Bruland waterfall.

River Jølstra is smooth and shallow with a fairly constant water level. There is bank casting and boat fishing. Waders are useful. Casting is facilitated by a number of wooden gangways built in strategic places. Fly, prawn, spoon. The season lasts from June 1 to Sept. 30. The best salmon season is in June and July with the best sea trout season in August. The fish is big, 30—40 pounders are often caught early in the season.

Centre: Førde.

Information and permits: The river is owned by a number of farmers. Contact the local river owners' ass. (Elveeigarlaget i Førde, 6800 Førde) for the first — and expensive — 7 weeks of the season. After that period contact Førde Jakt- og Fiskarforening (local angling and hunting ass.).

LOEN river, Loen, Nord fjord (B 11). Here is a river which affords more sea trout fishing than salmon fishing. Travel from Bergen by fjord steamer to Rysjedalsvika in 2 1/2 hours and then by bus to Loen in 5 hours. From Oslo by train to Otta in 4 1/2 hours and bus via Grotli in 4 1/2 hours. The road distance from Bergen via Vadheim is 171 miles, Oslo via Lærdal 355 miles. Map: 1318 I (Stryn).

River Loen drains the large glacier-fed lake Loen. The salmon water was only 1 km long between the fjord and Loenfoss waterfall. Here a fine salmon ladder with 19 rungs was completed in 1955, and the water enlarged to 3 km. The current is swift, and strong tackle is required. There is fishing for 3 rods. The season extends from June 1 to Sept. 30. The best salmon season is from mid-June to mid-July with the best sea trout season from mid-August to the close of the season. There is not so much salmon, but the sea trout fishing is said to be good.

Centre: Loen.

Information and fishing permits: The fishery is held by Bergens Sportsfiskere, fishing permits approx. kr. 200 per day.

NAUSTA river, Naustdal, Sunnfjord (B 11). Travel: see Jølstra. From Førde 15 mins. by bus or car to Naustdal. Map: 1218 III (Naustdal).

In recent years the Nausta has been one of the best small salmon rivers in Norway, and impressive catches have been made in the lower reaches of the river. This is where Hardy's Fishing School of Norway operates one-week courses with highly qualified instructors (contact Sunnfjord Hotel, 6800 Førde). In dry periods the rapids near the estuary are severely affected by tidal waters, but when the water level is normal this is an excellent fly fishing beat. In the pool above and below the next waterfall, fine fishing with spoons, prawns and worms for middle-sized salmon may be enjoyed. The open season starts on May 15. Fishing is best in June and July in the lower parts of the river and somewhat later further up the river. Sea trout mainly in Aug. From time to time the Nausta suffers from insufficient water.

Centre: Naustdal (not listed in «Where to Stay») and Førde.

Information and fishing permits: Førde Tourist Information and Sunnfjord Hotel will supply you with information concerning the lower and best part of the river. They co-operate with Hardy about leasing and fishing permits. Sunnfjord Hotel is also familiar with possibilities further up the river.

OLDENELV river, Olden, Nord fjord (B 11). A short and fast river between the fjord and lake Olden. Travel by steamer from Bergen to Rysjedalsvika in 2 1/2 hours and bus to Olden in 5 hours, alternatively by steamer direct in 19 hours. From Oslo, by train to Otta and bus via Grotli to Olden in one day. Road distances from Bergen via Vadheim 167 miles, from Oslo via Otta 322 miles. Map: 1318 I (Stryn).

Salmon and sea trout can be had over a stretch of 2,7 km up to Foss waterfall. The river winds and winds, and there are all types of fishable water, even when the river is high. The water is partly glacier-fed, but always clear enough for fly fishing. Three pools out of 20 are fished from a boat, otherwise there is bank casting. The water is reserved exclusively for rod fishing. June and July are the best months for salmon. The regular run of sea trout starts around August 1.

Centre: Olden.

Information: The river is owned by Olden Elveigarlag (Owners' Ass.) and tickets are sold in Aug. To the lower beats also in Sept. In June and July the river is leased. 4—6 tickets are issued for the whole river, the price per day and rod is approx. kr. 500—600, for the lower beats in September approx. kr. 100. Contact Rasmus Bruvoll, 6870 Olden.

OMMEDALSELV river, Hyen, Nord fjord (B 11). Also known as river Å or Hyen. Travel by steamer from Bergen to Florø and bus to Hyen in one day or by plane from Bergen to Sandane (50 mins.), bus to Anda

(10 mins.) and ferry to Hyen (1 hour). The distance by road from Bergen via Vadheim is 153 miles, from Oslo via Laerdal 346 miles. The village of Hyen lies at the head of the long and narrow Hyen fjord. Maps: 1218 I (Nordfjordeid) and 1218 II (Fimlandsgrend). There is fishing from both banks between the fjord and lake Å, a distance of 3 km including 4 pools. Lake Å is 500 yards long, and the river extends for another 500 yards between lake Å and lake Ommedal. A road runs alongside the river and both lakes. There is particularly good sea trout fishing in the lower part of the river, and good salmon fishing on the stretch between both lakes. Usually 3 to 4 rods. The salmon fishing is best in June and sea trout fishing in August.
Centre: Hyen.
Information: Enquiries should be directed to Sande Reisebyrå (Travel Agency), 6900 Florø.

STRYNSELV river, Stryn, Nord fjord (B 11). The Stryn is a well-kept river, said to hold more trout than salmon. Travel from Bergen by steamer to Rysjedalsvika in 2 1/2 hours and then by bus to Stryn in 5 hours. From Oslo by train to Otta 4 1/2 hours and buss via Grotli in 4 hours. Road distance from Oslo via Otta 310 miles, from Bergen via Vadheim 161 miles. The main road runs alongside the river. Map: 1318 I (Stryn).
The salmon water is 8—9 km long, between the fjord and lake Stryn. The current is smooth, interrupted by occasional rapids. Some pools are fished from a boat, but bank casting is the usual method. There are 5 boats. Waders are required. Salmon are caught with fly, spoon, spinner or prawn. There is no dry fly fishing for sea trout. Fishing for 5 rods. June is often best for salmon. August for sea trout, although the run of sea trout usually begins about July 20. There is a local hatchery, and the river has been stocked with salmon and sea trout annually since 1952. A fully furnished villa is usually included in the lease.
Centre: Stryn.
Information: The rivers is owned by the local farmers and leased for long periods. The present lease is held by an American, Mr. Morell.

MØRE AND ROMSDAL

In addition to the rivers described in the following sections one should make a note of the Korsbrekkelv river (also called Byg-daelv), which flows into the Sunnylven fjord at Hellesylt and for many years have yielded good sport with some very big salmon now and again. It is difficult to get hold of a beat here, as most of the river is on long-term

leases. *Moreover, in Sunnmøre the Valldal river is considered well worth trying too. In the Romsdal area one should make a note of these waters: The Tressa or Tresfjord river, Måna, Innfjordselv, Istra (tributary to the Rauma), Isa, Glutra, Vistdalselv and Oselv.*

SUNNMØRE AREA

STRANDAELV river, Stranda, Stor fjord (B 11). Travel by plane from Bergen to Ålesund (35 mins.) or Oslo (55 mins. and bus to Stranda (2 hours). Travel by coastal steamer from Bergen to Ålesund in 13 hours and bus to Stranda in 3 hours. From Oslo by train to Åndalsnes in 8 hours, bus to Linge in 2 1/2 hours and ferry to Stranda in 1 hour. Road distance from Bergen via Vadheim and Hellesylt is 210 miles, from Oslo via Dombås 385 miles. Map: 1219 I (Stranda).
River Stranda holds salmon over a stretch of 10 km up to Rødset waterfall. It is only about 15 yards wide with several rapids, interrupted by a number of placid pools. The water level fluctuates considerably, especially in spring and autumn. The river-bed consists of rocks and pebbles, with very clear water. There is bank casting everywhere and no boat fishing. Waders are useful. Mainly Devon spoon and prawn. The river is well looked after, and salmon fry are set out every year. The lower reaches are best in June and the upper reaches in July. A salmon will average about 12 pounds. Record salmon 39 pounds.
Centre: Stranda.
Information and fishing permits:
Contact the manager of Storfjord Hotel, Mr. Frode Holm Haagensen. Lately fishing has been divided in 3 periods with a short break at night, when no fishing is allowed. The price is approx. kr. 50 per rod for a 7 hour period. One day per week has been reserved for fly-fishing only. Fishing permits are in great demand, but if the hotel is contacted at an early date, chances for acquiring permits are good. Demand is greatest — and fishing at its best — at the end of June. Later in the season permits are easier to come by, especially for the lower reaches.

ÅHEIMSELV river, Åheim, Vanylven (A 11). Travel by coastal steamer from Bergen to Måløy in 9 hours and by bus to Åheim in approx. 2 hours. The distance by road from Bergen to Vadheim is 200 miles, from Oslo to Otta 376 miles. Motoring road along the east side of the river. Maps: 1119 III (Vanylven) and 1218 IV (Ålfoten).
The Åheim river is the lower part of the Gusdal system. It drains lake Gusdal and the salmon water between the lake and the fjord is approx. 3 km. The upper 500 metres are quite turbulent with small waterfalls, the lower 2,5 km are flat with sandy river bottom

and no pools (difficult to fish). Åheim is typical flood river in which both salmon and sea trout run.

Centre: Åheim.

Fishing permits: The river belongs to the local farmers. A limited number of fishing permits are sold through Åheim & Dalane grunneigarlag (Owners' Ass.).

BONDALSELV river, Sæbø, Hjørund fjord (B 11). This is another inexpensive river which has been very good for a number of years. Travel by boat from Bergen to Ålesund in 13 hours and from there by bus to Sæbø in 3 hours or by plane from Bergen to Ålesund (35 mins) or Oslo 55 mins). From Oslo by train to Åndalsnes in 7 hours and bus via Spjelkavik. The distance by road from Bergen is approx. 224 miles via Vadheim and from Oslo via Otta 355 miles. There are motoring roads on both sides of the river. Map: 1219 III (Hjørundfjord).

The river drains lake Rognstøylvatn and runs through the wild and beautiful Slettedal and Bondal valleys to enter the Hjørund fjord at Sæbø.

From Rekedal, where the river enters the Bondal valley, and down to the fjord at Sæbø fishing conditions are fine on both sides of the river. Open country on both sides with long stretches of artificial embankments which makes casting very easy (not many pools). Fishing is especially good at Rise and Hustad, at the mouth of the river, Kvistadhølen pool 3 km from the fjord and Berghølen pool at Rekedal 7 km from the sea. Large numbers of fry are produced annually by the river owner's hatchery. The river reacts quickly to warm weather and downpoor. The river holds plenty of salmon and some sea trout. The average salmon weighs approx. 6 pounds. Fishing with worms is the usual method, but in the lower reaches a few beats are reserved for fly-fishing. The best fishing season for salmon is from the middle of June to the middle of Aug. No fishing on Sundays between 9 a.m. and 1 p.m..

Centres: Sæbø and Ørsta.

Information and fishing permits: Bondalen Elveigarlag (owner's ass.) issues tickets, and they are available from camping sites and guest houses near the river. Both in the fly fishing zone, and a few kilometers up the river, fishing is divided into 3 periods of 6 hours each, with a closed period from midnight to 6 a.m. The price is approx. kr. 30 per rod and period and approx. kr. 50 in the fly-fishing zone. Further information from Mrs. Jorunn Hustad or from Mr. Anders Hustadnes, both 6180 Sæbø.

ØRSTAELV river, Ørsta, Ørsta fjord (B 11). Here is another fine and inexpensive river which has been fished with remarkable results over a number of years. Travel to Ålesund, see Bondalselv, and then by bus in 2 hours to Ørsta. Road distance from Bergen via Vadheim is 195 miles and from Oslo via Stryn 362 miles. There are motoring roads on both sides of the river. Map: 1119 II (Volda). Ørsta river, or Storelva as it is often called, is the result of the confluence of the Follestaddal river and the Åmdals river, 4,5 km from the fjord. It runs smoothly through magnificient country and is not difficult to fish. Both salmon and sea trout run in the Ørsta river, and there are definite possibilities of hooking big 'uns. The average weight of small salmons is 3 to 6 pounds, the average weight of bigger specimemns 9 to 16 pounds. The season extends until Sept. 15. The salmon fishing is best from the middle of June to the end of Aug., sea trout — average weight 1 pound — in Aug. Ørsta river rises quickly, especially in Aug. with the snow melting in the high mountains.

Centre: Ørsta.

Information and fishing permits: Viking Fjord Hotel, 6150 Ørsta will inform you about the river, which is divided into zones and each day into 4 periods of 6 hours each. Prices are reasonable, but there is a bag limit. Usually tickets will be available. These are sold in the hotel and also in J.J. Myklebust sportsforretning (sports shop) and the camping site 300 yards from the river.

STRAUMGJERDEELV river, Straumgjerde, Sykkylven (B 11). Also called Straumen or the shortest salmon river in Norway. Travel by boat (13 hours) or by plane (35 mins.) from Bergen to Ålesund and then by bus in 1 1/2 hours to Straumgjerde. Or by train to Åndalsnes in 7 hours and then by bus in 4 hours to Straumgjerde. Distance by road from Bergen via Vadheim 222 miles, from Oslo via Dombås 368 miles. Map: 1219 IV (Sykkylven).

Straumgjerde river drains lake Fetvatnet, which also holds salmon and sea trout, and reaches the sea after a run of approx. 100 metres. When the tide is high sea level and lake level are the same. The river is easy to fish with firm ground on both sides. Good runs of both salmon and sea trout. June and July provides the best salmon fishing, sea trout in August.

Centres: Sykkylven and Straumgjerde.

Fishing permits: Inexpensive tickets covering both the lake, the Velledal river and the Straumgjerde river are available from the Post Office, and the local shops, R. Dalseth A/S and B. Drabløs A/S in Straumgjerde.

STORDALSELV river, Stordal, Stor fjord (B 11). Travel by boat (13 hours) or by plane (35 mins.) from Bergen to Ålesund and then by bus in 2 hours to Stordal. Or by train from Oslo to Ålesund in 7 hours, and then by bus in 3—4 hours to Stordal. Road distance from Bergen via Vadheim and Stranda is 210 miles and from Oslo via Dombås 348 miles. Map: 1219 I (Stranda).

The Stordal river rises in the mountains above Langsetrene and flows down the entire Stordal valley to enter the fjord at Stordal village. Salmon run as far Jøsvoll, 7 km from the fjord, where the Stavdalfoss falls are an impassable barrier. The river may be divided into 9 zones. These are (from the fjord) Hove approx. 600 metres, Vinje 400 metres, Busengdal 50 metres, Kvammen — Kirkebø — Midbust 400 metres, Øvrebust 600 metres, Holt 600 metres, Storheim 700 metres, Mo and Vad 900 metres, and Jøsvoll (the last zone before Stavdalsfoss). Normally there is a good run of salmon, average size 11—17 pounds. Record salmon killed scaled 66 pounds.

Centre: Stordal.

Fishing permits: The river is owned by the farms (viz. the zones above) along the river. Each farm has the right to fish a certain number of hours per week. Stordal camping at the mouth of the river has at its disposal a certain number of fishing hours at Kvammen, Vinje and Hove and issues day tickets. Otherwise fishing can be negotiated with the farmers along the river. The Jøsvold beat is on a longtime lease.

ROMSDAL AREA
EIRA river, Nauste, Lang fjord (B 10).

A short but well known river between Nauste and lake Eikesdal. Travel by coastal express steamer from Bergen to Molde in 18 hours or by plane from Bergen or Oslo in 1 hour and then 2 hours by bus to Nauste at Eresfjord or to Øverås at the northern end of lake Eikesdal. From Oslo by train to Åndalsnes in 7 hours and then 3 hours by bus to Nauste or Øverås. Road distance from Bergen to Øverås via Vadheim and Geiranger 311 miles, from Oslo 341 miles. There is a car ferry across lake Eikesdal between Øverås and Reitan. Map: 1320 II (Eresfjord).

The Eira is only 9 km long and drains the beautiful lake Eikesdal. The watercourse is regulated by the Aura hydroelectrical works so that the water level is lower than it used to be. The salmon water is fairly wide with smooth currents and clear water. It is snow-fed and is often flooded in spring. There is boat fishing but mostly bank casting. Waders are required. Mainly fly fishing, but spoons, prawns and spinners are also used. The lower stretch is best in June and July, with the upper portion best in July and August. The sea trout fishing is best in August. The Eira salmon is heavier than in many other

rivers, with an occasional 50-pounder. The whole river is privately owned, but it is often possible to hire a stretch for shorter or longer periods. Tickets for some beats have been available at the camping site near the outlet. Lake Eikesdal holds sea trout, often of considerable size, later in the season. The best method is to fish with a spoon from a rowing boat.

Centres: Nauste and Reitan.

Fishing permits: See above. Fishing permits for lake Eikesdal are sold both at Øverås and Reitan.

RAUMA river, Åndalsnes, Romsdal fjord (B 10).

The river drains a great portion of the Dovre mountain plateau and flows through the town of Åndalsnes. Travel by coastal express steamer from Bergen to Ålesund in 13 hours and then by bus to Åndalsnes in 3 1/2 hours. From Oslo by train to Åndalsnes direct in 7 hours. The road distance from Oslo is 288 miles, from Bergen via Vadheim and Geiranger 259 miles. The main road runs parallel with the east bank of Rauma, and a local road runs along the west bank up to Fiva. Maps: 1320 III (Åndalsnes) and 1319 I (Romsdalen).

The salmon water is 42 km long, from the fjord to Verma waterfall. The water is greatly varied, with broad and narrow stretches, smooth and swift currents. Boat fishing and bank casting. Waders are often useful. Fishing starts May 15 and ends Aug. 31, in the upper reaches the Rauma is open to Sept. 15. The salmon season is best between June 15 and July 20. Sea trout season from the end of July until the close of the season, but is best in August.

Centre: Åndalsnes.

Information and fishing permits: Rauma is a popular river, and it is important to book fishing at an early date. Information and tickets are available from Åndalsnes Tourist Office, box 133, 6301 Åndalsnes, which also sells tickets to 5 smaller salmon waters and some mountain lakes. Most of the Rauma has been leased by Åndalsnes og Omegn Jeger- og Fiskeforening (local hunting and angling ass.), and its members have made great efforts in cultivating the river. The Rauma is divided into zones with a max. number of rods per day, which means that those who have secured tickets also will find it possible to fish. Fishing permits, as mentioned above, are issued by the tourist office and prices vary from approx. kr. 25 to kr. 400 for 24 hours. The last price includes 3 rods and a boat. The most expensive single ticket — in so-called zone 10 — costs approx. kr. 100, and in all zones where boats are needed, these are included in the price. Fishing starts at 1600 hours and continue to 1600 hours the following day.

NORDMØRE AREA
DRIVA river, Sunndalsøra, Sunndals fjord (B 10). Visitors travel by plane from Oslo or Bergen to Kristiansund in 1 hour and then 2 hours by bus to Sunndalsøra. From Oslo by train to Oppdal in 6½ hours and by bus to Sunndalsøra in 1½ hours. The motor road runs practically parallel with the salmon water. The distance by road from Oslo to Sunndalsøra via Oppdal is 308 miles, from Bergen via Otta and Oppdal 389 miles. Maps: 1420 III (Sunndalsøra), 1420 II (Romfo) and 1520 III (Oppdal).
The salmon water is 50 miles (80 km) long, from the fjord to the Oppdal waterfall, which lies at an altitude of 1,790 ft. Driva is a lively river, mainly fast running, with small waterfalls, affording good sport. The water is seldom too high or too low for fishing; this is a typical rod river and bank casting dominates. Waders are required. Mainly fly, spoon and prawn. Above Romfo the season extends to Sept. 10. The fishing is at its best from mid-June unntil the end of July. Average weight of salmon runs to about 18 pounds, sea trout about 1 pound. Sea trout fishing is most rewarding in Aug.
Centres: Sunndalsøra, Grøa, Fale, Gjøra and Oppdal.
Information and fishing permits: The river is owned by various farmers, who let their beats to private persons and the Sunndal Jæger- og Fiskeforening. The beats of the Sunndal Jæger- and Fiskeforening (Rod and Gun Club) extend to approx. 10 miles (15 km). Fishing cards (day or week) are sold to visitors at Sunndalsøra, Grøa, Fale and Gjøra. Heimstad Pension, Grøa and Fahle Farm, Fale have their own beats and enquiries can be directed to them. Information about the sale of tickets from Sunndalsøra Tourist Information.

SURNA river, Surnadal, Surnadals fjord (B 10). Travel by plane from Bergen or Oslo to Kristiansund in 1 hour and then by bus to Surnadal in 4 hours. From Oslo by train to Trondheim in 8 hours and bus to Surnadal in 2 hours. Road distance from Oslo via Berkåk 357 miles, from Bergen via Gudvangen and Otta 429, Kristiansund 59, Trondheim 80 miles. Maps: 1420 I (Snota), 1420 IV(Stangvik) and 1421 II (Vinjeøra).
The Surna holds salmon over a stretch of 40 km from the fjord to Rindal. The water is fairly wide with smooth current. Boat fishing or bank casting. Waders are necessary. June is best for salmon, July and August for sea trout. All river owners have organised themselves and formed angling clubs which sell fishing cards to anybody passing by. Each holder of a fishing card is allotted a beat, but if he grumbles, he can ask for a transfer beat.
Centre: Surnadal.
Fishing permits: Day and week tickets at reasonable prices from Surnadal Hotel and several places along the river.

SØR-TRØNDELAG
GAULA river, Melhus, Gaulosen fjord (C 9—10). A large river which joins the Trondheim fjord a few miles west of the city. The salmon water is reached by car from Trondheim, a distance of 15 to 35 km. Maps: 1521 I (Orkanger), 1521 II(Hølonda), 1621 III (Støren), 1620 I (Haltdalen) and 1620 IV (Budal).
The river holds salmon over a stretch of 95 km, between the fjord and Egga waterfall at Holtål. It is roughly 50 m wide with varied currents — smooth in the lower parts and swift in the upper parts. There is mainly boat fishing but also some bank casting. Waders are recommended. Fishing is quite good, especially between the mouth and Støren. The best salmon season is around July 1. The run of sea trout begins about July 20 and the fishing is best in August. A salmon will scale about 20 pounds, sea trout about 2 pounds.
Centres: Trondheim and Støren.
Information and fishing permits: Tickets are sold for practically the whole river from the fjord to above Støren. Day and weekly tickets are for sale at pensions, sports shops and petrol stations along the river. Enquiries can be directed to Trondheim Fisheries Administration (TOFA), Søndregate 20, 7000 Trondheim.

NIDELV river, Trondheim (C 9). The Nid drains lake Selbu and runs right through the city of Trondheim. The main road runs parallel with the river. Map: 1621 IV (Trondheim).
The stream is smooth and fairly wide. It holds salmon over a stretch of 12 km up to Nedre Lerfoss waterfall. There is boat fishing as well as bank fishing. The best salmon season is in July and August, when an average salmon will scale about 15 pounds. Sea trout from the end of July. There is fishing for about 20 rods.
Centre: Trondheim.
Information and fishing permits: Most of the fishery belongs to the city of Trondheim, but the management is left to Trondheim Fisheries Administration (TOFA), Søndregate 20, 7000 Trondheim, to whom enquiries may be directed. From Nidarø to the fjord fishing is free, but private properity along the river must be respected.

ORKLA river, Orkdal, Orkdals fjord (B 10).
This salmon water lies west of Gaula and is
reached by bus from Trondheim to Orkanger
in 1 hour, a distance of 27 miles. There is a
motoring road on either side of the river.
Maps: 1521 I (Orkanger), 1521 II (Løkken)
and 1521 I (Rennebu).
River Orkla has suffered badly from netting,
but seining in the river's mouth ceased in
1948, since when the river has been on the
way up. It is now a good river for fly fishing.
But hydro-electrical works are in progress
which may affect fishing.
Salmon can be had over a stretch of 70 km,
up to Toset waterfall in Berkåk. There is
boat fishing and bank casting. Waders are
required. The salmon fishing is best in July.
Centres: Orkanger, Meldal and Berkåk.
Fishing permits: Pools can often be hired on
the spot from river owners above Svorkmo.
Fishing permits are sold by pensions and
shops in Berkåk.

STORDALSELV river, Åfjord (B 9). Travel by ferry and bus from Trondheim in 3
hours to Åfjord. Distance by road from
Trondheim 56 miles. Local road along the
north side of the river. Maps: 1522 II
(Bjugn), 1622 IV (Åfjord) and 1623 (Roan).
The river drains lake Stordal to enter the
Åfjord after 20 km. 500 metres below lake
Stordal the Støvelfoss falls is overcome by a
ladder and salmon reach the Årbogfoss falls 5
km above the lake. The Stordal is a good little
river with a fair number of medium-sized
salmon.
Centre: Åfjord (not listed).
Information and fishing permits: Reasonable
tickets from Åfjord Turiststasjon. Enquiries
may be directed to Trondheim Tourist Office,
Dronningens gate 12, 7000 Trondheim.

NORDDALSELV river, Åfjord (B 9). According to reports from the last years this
river yields even more than the Stordal river.
Travel: See Stordal above. Highroad 715
runs along the river. Map: see Stordal above.
The Norddal river holds salmon — not big
fish — over a stretch of 15 km from the fjord
at Åfjord to Stoen waterfall.
Centre: Åfjord.
Fishing permits: Tickets may be bought from
Årnes Sport or the landowners. Enquiries
may be directed to the Trondheim Tourist
Office.

NORD-TRØNDELAG

*In addition to the rivers described in the
following sections the Mossa is also reported
to be good. It flows through the parish of
Mosvik on the west side of the Trondheim
fjord. There is no fishing in this river between*

Sundays at 1600 hours and Tuesday at 1600
hours. Fishing is also good in the *Årgårdselv*
with its tributaries Øyungsåa, Austerelv and
Ferja, as well as in the river Oksa further
west. The *Årgårdselv* river flows into the
Bang fjord south of Namsos. Several tickets
are available to this river and its tributaries.
Information from Sentrum Auto in Namdalseid. Salmon tend to be small, fishing depends
upon the water level.

*NAMSEN river, Namsos, Namsen fjord (C
8)*. Travel by plane from Oslo (50 mins.) or
Bergen (1 1/2 hours) to Trondheim and then
by train to Grong in 3 1/2 hours. From Oslo
by train to Grong in 15 hours. There is also
an air service between Trondheim and Namsos (35 mins.) The road distance from Oslo to
Grong is 475 miles, from Bergen via Gudvangen and Otta 566 miles. Maps: 1723 I
(Overhalla), 1723 IV (Namsos), 1724 II
(Skogmo), 1823 IV (Grong) and 1824 III
(Harran).
The Namsen offers some of the best salmon
fishing in Norway. The river is well-known
outside the country. Since 1830 British
sportsmen have visited Namsen. It is a wide,
and in many repects, special river, where
fishing is mostly from boats and with very
strong tackle. Namsen has lately yielded a
great number of 50-pounders, time and again
also fish in the 65-pounder class. Such giants
have become rarer, but one must always be
prepared for a big'un, especially in the early
season. Salmon will average less that 20 lbs.
In the Namsen salmon used to run 50 km to
the Fiskumfoss falls north of Grong. Here a
salmon ladder has been built and increased
the length of the run considerably.
The stream is broad and smooth with a fairly
constant level, and the fishing is not much
influenced by the weather. However, early in
the season or after heavy rain, the water may
be flooded for a day or two. There is mainly
harling, when two boatmen are required in
each boat for two rods. If only one man is
fishing, smaller boats with one boatman can
be used. Bank fishing is also feasible. The
usual bait is fly, spoon and wobbler. The best
season is usually from the beginning of June
until mid-July, and a little later in the upper
reaches. The river is very well looked after,
and is under constant supervision.
The salmon water is divided into a number of
zones. One looks much like the other, but as
one comes to know the river, one realizes that
they differ quite a lot. Some of these zones are
leased far in advance, and often to the same
person of firm. However, tickets are available
to several beats, both in the Overhalla and
Grong parishes. There are daily, weekly and
weekend tickets, prices vary greatly in accor-

dance with the size and reputation of the beats. Your first enquiry may well be directed to Nord-Trøndelag Tourist Association, Kongens g. 42, 7700 Steinkjer. Under «Information and fishing permits» we mention some places where tickets to certain beats can be bought. The Namsen has got several tributaries:

Bjøra tributary joins Namsen at Overhalla. It is only 6 1/2 km long, between the confluence and lake Eids. There are several pools. 3 boats. Fishing for 4 or 6 rods. Wading, bank fishing and some harling. Fly fishing, spinning and prawn. Best salmon season from mid-June to end July. Sea trout and grilse in late July and August. Local accomodation.

Eida tributary connects lake Eids with lake Grungstad. It is only 1 1/2 km long with fishing for 2 rods. Bank casting only. Waders are useful. There are 4 pools which are particularly good for sea trout. Season from May 1. Spoons and spinners are best early in the season, fly fishing from mid-June.

Sørå tributary feeds lake Grungstad and holds salmon over a stretch of 12 km to lake Flak. Mainly bank casting, but boats are used in a few pools when the water runs high. Altogether 40 pools. Waders are required. The best fishing is in June and early July, but August can be good for sea trout and grilse if there is sufficient rain.

At Grong the Sanddøla joins the Namsen. This river also contains some salmon and tickets are sold locally.

Centres: On the Namsen accomondation is available in Namsos, Overhalla, Grong and Fiskumfoss. Along the Bjøra, Eida and Sørå small guesthouses are found. Sanddøla is best fished from Grong.

Information and fishing permits: A day ticket for a good beat in Overhalla costs approx. kr. 100, with boat and boatsman approx. 500. Information on fishing and accommodation from Skogmo Gjestgiveri, 7864 Skogmo and Namsen Fishing Camp, 7863 Overhalla. In the parish of Grong tickets to the Namsen are sold for certain periods and for a limited number of rods. Generally prices are reasonable, but good beats incl. boat and boatsman will cost approx. kr. 500—700 per day. Some beats are for fly-fishing only. In the Bjøra tickets for the Himo beat and others are available from Skogmo Gjestgiveri. Tickets for the Sanddøla are sold by Paul Mediaa Eftf., Grong, Grong Tourist Information and Grong Samvirkelag (Co-op). In addition fishing may be acquired from Johannes Gartland in Jørum or Alf Ryan in Bergsmo. Tickets to the Namsen river are also sold at the NOROL petrol station in Harran, Fiskumfoss Gjestgiveri, Harran and in Grong from Ola Seem, Halvor Leksås and Harald Eriksen.

FIGGA river, near Steinkjer, Trondheim fjord (C 9). A small river which flows into the Trondheim fjord south of Steinkjer. Travel by train from Trondheim to Steinkjer in 2 hours, or 76 miles by car. Maps: 1723 III (Steinkjer) and 1722 II (Snåsavatnet).

The Figga holds salmon over a stretch of 20 km to lake Leksdal. The stream is smooth. Bank casting everywhere and no boat fishing. Rod fishing only. The Figgja is a good salmon and sea trout river, and salmon start running very early, at the end of May. Here are chances of heavy fish, the record is 37 pounds and the average salmon will scale from 17 to 26 pounds early in the season, to decrease somewhat in size later in the season. The best salmon beats are found along the middle and upper parts of the river with some very fine pools. In the lower part of the river there is a good run of sea trout from approx. July 20, later also sea trout in the upper reaches. The season starts on May 1 (elsewhere in Nord-Trøndelag on June 1).

Centre: Steinkjer.

Information and fishing permits: In O. Gartlands Sportsforretning and in Sportshytta, both in Steinkjer. From Sportshytta also reasonable sea trout tickets to certain zones are sold.

STEINKJERELV river, Steinkjer, Trondheim fjord (C 9). Here is an interesting salmon water which has been fished by British visitors, on and off since 1875. Travel by train from Trondheim to Steinkjer in 2 hours. Road distance from Trondheim 76 miles. Maps: 1723 I (Steinkjer) and 1723 II (Snåsavatnet).

River Steinkjer with its tributary the Ogna flows into the long and narrow Beitstad branch of the large Trondheim fjord. The main river and the tributaries are reserved for rod fishing only. There is no boat fishing, but fishing from both banks.

This is a popular salmon river, known for its big fish. Chances are best at the beginning of the season (June 1). Smaller salmon from approx. June 20, sea trout from approx. July 20. The salmon water is 2 1/2 km long and divided into 3 zones.

Centre: Steinkjer.

Information and fishing permits: The river is administered by Steinkjer Jeger- and Fiskerforening (local hunting and angling ass.). Tickets are sold to both banks. Zone 1 is reserved for flyfishing only from June 15 to the end of the season. In zones 2 and 3 flies, spoons and worms are permitted. 5 day tickets are issued to zone 1, 10 to both of the other zones. In addition sesonal cards are sold to locals. Prices are reasonable. Tickets are available from Sportshytta, Sakshaug Sportsforretning, O. Gartlands Sportsforretning and Gullbergaunet Camping, all in Steinkjer.

OGNA, Steinkjer (C 9). Travel and maps: See Steinkjerelv. The Ogna flows into the Byaelv river at Guldbergaunet in Steinkjer. The river holds a good stock of salmon, which is helped by salmon ladders in the Brandsegg-foss, Støafoss and Hyttfoss waterfalls. Many fine pools for flyfishing. Upon the whole a relatively rapid river, where rapids and falls alternate with pools. To spread out fishing, the Ogna has been divided into 15 zones with partly limited sale of tickets. The water level changes considerably, from almost «dry» to spate periods. Open season from June 1. Between June 1 and June 10 salmon passes the Brandseggfoss and between June 20 and July the Støafoss. Above Hyttfoss no fishing is allowed.
Centre: Steinkjer.
Information and fishing permits: Day and season tickets are sold at reasonable prices in most zones, with the exception of a few, which are on long-term leases. Contact Nord-Trøndelag Tourist Office, Kongensgt. 42, 7700 Steinkjer.

STJØRDALSELV river, Trondheim fjord (9). The Stjørdal originates in Sweden and terminates in the huge basin of the Trond-heim fjord. It also includes the Førra tribu-tary. Travel by local train from Trondheim to Hegra in 1 hour. Road distance from Trond-heim to Hegra is 28 miles. Maps: 1621 I (Stjørdal), 1721 I (Meråker) and 1721 IV (Flornes).
The Stjørdal is a fair-sized river with me-dium current. The water is never too low for fishing. It is reserved mainly for rod fishing. There is fishing from bank or boat. Waders are required. The salmon water is 50 to 60 km long. 3 zones: Zone 1 covers the lower reaches from the estuary to the Hegra bridge, or approx. 10 km. Zone 2 goes as far as the Flornes bridge, or approx. 21 km, and zone 3 runs to Nustadfoss falls in Meråker, approx. 20 km. Fishing from both banks with flies and spoons, prawns are not allowed. Salmon fishing is best in June and the first half of July, sea trout in Aug. Big salmon (20—40 lbs.) are mostly killed in zone 2. In zone 1 smaller salmon and sea trout are landed.
Centres: Near the river accommodation in many farms, pensions and camping sites with chalets.
Information and fishing permits: Great parts of the river is administered by Stjørdal Jeger og Fiskerforening (local hunting and angling ass.), for other parts local owners must be contacted. Some beats are reserved for flyfish-ing only at certain periods. Tickets are sold in sports shops in Stjørdal and Meråker, as well as from pensions and camping sites and farms

along the river. Further information from the tourist information offices at Stjørdal and Meråker. Day permits — in July only — are approx. kr. 150, week permits approx. kr. 600. New prices are stipulated every year. When buying your ticket, you will also re-ceive detailed information of the the regula-tions in force in your zone.

VERDALSELV river, Verdal, Trondheim (C 9). It joins the Trondheim fjord at Ver-dal, which is reached by train from Trond-heim in 2 hours, or 58 miles by road. Maps: 1722 IV (Stiklestad), 1722 I (Vuku) and 1722 III (Feren).
The salmon water is 25 km long, from the fjord to Grundfoss waterfall, where a salmon ladder is planned, thereby opening up ano-ther 10 km of ideal spawning grounds, up to Granfoss waterfall. The river is divided into zones. Possibilities are best between Stiklestad and Vuku, but also between Vuku and the Inna outlet in the Verdalselv fishing is quite good at times. In rainy weather the river becomes muddy because of the clay-bed. Everywhere access to the river is easy. Spoons, worms and flies are used.
Centre: Verdal.
Information and permits: For tickets — at reasonable prices — apply to the Ekle, Volen, Vestre Efskind (Auskin) and Øksnes farms.

NORDLAND
In addition to rivers mentioned below we should like to draw your attention to the Drevja. This is a good salmon river, 19 km long, that empties into the Vefsn fjord north of Mosjøen. Fishing is best at the end of June, but it depends upon the water level. Salmon average 2 to 6 lbs. In July and Aug. also sea trout.

BEIARELV river, Beiarn, Beiarn fjord (C 6). This is an interesting river which holds both salmon, sea trout and migratory char. Travel by boat from Bodø to Beiarn in 3 1/2 hours. The road distance from Bodø — ferry Vågan to Skjerstad — to Beiarn (Storjord) is 45 miles. There is a motoring road along the river. Maps: Bodø and 2028 I Beiardalen.
It rises in the neighbourhood of the great Svartisen glacier and receives several tributa-ries before it enters the fjord. The lower part of the river runs calmly over a sandy bottom for several kilometres. Gradually the river becomes more turbulent, forming rapids and pools, until Høgefossen 30 km from the fjord. These falls are an impassable barrier for the salmon. The lower reaches are best, with smooth current and crystal-clear water except when in flood. The upper reaches are cram-med with large boulders, which often make

28

casting difficult. There is no boat fishing. As
the water is often muddy until the end of
July, it is customary to fish with a spoon
until the water clears and then switch to flies.
Salmon starts running in the beginning of
June and continues most of the summer. No
serious fishing takes place before the middle
of June, and fishing is best around the middle
of Aug. Salmon will scale from 6 to 12
pounds. Record salmon caught in the river
weighed 70 pounds. The Beiar is predomi-
nantly a salmon river, but the results wary
greatly from one season to the next. Late in
the summer sea trout run in great numbers.
Average weight 1 pound, record fish 15
pounds. The migratory char usually scale one
pound, but may weigh as much as 7 pounds.
The Arstadåga tributary, only 400 metres
from the confluence to the beautiful Arstad-
foss waterfall, has a fine run of migratory
char and some sea trout. Some migratory
char also enters the Eiteråga tributary but sea
trout rarely. Tollåga is the main tributary of
the Beiar river. The salmon water here is
approx. 3 1/2 km.
Centres: Moldjord and Strand, both with primitive lodgings.
Information and fishing permits: It is said
that the owners (farmers) along the river are
most agreeable to sublet on reasonable terms,
but is difficult to make arrangements in advance. The best idea is to direct
enquiries through the Bodø Tourist Office,
8000 Bodø. Tickets also available at the
Moldjord post office.

ÅBJØRA river, Åbygda, Bindal fjord (C 8).
A good salmon water, also known as river Å,
situated in a beautiful but isolated district.
Travel by coastal express steamer from Bergen to Brønnøysund in 50 hours or from
Trondheim in 14 hours, then approx. 4 hours
by bus to Terråk. The distance by car from
Steinkjer is 124 miles, from Trondheim 200
miles. Map: Bindal.
The Åbjøra is about 15 km long. With one
exception (Nordfoss pool) all fishing is from
boats, of which there are 5 or 6. Excepti-
onally — when the river is very low in
August — there are some pools that can be
fished by wading from shingle banks, but even
then a boat is necessary to reach them. With
normal levels of water, fishing is all with wet
fly. Spinning is not encouraged (nor prawn
fishing), except when the water is too high
and coloured to permit fly fishing. Dry fly for
sea trout may be useful in August. Owing to
water power installations the outlook for the
Åbjøra is uncertain.
Fishing does not start normally till early
June. The larger salmon — up to 20 pounds
— run in June, grilse and small salmon in
July. From July 15, sea trout start to run,

size up to 10 pounds and continue to run
through August, but smaller in size — with
the odd salmon. There is also some migratory
char in the lower reaches of the river. Excellent fjord fishing.
Centre: Terråk.
Fishing permits: Contact Terråk Gjestegård.
The fishery is divided among several owners.
Some of them sell day tickets.

*ELVEGÅRDSELV river, Bjerkvik, Ofot
fjord (C 5).* This river is also known as the
Bjerkvik river and lies on the Nord Cape
road north of Narvik. It is reached in less
than an hour by bus from Narvik, road distance 20 miles. Map: Narvik.
The water is fairly narrow and only 4 km
long, up to lake Hartvik. Open season: June
16—Sept. 30. Salmon run in June — July,
average weight 12 pounds, sea trout in Aug.
Sea trout may weight as much as 3,3 pounds,
but usually smaller.
Centres: Bjerkvik and Narvik.
Information: Narvik Tourist Office, 8500
Narvik. The fishing is owned by local farmers. Acquiring fishing rights in advance is
hardly possible.

*FUSTA river, Mosjøen, Vefsn fjord (B/C
7).* This river lies 9 km north of Mosjøen
which is reached by train from Trondheim in
6 hours. The distance by road from Trondheim to Mosjøen is 255 miles. Maps: Mosjøen and Røsvatn.
The salmon water used to be only 7 km long,
from the fjord to lake Fust. Now the system
holds salmon nearly to lake Luktvatn. Between lake Luktvatn and lake Fust there are
two other lakes, Ømmervatn and Mjåvatn.
Between lake Fustvatn and the fjord the river
flows gently for about 4 km to the Forsmofoss
waterfall, where there is a salmon ladder.
Below the waterfall there is a long, quiet pool
where salmon gather waiting for suitable water condition in the ladder. The rest of the
Fusta down to the fjord is a swift and turbulent river with stony river bed. The salmon
are usually less than 10 pounds.
Centre: Mosjøen.
Information and fishing permits: The best
beats are on long term leases, but as the river
is owned by a number of farmers, it is usually
easy to get to terms on less prominent stretches of the river. Enquiries should be directed
to Helgeland Tourist Office, 8650 Mosjøen.
Day tickets are sold from some camping sites
and by some farmers along the river and
lakes.

*KOBBELV river, Sørfold, Leir fjord (C
5—6).* A salmon water, which may provide
good sport. It flows into Leir fjord, north of
Bodø. Travel by plane from Oslo or Bergen to

Bodø in 1 1/2 — 3 hours and then by bus and ferry to Bonnåsjøen in 3 hours. From here a taxi must be rented to the river's mouth at Elvekroken. Map: Sørfold.

River Kobbelv is 7 km long up to lake Kobbvatn which is 5 km long. It then holds salmon for another 2 km beyond the lake up to Gjerdal waterfall. Among the best salmon spots from the fjord and up are Hammeren, which is a stretch with swift current, and some rapids called Fossen, and another series of rapids named Langfossen, followed by Lenningen pool. There is also a good pool at the confluence with Inderelv and finally a good spot at the outlet from lake Kobbvatn. Salmon start running in June, but fishing is best in July and Aug., when there are salmon of 8 to 10 pounds (record fish 35 pounds). Sea trout occur in Aug. Rumour has it that the record sea trout weighed almost 20 pounds, but the average specimen will be around 2 pounds. Migratory char in large number appear in August.

Centre: Nearest hotel accomodation in Fauske. Fauske Jeger- og Fiskeforening owns a cabin with 6 beds situated on the river below the lake. Provisions must be bought at the nearest local shop or brought along.

Fishing permits and information: Fisheries are divided among a number of owners. Fishing rights may be acquired through the local fishing administration. Enquiries should be directed to Fauske Tourist Office, 8200 Fauske.

RANA river, Mo i Rana, Rana fjord (C 7). The Rana drains a vast network of lakes and rivers through the Dunderland valley and reaches the sea at Mo i Rana. Travel by train from Trondheim to Mo in 7 1/2 hours. The distance by road from Trondheim is 314 miles. Maps: 1927 I (Mo i Rana).

Owing to water power installations and irregular flow of water Rana is an unreliable river. At present it holds salmon between the fjord and the Reinfoss waterfall, a distance of 14 km. A dam has been built across the fall which has reduced the water below it considerably. Between the Reinfoss and the fjord is the Kobbfoss with a salmon ladder. A giant salmon ladder was built at Reinfoss waterfall which is 28 m high, situated 12 km from the fjord. Once hopes were great of converting the Rana above Reinfoss into a fine salmon river. One might well say that these prospects have been considerably dimmed by the Reinfoss dam. Below the Reinfoss there is some salmon, sea trout and migratory char. Salmon will scale from 10 to 20 pounds. Salmon enters the river at the end of July, sea trout in the middle of Aug.

Centre: Mo i Rana.

Information and fishing permits: Day tickets to the Rana are sold by sports shops in Mo i Rana. Enquiries may be directed to Rana Tourist Office, 8600 Mo.

RØSSÅGA river, Korgen, Rana fjord (C 7). The Røssåga flows into the Rana fjord at Røsså which is reached by train from Trondheim in 7 hours. The distance by road from Trondheim to Korgen is 290 miles. Map: Rana.

The Røssåga is regulated by the Røssåga power stations. Below the last power station at Korgen the river has plenty of water. From here to the fjord, a stretch of 14 km, the Røssåga holds a fair amount of salmon. Smooth stream with muddy water. Mainly boat fishing, also some bank fishing.

Centres: Korgen and Bjerka, both with camping huts (not listed in «Hotels in Norway»).

Fishing permits: Available from Korgen camping to some beats in the vicinity.

SALTDALSELV river, Rognan, Skjerstad fjord (C 6). This salmon water includes a great network of rivers. The Arctic Highway and the Nordland railway run parallel with the river between Lønsdal and Saltdal (Rognan) stations, reached by train from Trondheim in 9 1/2 hours. Lønsdal station on the «Artic Circle» lies 13 km south of Storjord. Saltdal railway station lies at the river's mouth. The distance by road from Trondheim to Rognan is 408 miles. Maps: Saltdal and Junkerdal.

The Saltdalselv river is richly endowed with all the trimmings which tend to make a grand salmon water. Practically all fishing is by rod only, but the local sportsmen complain bitterly of the intensive netting which goes on in the narrow sounds of Salta fjord and Skjerstad fjord.

The main *Saltdalselv* river is 40 km long between the fjord and Storjord. The Arctic Highway runs parallel with the river. The current is swift and the water is crystal-clear. The river bed consists of large pebbles. Storjord, where the Saltdal is formed by the confluence of the Junkerdalselv and Lønselv river, is one of the best beats on the river. Salmon proceed for another 5 km in the Lønselv river and approx. 15 km in the Junkerdal river. Bank casting only. The open season extends from June 1 to Sept. 15. The river holds sea trout and migratory char in August.

Centres: Lønsdal, Røkland and Rognan.

Information and fishing permits: The lower reaches from the fjord to Berghulnes bridge are owned by farmers, and locals say it is easy to obtain salmon fishing on the spot. From Berghulnes to Storjord (5 km), the river is state-owned, day tickets are sold by hotels and shops along the river, as well as from the forestry inspector at Storjord, at reasonable prices. Information from Salten Tourist Office, 8200 Fauske.

SKJOMAELV river, Skjom fjord (C 5). This river which is also called Elvegård, lies south of Narvik at the head of the narrow and beautiful Skjom fjord. Travel by bus from Narvik to Elvegård in an hour. The distance by road from Narvik is 22 miles. Map: Skjomen.
The salmon water is 14 km long between the fjord and Lillefall waterfall at Tangen farm. Gravel or stony river bed, sandy in parts, several rapids and pools. Salmon run in June and July, average weight 10 pounds, 32-pounders have been killed. Best fishing in Aug. Usual weight 2—4 pounds, but it is possible to hook six-pounders. To day the Skjomen river is regulated by a power station, and fishing has deteriorated thanks to the low water level.
Centre: Narvik.
Information and fishing permits: The river is owned by a number of farmers. They usually agree to let visitors fish for a day or a week at a reasonable cost. Enquiries may be directed to Narvik Tourist Office, 8500 Narvik.

VEFSNA river, Mosjøen, Vefn fjord (C 7). The Vefsna provides the largest salmon water in the province of Nordland. Travel by train from Trondheim to Mosjøen or Hattfjelldal. Motoring roads makes the Vefsna and its tributaries easily accessible. Maps: Mosjøen and Hattfjelldal.
The *Vefsna itself* holds salmon over a stretch of 44 km, from the fjord to Trofors, but if the various tributaries are added, the total distance is many times more. The river is fairly broad — from 40 to 150 metres — and the current is equally varied. The river bed consists of gravel, pebbles and rocks. The water is generally gin-clear, but is muddy when in flood. The water level can vary up to 1 1/2 metres. There is mainly boat fishing, but bank fishing is feasible in places. Waders are recommended.
There are 3 salmon ladders in the main river between the fjord and Trofors. The lowest ladder lies 16 km from the fjord at Forsjord waterfall (5 m high). Then follows the ladder at Laksfors (15 m high), situated 29 km from the fjord, and the ladder at Fellingsfors (5 m high), situated 42 km from the fjord. The best fishing is between the fjord and Trofors starring such pools as Forsjord and Laksfors. Salmon start running in the Vefsna from approx. May 20. Fishing starts on June 1. Flood conditions may keep the fish away from the ladders at Forsjord and Laksfors, and fishing in the upper parts of the river may be considerably deterred. Salmon only

occur in late June and early July in the uppermost reaches of Vefsna and its tributaries. Some sea trout is caught in the lower parts, near the Vefsn fjord, in Aug. At Trofors, 44 km from the fjord, the Svenningdal river joins the Austervefsna to form Vefsna.
The Austervefsna extends eastwords towards Sweden and holds salmon over a stretch of 47 km between Trofors and the confluence with river Unker. There is a salmon ladder at Storfossen (5 m high), situated 4 km east of Trofors. This salmon water is generally narrower than the main river and the season commences later. All lakes and rivers in this area are good for brown trout.
The *Svenningdal* tributary holds salmon throughout its length of 17 km between Trofors and Brenna. There is a salmon ladder at Storfossen (5 m high), situated 5 km south of Trofoss. The Svenningdal is joined by 2 tributaries at Brenna — the *Vass* which holds salmon up to Kvernfoss waterfall, and the *Holmvass* which holds salmon up to Engifoss waterfall.
Centres: Mosjøen, Trofors and Hattfjelldal.
Information and fishing permits: From the mouth of the river to where the Bjønnåga river joins the Vesna, the municipality of Vefsn owns the east bank of the river and fishing is free for everybody. The middle and best part of the river — between Forsjord and Laksfors is privately owned. The Laksfors fisheries is now owned by Norges Vassdragsvesen (Norway's Hydroelectrical board). Middelthuns gate 29, Oslo 3 with whom the sub-letting of this beat may be negotiated. Inexpensive fishing permits are sold by Fellingfors Gjestgiveri (Guest House) and Esso Petrol Station, Trofors. In the Svenningdal and Austervefsna area (to the Hattfjelldal border), the State owns considerable river stretches to which fishing permits are sold by Nesbrugets Skogforvaltning, Mosjøen or the local forestry inspectors. Fishing permits to state-owned river stretches in Hattfjelldal can be bought from Sør-Helgeland Skogforvaltning, Mosjøen or the local forestry inspectors.

TROMS
LAUKHELLE-LAKSELV, Senja, Solberg fjord (B 4). This is one of the best rivers in Troms. Travel by coastal steamer to Finnsnes from Trondheim in 48 hours. Or by plane from Oslo or Bergen to Bardufoss in a few hours and then by bus to Finnsnes in one hour. The distance by road from Trondheim to Finnsnes is 666 miles. From Finnsnes there is a bridge to Senja. There is a motoring road along the river. Map: Tranøy.
Including the Svanelv river, the Lakselv is 27 km long. It forms a number of lakes and holds salmon, sea trout and migratory char and, of course, trout and red char. In the

Svanelv there are some good beats and pools, for instance Hellevaet and Lillefossen, 3,5 km above Svanelvmo the Svanelv joins the Kaperelv river and forms the Lakselv. Salmon and sea trout run only a few kilometres up the Kaperelv, as far as the Kaperfoss waterfall. The Lakselv drains lake Almenningsvatn, lake Trollbuvatn and lake Hellevatn. The first two lakes are reputed to be very good. There is also a fine beat at the outlet of Hellevatn, called «Kroken». From here down to the Hellefoss waterfall, a distance of a few hundred yards, the river is rather rapid. The Hellefoss is a long waterfall where natural pools for salmon, sea trout and migratory char provide good fishing. After Hellefoss the Lakselv drains lake Mevatn and lake Gamvatn. The rapids between those lakes, a couple of hundred yards, contains well-known pools such as Stenghølla, Langstrokket, Gammelstenget og Albertholla. Between lake Gamvatn and the fjord the river runs slowly and this broad stretch of river is of no particular interest to anglers with the exception of the Sjøfoss waterfall where the river literally jumps into the sea. The salmon season starts in early June when spoons, prawns and worms will do the trick. After Midsummer the fish will take to flies, especially the smaller sizes. The migratory char fishing is considered to be best in the first fortnight of July, but can be quite good later in the season too. Sea trout run in July and especially in Aug. Salmon is seldom heavier than 25 pounds, average weights are 7 to 14 pounds. Sea trout of 6 to 9 pounds occur, but it is much more usual to kill 1 and 2-pounders, and migratory char weights around 1—2 pounds.
Centre: Finnsnes.
Fishing permits: Fishing permits are sold by the owners' association — A/L Lakselva, 9300 Finnsnes — but apart from the lakes there are few beats and there are plenty of anglers around when the fishing is good.

MÅLSELV river, Målselv, Malangen fjord (C 4). This is one of the largest salmon rivers in Arctic Norway, situated on the 69th parallel. Travel by air from Oslo to Bardufoss in a few hours or by coastal express steamer from Trondheim to Finnsnes in 48 hours and then 2 hours by bus to Målselv. Distance by road from Narvik 78 miles, from Trondheim 653 miles. Maps: Målselv and Bardu.
The Målselv is the biggest river in Troms and the best known salmon water. It is a long and broad river with mainly smooth current. The lowest stretch is to deep for fishing. 40 km from the fjord it receives the Bardu tributary, and 1,5 km above the confluence follows the finest beat on the whole river, the Malangsfoss beat, which lies below the famous

Malangsfoss waterfall. A giant salmon ladder was built here in 1910, and this allowed the salmon to proceed to the upper reaches of Målselv. In fact salmon run nearly 70 km above the Målselv system until its stopped by the Divifoss waterfall in the Divielv tributary. This makes the total length of the salmon water 110 km. Some of the other tributaries hold salmon too, but in small numbers. The Barduelv used to be a fine sporting river before the power station at Bardufoss was built. 50-pounders have been killed on the Målselv, but the average is 12 to 15 pounds. Salmon occur already in May, but the big run is later. July is considered to be the best month in the lower reaches and the Malangsfoss pool. There is bank fishing at a number of places, especially in the tributaries and upper reaches, but boat fishing is more usual. Waders are always required. Flies, spoons and prawns are used.
Centres: Bardufoss and Målselv.
Information and fishing permits: The fisheries below the Malangsfoss belong to local owners. Above the waterfall the State owns most of the river as far as Høgskaret in the Dividal valley. There are a few private owners here too. The famous Malangsfoss pool has been leased to a foreign businessman. The Rundhaug Hotel and some private farmers sell day tickets to beats above Malangsfoss, and a limited number of tickets to the State's fisheries are available from the local forestry inspector — Statens Skogforvaltning, 9220 Moen i Målselv.

REISAELV river, Nordreisa, Reisa fjord (C 3). A long and large river, also called Nordreisa, which reaches the fjord at Sørkjos in Nordreisa. Travel by express bus from Narvik (11 hours) or Bardufoss (5 hours) to Sørkjos. Road distance from Trondheim to Sørkjos 729 miles, Narvik 173, Tromsø 122 miles. There is a motoring road along the river from Sørkjos to Bilto, a distance of 54 km. The river is navigable by motor boat right up to Imo waterfall, and several river boats are available for short trips as well as for longer terms. Charges are made according to a fixed tariff which is said to be reasonable. Maps: 1734 III (Reisadalen) and 1733 IV (Raisduoddar-Hal'di') and 1733 I (Mållesjåkka).
The Reisa holds salmon over a stretch of 90 km between the fjord and Imo (or Reisa) waterfall. The salmon water is between 40 and 50 metres wide with varied currents, mainly smooth but rather swift. The river bed consists of rock, pebbles and sand. Very clear water except when in flood. There is boat fishing in the lower parts, but mainly bank fishing in the upper parts. Waders are recommended. The fish will take spoon, fly or

The Vosso river deserves your attention, especially the lower part which is called the Bolstad river. In 1977 the average weight of salmon caught in the Bolstad river was 27 lbs., perhaps the highest in the world as far as Atlantic salmon is concerned.

Photo: Flyspesialisten.

Angling in Norway is a family sport. Anglers are said to form the country's biggest party. There are more than 300,000, and many more if you include sea fishing.

Photo: Thorbjørn Tufte.

The Hardangervidda is a vast mountain plateau — 3,300 to 4,300 ft. above sea level — and divided between the counties of Buskerud, Telemark and Hordaland. The whole plateau lies above the timber-line and is «inhabited» by large herds of wild reindeer. It is also rich in rivers and lakes and offers great possibilities to anglers who are not adverse to hiking to the most rewarding places.

Photo: Torbjørn Tufte.

There are more than 200,000 lakes in the country, plus a multitude of rivers and streams, most of which contain trout. Theoretically there should be a lake or a brook for every angler, but actually they tend to flock to the more popular and easily accessible waters. But it should not be difficult to find lakes which you may enjoy all for yourself.

Photo: Johan Berge.

prawn. The salmon season is usually best from July 10 to August 20. The sea trout season is best during the last week of Aug. in the lower parts, there is not much sea trout in the upper part. An average salmon will scale about 18 pounds early in the season, but considerably less later on. Sea trout of 2 to 4 pounds.

Centre: Sørkjosen.

Fishing permits: The Reisa is privately owned from the fjord and 15 km inland, the following 35 km belong both to the State and private owners, whereas the upper reaches is State property only. Private owners may be approached on the spot and are often willing to come to reasonable terms. The States fisheries have been leased by the local hunting and angling association, Nordreisa Jeger og Fiskerlag. Day tickets, approx. kr. 50 per day, are available at Sørkjos Hotel, Sappen Samvirkelag (co-operative store) and several places along the river.

SALANGSELV river, Sjøvegan, Salang fjord (C 4). River Salangselv lies north of Gratangen, which is reached by bus from Narvik in 1 1/2 hours. Road distance from Trondheim to Gratangen is 573 miles, Bodø 183, Narvik 17, Tomsø 132 miles. Maps: Salangen and Bardu.

The salmon water is 20 km long between the fjord and Langfoss falls. The river is 0,7 km long from the fjord to lake Nervatn which is 1 1/2 km long. Then follows a stretch of 1 1/2 km to lake Øvrevatn which is 2 km long. There is a river stretch of 10 km between the lake and Kistefoss salmon ladder and finally 5 km to Langfoss. There are altogether 5 salmon ladders. Below the Kistefoss falls the Salang river has one of the finest salmon waters in Troms where 42-pounders have been killed. Here — as in most salmon waters in North Norway — the run of big salmon is not what it used to be, whereas there is still a good run of small salmon, sea trout and migratory char. The char will weigh from 2 to 6 pounds. The best season for salmon is late May and June, for sea trout and migratory char July — Aug.

Centre: Sjøvegan.

Fishing permits: The river is privately owned. Fishing permits are available at Sjøvegan.

SIGNALDALSELV river, Storfjord, Lyngen fjord (C 4). It flows into Lyngen fjord at Oteren. Traved by bus from Narvik in (7 hours), Bardufoss (2 hours) or Tromsø (4 hours). Road distance from Trondheim to Oteren 677 miles, Narvik 121, Tromsø 60. There is a motoring road along the river. Map: 1633 III (Signadalen).

The salmon water is 27 km long with, fast current. Bank fishing everywhere although casting is somewhat tricky at several places. The Signaldal holds salmon, sea trout and red char.

Centre: Oteren.

Fishing permits: Tickets are sold locally at Storfjord Samvirkelag (co-op), Kvesmenes.

SKIBOTNELV river, Skibotn, Lyngen fjord (C 4). This water lies immediately north of the Signaldal river. Map: 1633 I (Storfjord). It holds salmon over a stretch of 17 km to Lulle waterfall. The river has undergone changes during recent years and the fishing has deteriorated. The fishing, however, is better than in the Signaldal river.

Centre: Skibotn.

Fishing permits: These are available at Skibotn.

FINNMARK

ALTAELV river, Alta fjord, Finnmark (C 2). Here is one of the best salmon rivers in the world. It drains a network of lakes on the Finnmark mountain plateau and reaches the fjord at Alta. This little village can be reached in 3 hours from Oslo when travelling by air. Otherwise, there is a journey of 4 nights by coastal express steamer from Bergen to Hammerfest and then 5 hours by bus to Alta. The road distance from Oslo by the Arctic Highway is 1,206 miles, Trondheim 860, Narvik 304, Tromsø 243 and Hammerfest 84 miles. Maps: 1834 I (Alta) and 1934 IV (Gargia). The river holds salmon over a distance of 27 1/2 miles. There is no glacial water. Floods are caused by melting snow in springtime, but the river water is warmer than the sea water, which probably makes it easier for the salmon to find the river's mouth. The bed consists of large pebbles and gravel. In the upper reaches, there are also some large boulders. The water is fairly broad and all fishing takes place from boats except in two pools on the Sautso beat, where bank fishing is preferred. The salmon water affords a continuous series of pools and rapids. All pools are ideal for fly fishing. It is a well kept river, where almost fly fishing only is allowed (at certain times also spoons). The season extends from June 1 to Aug. 31. Only people from Alta are allowed to fish in August.

The river is divided into zones with a limited number of rods, in all 6.

(1) *Raipas beat,* 14 km, from the fjord to Jøraholmen. This is the broadest part of the river with several islands and large pools. Both banks are reached by car, only 2—3 km from Alta.

(2) *Jøraholmen beat,* 7,5 km, to Detsika seter, also including the confluence with the Eiby tributary. The road runs almost parallel with the river.

(3) *Vinas beat,* 8 1/2 km, to Battagoski waterfall. The road runs close to the central section of the beat.

(4) *Sandia beat,* 9 km, a narrow stretch from Battagoski and Gilvo rapids to Steinfoss rapids. Access by river boat from Alta (or meet boats by car along river).

(5) *Sautso beat,* 7 km, from Gabo rapids to Langfoss waterfall. The surroundings are rugged but beautiful, with steep mountains and rich vegetation. Access by river boats. When punting upstream, the Gabo rapids cannot be negotiated, and the boats are here hauled overland. Above Gabo, however, the stream is smooth and rowing is possible.

From 1860 to after World War 2, the Alta was fished mainly by British noble families and their friends. Today most of the fishing permits are sold to the people of Alta. The angling rights belong to Alta Laksefiskeri Interessentselskap (owners' ass.), which also administers the river and leases the beats.

Fishing records have been kept for centuries — the oldest known record is dated 1567 — and there are several fantastic tales about giant catches throughout the ages. The heaviest catch ever recorded was made by the Duke of Roxburghe in 1860, when he landed 39 salmon and grilse in one night on the Sandia beat. Fish is not quite so heavy as those of the Tana, Namsen and Årøy rivers, but 50- and even 60-pounders have been landed.

Centre: Alta.

Information and fishing permits: Please direct all enquiries (in good time) to the chairman of Alta Laksefiskeri Interessentskap, Mr. Osvald Møllernes, 9510 Elvebakken. For foreigners there is fishing from June 24 to Aug. 3, and day tickets cost between kr. 150 and kr. 1 500. In addition there are week tickets. What makes the Alta expensive, is the fact that almost everywhere you will need a boat and a boatsman, which is not to be had for less than kr. 500 per day. From the start of the season to Aug. 1 there is fishing between 6 p.m. and noon on the following day, and than there is a 6-hour break for the salmon. Most fish are caught at night, but because of the Midnight Sun it is daylight round the clock. The Eiby river, which flows into the second zone of the Alta, holds salmon for several kilometers. Reasonable day and week tickets are sold from Eiby Kafé.

BERGEBYELV river, Nesseby, Varanger fjord (D 2). This river may now be worth a visit, since it has improved after a salmon ladder was built in 1955 at Bergebyfoss waterfall, 1 km from the fjord. Travel by plane to Kirkenes in 4 hours and go by bus to Varangerbotn in 3 hours. You may also go by coastal steamer from Trondheim to Vadsø,

which lies only 22 miles east of the river. The distance by car — if you should consider it — is staggering: 1349 miles from Oslo. Map: Nesseby.

The Bergeby river is 35 km long with a number of tributaries. The lower part is stony with some rapids. The river bed higher up is sandy with some fine pools. Salmon, sea trout and migratory char run in the lower reaches. The average salmon will scale 6 to 7 pounds. Prawns are forbidden, spoons are permitted, not after July 10 when only flies and worms are allowed. The fishing in best in July — August.

Centre: Vadsø.

Fishing permits: ˙For foreigners there are combined tickets for the Bergebyelv and the Vesterelv. These are available locally and cost approx. kr. 50 per day and kr. 250 per week.

BØRSELV river, Børselv, Porsanger fjord (D 2). It has a great number of tributaries and drains a large part of the Finnmark mountain plateau. Børselv village lies on the Arctic Highway and is reached by bus from Lakselv in 1 hour. Lakselv again is only 4 hours by plane from Oslo. Maps: 2035 I (Børselv) and 2135 IV (Vieksa).

River Børselv is fairly wide but shallow, and the water is clearer than in any Finnmark river. The river bed is white because Børselv runs through chalk formations. It is a fine river with bank casting everywhere. The Børselv is very good for fly-fishing, especially in the upper reaches. Salmon and migratory char will normally not run beyond the Badnitsjakfoss waterfall. Most salmon are killed between Børselv bridge and Aiteråtto. Good pools below the Silfarfoss, where the Vieksa joins the main river, and at Aiteråtto. The best season for salmon is July. After July 31 there is no salmon the river, but sea trout start to run in the middle of Aug. According to locals this sport is good too. Average weight of salmon 15—20 pounds but 25—30 pounders are not rare. Also fine migratory char fishing in August. The char will often take dry flies, or very small wet flies. Usually, small flies (size 2—6 or smaller) are best in all smaller Finnmark rivers. The red char may scale up to 6 pounds, but the average is 2—3 pounds.

Centre: Lakselv.

Fishing permits: Day tickets are available from Samvirkelaget (Co-op), Børselv, approx. kr. 30 per day.

FUTELV river, Gamvik, Skitten fjord (D 1). A small river on the Nordkinn peninsula east of Mehamn. Reached by coastal steamer from Trondheim or Bergen to Mehamn or Gamvik. Or by plane to Mehamn in 6 hours. The Nordkinn peninsula is linked by road and ferry to Highroad 6. The distance by car from Lakselv (see below) to Mehamn is 106 miles, Gamvik 117 miles. Maps: Nordkinn and Hopseidet.

The Futelv offers a good run of migratory char and some salmon. The char may weigh up to 4 pounds and the salmon will scale 9 to 11 pounds.

Centres: Gamvik and Mehamn.

Information and fishing permits: Available from Sør-Varanger Jeger- og Fiskerforening (hunting and angling ass.), 9900 Kirkenes, approx. kr. 50 per day and kr. 250 per week.

GRENSE JAKOBSELV river, Kirkenes, Varanger fjord (E 2). This is Norway's easternmost river which also forms the frontier with Soviet Russia. The distance by car from Kirkenes to the mouth of the river is 40 miles. Kirkenes is reached by plane from Oslo in 4 hours. The distance by road from Oslo 1610 miles. Maps: Jarfjorden and Karpelv.

It is a river which yields good sport and it is rather heavily fished by anglers from Kirkenes. The average weight is 10 to 14 pounds, but heavier fish of up to 25 pounds are landed every summer. The best season is from June 20 to the end of July, but fishing also takes place during August. The water is fairly shallow with a number of fine salmon pools. Bank casting everywhere. There is a very fine salmon pool at the spot where the river from Grensevatn flows into Langvatn. The current is very swift, and strong tackle is required.

Centre: Kirkenes (no accommodation near the river).

Fishing permits: Available at Kirkenes. Only Norwegians are permitted to fish in this border river.

KARPELV river, Kirkenes, Varanger fjord (E 2). A small river, 23 km east of Kirkenes, reached by car. Map: Karpelv.

It holds salmon over a stretch of 18 km with fish of 8 to 10 pounds. Bank casting. Season from mid-June until late August. The salmon season is best in July, sea trout in August.

Centre: Kirkenes.

Fishing permits: The river has been leased by Sør-Varanger Jeger- og Fiskerforening, 9900 Kirkenes. Tickets are sold, approx. kr. 50 per day and kr. 250 per week.

KOMAGELV river, Vardø, Varanger fjord (E 1). A good sporting river between Vadsø and Vardø. Travel by coastal express steamer from Bergen to Vadsø or Vardø and then by bus to the Komag in approx. 1 hour from either town. Or take the plane from Oslo to Kirkenes in 5 hours. Road distance from Trondheim to Vadsø is 1304 miles, to Vardø

1349 miles. Maps: Kiberg, Vadsø and Båtsfjord.

River Komagelv is 45 km long and holds salmon for about 35 km to Øvre Via. There are no waterfalls or rapids of any considerable size. The water is fairly shallow, and after the end of July it is usually feasible to wade across at several points. There are no trees, only a few bushes here and there. There are many fine pools with ideal casting conditions. There is rod fishing with flies or worms only. Not more than 2 flies per line is permitted. Waders and boats are not allowed. No fishing in the Skjærkulpen pool. The salmon is rather small, from 4 to 8 pounds, but there are plenty of them. The season is best between July 10 and August 10. There are very few sea trout, but excellent migratory char fishing in August (often even at the end of July), of a similar kind as in river Børs.

Centres: Vardø and Vadsø (no accommodation but fine camping possibilities on the river).

Fishing permits: The fishery is controlled by the local angling association (Komagvær Fiskerforening). Fishing cards are available from Mr. Benjamin Hagala, 9863 Komagvær.

KONGSFJORDELV river, Berlevåg, Kongsøy fjord (D 1). A good sporting river on the northern fringe of the Varanger peninsula. Travel by coastal steamer from Trondheim or Bergen to Berlevåg. Or take the plane from Oslo to Berlevåg in 5 1/2 hours and go by bus to Kongsfjord or Berlevåg. The distance by car from Trondheim to Berlevåg is 1347 miles. Map: Tana.

8 km from the fjord there are two waterfalls. Before 1958 only few salmon passed this barrier, but after salmon ladders were built in 1958 some fish have run further up the river. The best beats on the Kongsfjordelv are between the waterfalls and the sea. The river holds a fair amount of salmon, some trout and offers a fine run of migratory char. Salmon will scale from 8 to 16 pounds, but much bigger fish have been killed. The average weight of the migratory char is 1 pound. Rod fishing only. Spoons permitted.

Centre: Berlevåg. No accommodation on the river but fine camping possibilities.

Fishing permits: The fishery is controlled by the local hunting and angling association — Berlevåg Jakt- og Fiskerforening, 9980 Berlevåg — and tickets are sold in Berlevåg and by the river warden, approx. kr. 40 per day.

LAKSELV river, Lakselv, Porsanger fjord (D 2). A large river which joins the fjord at Lakselv village. Travel by plane from Oslo to Lakselv in 4 hours. Or go by coastal steamer

to Hammerfest from Trondheim and then take a bus to Lakselv in 3 1/2 hour. The distance by road from Trondheim is 1000 miles. Maps: 2035 III (Lakselv) and 2034 IV (Skoganvarre).
River Lakselv holds salmon over a stretch of 32 km, from the fjord to Savnja waterfall. A tributary called Vuolajokka also holds salmon. Between Nedrevatn lake and Revfossnes, a distance of approx. 5 km, the difference in height is 132 ft., the rest of the river combines rapids with smooth water. Dense vegetation along the banks makes casting difficult, but the Lakselv is navigable by riverboat. Extensive netting and indiscriminate rod fishing has reduced the sporting values of the Lakselv. The river holds some salmon, which on the average will scale 7 to 22 pounds, but 68-pounders have been killed. Variable runs of sea trout and migratory char. Best salmon season at the end of June and beginning of July. Sea trout and migratory char in Aug.—Sept.
Centre: Lakselv.
Fishing permits: Day tickets, approx. kr. 50, are sold by Banak Hotel, Lakselv Gjestgiveri and Greiners Sport, Lakselv.

LANGFJORDELV Langfjorddalen (D 1). The upper reaches of the river is reached on foot from Highway 6 between Ifjord and Vestertana. The river flows into the Lang fjord (a branch of the Tana fjord), and the salmon run is approx. 14 km. Only a few pools, but good angling all the same. A fine river for salmon, biggest fish on record 36 lbs. Migratory char in great numbers. Fishing is best from the end of June to Sept. 1.
Information and fishing permits: The river has been leased by Gamvik Sportsfiskerforening (local angling ass.). Reasonable tickets are available in Gamvik, Mehamn and from the river warden. Spoons are allowed to July 1. After that date flies and worms only.

MUNKELV river, Neiden, Munk fjord (E 2). A minor salmon river 20 miles west of Kirkenes. Travel by plane to Kirkenes in 4 hours and by bus to the river in 1/2 hour. The distance by road from Oslo to Kirkenes is 1561 miles. Map: Svanvik.
The Munkelv in Norway is 15 km. There is another 20 km of the river in Finland. It can hardly be recommended for salmon fishing, but is does afford some good sea trout fishing, particularly at the river's mouth. The best sea trout season is from mid-August and onwards, when sea trout of 3—4 pounds are landed with dry or wet flies.
Centres: Kirkenes or Neiden (5 miles west of the river).
Fishing permits: Mikkola's Kafé.

NEIDENELV river, Neiden, Neiden fjord (E 2). Travel: See Munkelv above. Map: Neiden.
Approx 27 km of the Neiden river lies in Norway. The river is broad and shallow in many places and alternates between rapids and pools and smooth water. The lowest part flows parallel with the highroad. From the Kobbfoss waterfall to St. George's Chapel boats are used, otherwise bank casting only. Rod fishing is not permitted between the bridge and the Skoltefoss ridge. The Käppällää pool below the Skoltefoss waterfall is netted by the locals. This fishing starts around Midsummer. The usual week-ban applies to the Käppällää fishing.
From June 1 to approx June 25 there is fishing between the Kobbfoss and Skoltefoss waterfalls. After that day the river may be fished to the Finnish border. Usually big salmon enters the river first, smaller fish somewhat later. Average weight is 10—27 lbs, 35 to 45-pounders have been killed. With the exception of the Käppällää fishing only rod fishing is permitted. In the Skoltefoss only flies and rods of minimum 10 ft. Prawns and worms are not allowed in the Neiden. Moreover only local boats may be used. An unlimited number of day tickets are sold, valid from 1800 to 1600 hours the following day.
Centres: Neiden and Kirkenes.
Fishing permits: Neidenelvas Fiskefellesskap — the local fishing co-operative — controls the fishery. Tickets are available from Neiden Camping, Neiden Fjellstue and O. M. Abrahamsen, Neiden. Day tickets cost approx. kr. 125. Prices and regulations can be changed every year.

ORDOELV river, Båtsfjord, Sylte fjord (D 1). An attractive river also known as Vesterelv or Syltefjordelv. Travel by coastal steamer from Trondheim or Bergen. Or take the plane from Oslo to Berlevåg in 5 1/2 hours and go by bus to Båtsfjord or Syltefjord. The distance by car from Trondheim to Syltefjord is 1343 miles. There is a motoring road along the lower third of the river. From the main road at lake Magistervatn there is a local road to lake Ordovatn. Map: Båtsfjord.
From lake Ordo to the fjord the length is 38 km. The river runs smoothly with many pools. Down to the confluence with Skogåselv the river is usually called Ordoelv, between this point and the sea Vesterelv or Syltefjordelv is the more common name. For most of its course the river bed is dark, but the last 3 km before fjord the river bed is sandy and light. At the mouth the river widens into lake Syltefjordvatn. The Ordo holds a fair amount of salmon and migratory char, both can run as far as lake Ordovatn. Unlike the salmon,

the migratory char also run in the tributaries. Salmon will scale from 3 to 12 pounds, the average migratory char nearly 2 pounds. The sea trout run does not amount to much. Best fishing season: July—Aug. Rod fishing only. *Centre:* Båtsfjord (23 miles west of the river). Good camping conditions along the river.

Fishing permits: Ordo Fiskerforening, 9990 Båtsfjord controls the river, which is mostly State property. Tickets are available from among others Båtsfjord Materialhandel and Båtsfjord sports shop. Day tickets cost approx. kr. 30, in addition kr. 30 must be deposited. At lake Ordovatn, where red char fishing is fine, tickets can be bought from the warden.

REPPARFJORDELV river (C 2). Here is a good salmon river, well looked after. Travel by coastal express steamer from Bergen or Trondheim to Hammerfest in 1 1/2 hours, or by plane to Alta in 3 hours and then 2 hours by bus to Skaidi. Road distance from Trondheim is 1300 miles, Oslo 946 miles. Maps: Repparfjord, Komagfjord and Stabbursdal. The Arctic Highway runs parallel with the river.

The Repparfjord drains a network of lakes on the Porsanger peninsula, and the salmon water is 45 km long. Until 1956, the salmon stopped at Aisaroaivve waterfall, 25 km from the fjord, but now that the salmon ladder is functioning the stretch beyond the waterfall has turned out the best part of the river. The water is fairly shallow and the current is swift. There are few pools and many rapids. Waders are essential. When the river is flooded, casting may be difficult. There are some wooden bridges to facilitate crossing from one side to another. The open season lasts from June 1 to Aug. 31, the proper fishing season from June 20 to Aug. 15. There are salmon of about 12 pounds with some heavier fish of up to 40 pounds, but there are practically no sea trout.

This river has been supervised by Vest-Finnmark Fiskerforening of Hammerfest since 1928. This is a very active angling club with many keen members. By joining hands with experts, they have succeeded in weeding out netting. Only rod fishing is allowed. It is illegal to use a spinning rod and it is forbidden to fish from boat or bridge. The fishing card is valid for the whole river. There are a few private pools in the lowest 5 km, but only on one bank.

Centre: Skaidi.

Fishing permits and information: Visitors are advised to book both fishing and lodging well in advance. Bookings should be directed to Skaidi Gjestehus 9626 Skaidi. Day tickets cost approx. kr. 50.

RISFJORDELV river, Gamvik, Nordkinn (D 1). This is a good little river which deserves further exploration. Travel: See Futelv river, page 37. From Gamvik by motor boat to the river's mouth at Risfjord. Map: Hopseidet.

The river is only 3,5 km long, but it holds a fair amount of salmon. 7 to 8 fine pools, stony river bed with moss. Salmon will scale from 6 to 10 pounds, record salmon weighed 25 pounds. Good runs of sea trout and migratory char which go as far as lake Koifjordvatn. When the tide is in, the mouth of the river is enlarged and one can watch the salmon entering the river. Spoons are allowed before July 1, after that fly fishing and worms only. Best season: Midsummer to the end of August.

Centre: Gamvik. Camping along the river is feasible.

Fishing permits: The river is controlled by a local angling club, Gamvik Sportsfiskerforening, and day tickets approx. kr. 35, are available at Mehamn (Sigurd Fermann) and Gamvik.

SANDFJORDELV river, Gamvik, Nordkinn (D 1). This river runs parallel with the Fut river and enters the sea at Sand fjord. Travel: See Futelv, page 37. The road between Mehamn and Gamvik runs across the river mouth. Maps: Nordkinn and Hopseidet.

The Sandfjordelv is approx. 30 km long with several pools. The river bed is stony and the current is rapid. Fishing is not allowed in the Sandfjordfoss waterfall, and the pool below it, during the summer. There are a fair number of salmon in the river, weighing from 2 to 17 pounds. Spoons are allowed before July 1, after that date fly fishing and worms only. Fishing is best from Midsummer to the end of July.

Centre: Gamvik.

Fishing permits: The river is controlled by Gamvik Sportsfiskerforening, 9975 Gamvik. Day tickets — approx. kr. 35 — are available at Mehamn (Sigurd Fermann) and Gamvik.

SANDNESELV river, near Kirkenes, Langfjord. Travel by boat from Bergen or Trondheim to Kirkenes or by plane from Oslo in 4 hours. Distance by road from Oslo 1575 miles. Map: Svanvik.

This river is 12 km long from lake Sandnesvatn to the fjord. The river drops 275 ft. between the lake and fjord and forms several rapids and a few long pools. The river is under cultivation. Salmon fry and fingerlings have been planted annually since 1953. Very few salmon, but the sea trout fishing is quite good.

Centre: Kirkenes.

Fishing permits: The river is controlled by

Sør-Varanger Jeger- og Fiskerforening, 9900 Kirkenes. Fishing cards — approx. kr. 25 per day — are available through Kirkenes Tourist Office.

SKALLELV river, Vadsø, Varanger fjord (E 1). This river enters the sea 20 miles east of Vadsø, or 7 miles west of the Komagelv river. Travel: See Komagelv, page 38. Highroad 98 between Vadsø and Vardø runs across the mouth of the river. Map: 2435 II (Ekkerøy). The Skallelv is approx. 25 km long. 5 km from the fjord it is joined by the Ridelv tributary. The river holds only a few salmon above this point, but in the Ridelv tributary salmon run as far as lake Vasavatn. The migratory char run as far as Skallelvskaret in the main river, and to lake Vasavatn in the Ridelv. The river holds very few sea trout in the open season, but some are caught in spring at the outlet. Both the Skallelv and the Ridelv are good, sporting rivers with several rapids and enticing pools. Prawns are forbidden, spoons are allowed up to July 10, after that fly fishing and worms only. The best fishing occurs in July and Aug.
Centre: Vadsø. Fine camping possibilities near the outlet of Skallelv.
Fishing permits: This river is controlled by Skallelv og Vadsø Jeger- og Fiskerforening. Day tickets — kr. 25 — available from Skallelv Samvirkelag (Co-op) on the spot, Leif Bjerk, Vadsø and Vadsø Hotel.

STABBURSELV river, near Lakselv, Porsanger fjord (C 2). A long and smooth river on the west side of Porsanger fjord. The Arctic Highway leads across the river's mouth, 7 miles North of Lakselv. Travel: See Lakselv, page 38. Map: Stabbursdalen.
Salmon, sea trout and migratory char run to the Stabburfoss waterfall, where a salmon ladder has been built. This ladder has added another 15 km of ideal spawning ground to the river. Best salmon season end of June — beginning of July, sea trout and char in Aug.—Sept.
Centre: Lakselv.
Fishing permits: Day tickets, approx. kr. 50, available from hotels in Lakselv and the camping site by Stabburselv bridge.

STORELV river, Kunes, Lakse fjord (D 2). The Arctic Highway runs along this river for miles on end. Kunes at the river's mouth lies 55 miles east of Lakselv. Travel: See Lakselv, page 38. Maps: 2135 I (Adamsfjord), 2135 II (Ullugaissa), 2135 III (Retkajakskaidi) and 2135 IV (Vieksa).
The Storelv or river Kunes, as it is often called, drains the Finnmark mountain plateau, and consequently the season is later than in most other Finnmark rivers. There is

salmon after July 10 and sea trout after Aug. 1. It holds salmon up to the suspension bridge where the Arctic Highway crosses the river. A fine salmon pool is located just below the bridge.
A fairly small river east of Kunes — the Østerelv river — holds no salmon, but is said to yield fair sea trout during late June and all of August.
Centre: Kunes (primitive accommodation).
Fishing permits: Fishing cards are available locally.

TANA river, Tana, Tana fjord (D 2—3). River Tana with a great network of tributaries is a real tourist attraction on its own merit. It forms the most extensive salmon water in the whole of Norway and covers a distance of approx. 320 km or 200 miles. If all tributaries are included, the total length is over 800 km or 500 miles. The Tana is known outside Norway for the giant salmon caught here. The world record was set in the Tana in 1929 when an 81-pounder was landed. In the fifthies some 75-pounders were killed, and in recent years 50-pounders have quite often been caught.
Travel by plane from Oslo to Lakselv in 4 hours and then by bus to Karasjok in 2 hours. Or by plane to Kirkenes in 4 hours and bus to Skipagurra in 3 hours or Levajok in approx. 6 hours. The distance by road from Trondheim to Karasjok is 1060 miles, to Skipagurra 1130 miles and to Levajok 1190 miles. Maps: Tana, Nesseby, Polmak, Bievra, Rastigasissa, Halkkavarre and Karasjok. For parts of the river also newer 1:50 000 maps are available.
Salmon fishing. In spite of the great output of salmon in river Tana, most of it is caught by netting — legally or illegally. Probably less than 10 per cent of the total catch is landed by rod. There is bank casting and boat fishing. Waders are generally required. The stream is swift and requires heavy tackle. The river bed mostly consists of pebbles. The salmon start running at the end of May and go on to the end of Aug. Fishing is best from June 10—15 to the beginning of July, and in the beginning of Aug. But flood conditions affects these periods. Moreover fishing in the lower reaches start much earlier than in the upper parts.

Fishing places on the Tana.
As the whole river is available to anybody who has bought a fishing card, there are no fixed beats. Visitors are only permitted to fish with rod and handline from the bank at following places: The river's estuary, the upper part of the Storfossen rapids, the Aile rapids and Matinköngäs (in compliance with the notice boards here), the Anarjokka river

above Matinköngäs and the whole of the Skiettjamjokka river. Elsewhere boat fishing only. Trolling is allowed only from boats registered in the Tana valley. Below is a list of promising beats from a sportsman's point of view:

(1) *Rustefjelbma.* This is a small village on the Arctic Highway, about 14 km up river. There are not many salmon but quite good sea trout fishing at the river mouth, with specimens of up to 4—6 pounds. From the estuary to Langnes it is not allowed to use rods and handlines between July 14 and Sept. 1. Above Langnes fishing starts on June 1 and continues to Sept. 1. Fishing is best between June 15 and July 20. A motoring road leads along the river right to the fjord.

(2) *Tana bridge* is a popular fishing place for salmon. The Arctic Highway runs across the bridge which lies 23 km above Rustefjelbma and 5 km below Skipagurra.

(3) *Skipagurra* is a small village where the Arctic Highway turns away from the river.

(4) *Polmak* lies 18 km above Skipagurra, near the Finnish frontier, which is marked by cairns on either side.

(5) *Nedre Storfoss* is a series of rapids, some 8 km long. A very good spot for rod fishing. This is where the heaviest salmon are landed. Several Norwegian and Finnish anglers are usually encamped here.

(6) *Sirma* lies 17 km above Nedre Storfoss. So great is the river here that the only fishing method is to harl, although bank fishing is possible at one or two places. The fishing is best during the last week in June and the first three weeks in July. Most fish are caught on large spoons by harling in June. But fly also fishes well later on in July and August.

(7) *Øvre Storfoss*, also called the Aile rapids, consists of three series of rapids which cover a stretch of 5 km and affords some fine salmon fishing.

(8) *Levajok* is a well-known fishing centre on the Tana with its own fishing school. However, it lies rather far up the river for salmon in the early season.

The rapids may be fished from the banks, otherwise boat fishing is the usual way. Above Port there is not much salmon.

Tributaries to the Tana.
Fishing cards for the Tana also apply to most of the tributaries. Sportsmen from abroad, however, are not permitted to fish in the tributaries with the exception of the Karasjokka below the Jiesjokka. Here are some of the tributaries:

(a) *Maskejokka* (Rapp) *tributary* is a smallish river of 30 km, which joins the Tana 15 km above Rustefjelbma. Only rod fishing is allowed, although it is fairly well known that illegal netting often takes place. There are

many fine pools. The Arctic Highway leads across river Masjok near the confluence with Tana.

(b) *Dunkratt tributary* joins river Maskejokka and affords particularly good fishing below a waterfall of 15 ft. where there are nearly always some big salmon.

(c) *Lavsejokka* (Laksejokka) *tributary* joins the Tana just above the Storfoss rapids. It holds small-sized salmon of about 8 pounds. It also has a good run of sea trout in August. This river provides some entertaining rod fishing, particularly below a waterfall higher up. Fishing cards for Tana do not apply to Lavsejokka.

(d) *Levajokka tributary* is a river which reaches the Tana near Levajok Fjellstue. It is a fast river with several fine pools of crystal-clear water.

(e) *Anarjokka tributary.* From the confluence with river Karasjokka, the main river is no longer called Tana, but is named Anarjokka. It holds salmon over a stretch of 150 km from the confluence and up. There is some good salmon fishing on both sides of the bridge which carries the road into Finland and lies 23 km east of Karasjok. Fishing cards for Tana also apply to Anarjokka.

(f) *Karasjokka tributary* holds salmon over a stretch of 120 km. It runs through Karasjok, which is one of the Lapp villages in Arctic Norway.

(g) *Jiesjokka tributary* joins river Karasjokka, the confluence being 15 km west of Karasjok. It holds salmon over a considerable distance right up to lake Jiesjavre. Some good salmon fishing takes place from Assebakte seter which lies just below the confluence, and up the Jiesjokka. There is mainly bank fishing, but also boat fishing. The season is from June 15 to Sept. 1, but June and July are best. There is salmon of 5 to 40 pounds and the average weights is said to be 20 pounds.

Centres: Rustefjelbma, Skipagurra, Levajok and Karasjok. Polmak and Sirma are not listed in «Hotels in Norway».

Fishing permits: The river is stateowned and tickets are sold by the local bailiffs, petrol stations, local shops, hotels, guest houses, camping sites as well as by the river wardens. There are 2 different tickets: Yellow cards for the Norwegian salmon water and green cards where the river forms the boundary with Finland. For Norwegians the yellow card also covers the Norwegian tributaries. Day tickets cost approx. kr. 75 for Norwegians and kr. 150 for foreigners. Prices can be adjusted every second year.

VESTRE JAKOBSELV river, Vadsø, Varanger fjord (D 2). This promising river lies 11 miles west of Vadsø. Travel: See Komagelv river, page 38. Map: Vadsø.

In the lower reaches of Jakobselv, 3 to 10 km from the river's mouth, there are 4 waterfalls. In all 7 salmon ladders have been built allowing the fish to enter the upper reaches. But they have not quite had the desired effect. Below the First waterfall (literally called First Fall) there are some fine pools, also between the Second waterfall and Jakobselv-kroken (where the river turns) large and small pools are found. In the tribuary Nedre Flintelv there is a waterfall 2 km up the river. Jakobselv holds a fair amount of sal-mon considering that only the lower 3—4 km contain salmon. There are not many sea trout or migratory char. Prawns are forbidden. Spoons are allowed to July 10, after that date flies and worms only. Best season is July—August.

Centre: Vadsø.

Information and fishing permits: Most of the river is administered by the fishing and hunting association of Vestre Jakobselv and Vadsø. Tickets are sold both in Vadsø and Vestre Jakobselv.

TROUT AND OTHER FRESHWATER SPECIES

Norway has excellent natural conditions for most kinds of flyfishing. There are more than 200,000 lakes in the country, plus a multitude of rivers and streams, most of which contain trout or other fish of interest to the angler. In numerous parts of the country good fishing can be had for very little financial outlay, but in the more obvious spots competition may be heavy. On the other hand the area included in a fishing permits is generally large, and away from the beaten track there are good chances of satisfactory catches. Stocks of fish in many waters are not very large, but for the fisherman compensation can often be found in the good average quality and size of the fish caught in these areas, and in the fact that they are very active at certain times of the year.

The influence of weather conditions and water levels is of more importance in Norway than further south. A late spring and a cold or rainy summer can make fishing, especially fly fishing, a difficult and chancy sport for much of the season, even if there are plenty of fish in the waters. It is therefore important for the angler to be able to vary his technique accordingly.

Seeking out the best waters and judging them for the best sport and the right technique will be an important part of your fishing holiday in Norway. The possibilities are legion.

Trout fishing is best for the sportsman in the mountainous areas close to and above the timber line. The quality and the size of the fish in the lakes and rivers of these areas are usually better than fish from the lower-lying country. Almost all the higher-lying lakes and rivers have only trout, but with some char in certain places. The height of the timber line varies, of course, quite considerably, more or less in keeping with the latitude of the area. Thus in Southern Norway it usually varies from an altitude of 1,800 to 3,300 ft., in Nordland (a northerly county, which is cut by the Polar Circle), trees don't grow much above 1,200 ft., and in the far north, in Finnmark county, trees give up the struggle at 600 ft. or even less. The further north you travel the better the trout fishing waters in lower-lying areas.

The massive Langfjellene (the Long Mountains) mountain formation which runs from just above Kristiansand (the Setesdal uplands) in the very south of the country all the

way, in a continuous chain, to the north-east of Røros (the Sylene Range) provides the best fishing waters in the southern part of Norway. In this area lie the lakes and rivers of the valleys of Østerdalen, the Gudbrandsdal, Valdres and Hallingdal (Bergen Railway) with tributary valleys, in the northerly reaches the Femund area and westwards the Hardanger mountain plateau. The mountain areas between the Østerdal and Gudbrandsdal valleys have few lakes or rivers. Generally, fishing is best in the lakes and rivers which lie a little off the beaten track.

Trout fishing in the lower-lying areas of Southern Norway is, generally speaking, a chancy game. But there are a number of forest lakes with mixed stocks of trout and perch which offer the angler attractive fishing. The Østerdal valleys, moreover, have in various places good stocks of trout as low as 1,200 to 1,800 ft. and the major rivers of this area offer good sport. In the other main valleys fishing is undoubtedly better at higher altitudes, but there is always the chance of big fish in some reaches of the rivers.

Along the South Coast (Sørlandet), there is a multitude of lakes, both large and small, but the fish are small and often of poor quality. Moreover pollution — sulphurous downfall from abroad — has greatly affected the area and killed the fish in many rivers and lakes. In the low-lying waters of the Fjord Country (Western Norway) there is often plenty of small trout of inferior quality, but here also the higher-lying lakes offer excellent sport.

The mountain areas of Trøndelag offer mostly good fishing, and in the most northerly parts of this county and in North Norway in general are to be found some of Norway's best finshing districts. There are fewer small trout even in the low-lying waters. In the mountain lakes the char often run to considerable size. There are good fishing lakes also along the coast, but the best areas for trout fishing are near the Swedish border. The word Finnmarksvidda, the Finnmark plateau, sounds especially sweet in a fisherman's ear. Here, even today, can be found lakes and rivers seldom, if ever, visited by people, and offering really splendid sport. Naturally such waters are becoming rarer and, in most cases, they are found far off the beaten track.

Fishing seasons.
The time of the year when you will get best results and greatest enjoyment from your fishing depends very much on where you have thought of doing your fishing and what kind of fish you are after. Ordinary trout fly fishing in the low-lying waters of the South Coast (the most southerly areas) and in the Fjord country opens as early as April, and fishing is at its best in May and June. The water here often becomes too warm in the middle of the summer for good fishing, especially in Sørlandet. The fishing improves again in the autumn and the season closes in September. A general rule for trout fly fishing in Southern Norway is that it is seldom good before June. This is also true of the forest tracts of Østlandet (the eastern counties), and the waters of the valleys which lie below about 1,200 ft. A general «dead» period in all these waters normally occurs in July. Then comes an upswing again in August, and in normal summers the season ends about the 15th September. If you want to fish in waters lying higher than 1,200 ft. then you would do best to wait until after 15th June. In the mountain waters, i.e. lakes and rivers more than 2,400 ft. above sea level, the fishing season is normally reckoned to run from 15th July to 30th August, but there are, of course, exceptions to this rule too.
Good fly fishing cannot be expected in North Norway before about 1st July and often not before 15th July. The higher the altitude and the further north you go the later you must wait before the fishing seasons opens. If you are travelling to Finnmark for the sole pleasure of trout fishing it would be wise to wait until August.

Tackle.
Both glass fibre and split bamboo are used as material for rods and may prove equally good according to personal taste. Norwegian split bamboo rods are recommended. They are just as good as more expensive rods made in other countries. Rods between 8 1/2 and 9 1/2 ft. will prove adequate for flyfishing in most Norwegian rivers and lakes. Double tapered lines are preferred to forward tapered lines by Norwegian anglers who still stick to silk lines. Leaders ought to be of nylon to provide maximum strength, and reels — though light — should have a capacity of 30 yards of double tapered line and 50 yards of backing. With this kind of equipment one can use wet or dry flies, nymphs and other imitations, streamers and worms. Some flies have turned out so well in Norway that they have become all-rounders. They include the following wet flies: Butcher, Coachman, Dusty Miller, Greenwells Glory, Heggeli, March Brown, March Brown Silver, Red Tag, Teal and Red, Wickhams Fancy, Zulu Silver and do not forget Silver Doctor and Black Zulu. Dry flies: Black Ant, Black Grant, Brown Ant, Butcher, Coachman, Coch y Bondhu, Greenwells, Quill, Humla, March Brown Silver, Red Quill and Tups Indispensable. The usual size for wet flies is 10, but size 8 is considered better at night, and size 12 when trout are easily scared. Size 12 is the usual dry fly.

Fishing rights.
As already mentioned all persons over the age of sixteen years wishing to fish for any species of fresh-water fish must pay a fishing duty to the State. This duty amounts to N. kr. 30 and is payable at all post offices. A great many tourist offices, hotels, travel agents and persons issuing local fishing permits, also sell National fishing licences.
In addition to the compulsory licence persons wishing to fish in Norway must obtain a local permit. Rates vary, and are shown for each locality. In the case of trout fishing the price is not as accurate a guide to quality as it is for salmon fishing. Some of the best trout fishing in the country is very inexpensive though, this will generally involve trekking on foot a dozen miles or so.
At all the places mentioned in these pages fishing rights can be bought or arranged without difficulty. A general review of arrangements governing fishing rights may, however, be useful to the tourist.
In addition to privately owned rivers and lakes there are large areas owned by the state common ground, the rural common ground, private common ground or various forms of purely private cooperative ownership. Where there is a private monopoly of fishing rights, individual agreement must be made with the owner. In the inland districts many private owners or associations of owners issue fishing permits. If permits are not issued, then a special agreement must be made with the owners.
In rural common grounds non-locals may only fish in the waters owned by the common ground if fishing permits are issued to them, in the same way as in private common grounds and jointly owned waters.
In the purely state owned tracts (most of the larger areas lie in the north) fishing permits are normally issued. A very large part of Finnmark county is state property. Here all Norwegian citizens, under the terms of the law, are nominally entitled to fish free of charge.
Non-Norwegians can obtain fishing permits in the same way as Norwegian citizens from private owners, in the rural common grounds and in private common grounds and co-operatively owned waters.

Fishing Regulations.
The most usual provisions in the fishing regulations are the fixing of the closed season, a ban on the use of specified gear, or of specified ways of using fishing gear, plus rules as to minimum size (usually 8" to 10"). The most usual closed season is from some time in September until the end of October or beginning of November; fairly frequently fishing is closed from the middle of September to the middle or end of October. But there are many exceptions, and in some places the closed season begins as early as August and lasts till late spring.
As regards the ban on the use of certain equipment, what is of greatest interest to anglers is the tendency to prohibit the use of spinners.
In addition to the public regulations, private owners and fishing boards may fix special rules applicable to their local districts.

Other freshwater species.
The Trout Fishing section includes such freshwater species as red char, grayling, gwyniad, pike and perch. Red char resembles trout, tastes as good, and will rise just as readily to your fly. Moreover in regulated waters, where trout fishing has deteriorated, red char is often more plentiful than ever. The grayling is a very game fish, though not as sporting as trout. In Scandinavia perch and pike are often taken on a spoon or spinner, or on a hook baited with a worm. Live fish is not allowed as bait in Norway.

How to use this part of the booklet.
The information contained in the Trout Fishing section is arranged by counties and rural municipialities. Under the respective municipialities fishing areas are described. The centres from which these areas can be fished and places where fishing permits can be bought are also listed. Quite a few of the centres included in the following pages are mountain lodges accessible on foot only. These are not postal addresses and will not accepted advance bookings. Only a few are included in Norway Travel Association's «Hotel prices in Norway».
The prices of fishing permits are constantly altered and always upwards. In this book we have therefore often used the expression "reasonable" to indicate that a ticket costs less than kr. 25 per day or kr. 50 per week. Often, in fact, they cost considerably less.

OSLO

Oslo — Norway's capital — is a separate county and also a municipality. In the wooded hills called Oslomarka stretching for miles behind Oslo there are a number of woodland lakes which offer quite good fishing. In most of the 250 lakes fishing is permitted. Great quantities of fry are produced and lakes are stocked by the Oslomarka Fishing Administration. The annual catch is estimated to approx. 6 metric tons. Fishing is considered to be middling, with periods of excellent fishing in between.

NORDMARKA, Kobberhaughytta area (D 12). Suburban tram from Oslo to Frognerseteren in 3/4 hours. On foot 6 miles along marked path to Kobberhaughytta. Map: Oslo Nordmark.
Fishing in the lakes Kopperhaugtjern, Blankvatn, Øyvatn, Fiskeløstjern, Sulutjern, South end of Bjørnsjøen and Skjærsjødammen. The stock of fish in Oslomarka is well managed, but fishing demands skill because the lakes are heavily fished. Fish are mediumsized, averaging from 6 to 10 ounces, but each year big fish are caught in most lakes. The lakes are well suited for fly fishing. The fishing is done from the banks. Seasons is from the end of May to the end of August.
Centres: Kobberhaughytta (forest lodge) or Oslo. Booking for Kobberhaughytta at Speidersport, Stortingsgt. 12, Oslo.
Fishing permits: Oslomarkas Fiskeadministrasjon's fishing permit is available at Kobberhaughytta and sports shops in Oslo, kr. 30 per season.

NORDMARKA, Kikutstua area (D 12). Suburban tram to Frognerseteren and 3 hours on foot along marked path. By bicycle from Sørkedalen school in 1 1/2 hours. A bicycle is very useful for anglers in Nordmarka. Cars are not allowed in Oslomarka. Bicycles may be hired from Gresvig A/S, Storgt. 20, Oslo. Map: Oslo Nordmark.
Fishing in parts of Bjørnsjøen and Fyllingen and in a number of smaller lakes near by. Boats may be rented in Bjørnsjøen at Kikutstua.
The stock in Bjørnsjøen and in East and West Fyllingen is trout. In these lakes there is a chance of catching fairly large fish. (See also under Kobberhaughytta.)
Centres: Kikutstua (forest lodge) or Oslo. Booking for Kikutstua at Skiforeningen, Skippergt. 40, Oslo.
Fishing permits: Oslomarka Fiskeadministrasjon's fishing permit is available at Kikutstua and sports shops in Oslo, kr. 30 per season.

KROKSKOGEN, Løvlia area (D 12). Krokskogen is actually part of the county of Buskerud, but for recreational purposes it belongs to Oslomarka. Bus from Oslo to Åsa in 2 hours, and 2 1/2 hours walk to Løvlia. Many of the Krokskogen lakes can be reached

Quite a few Norwegian hotels offer free fishing to resident guests. Hotels which provide such facilities are mentioned under the rivers and fishing areas in this guide. Our picture shows Seljestad on the E 76 in the Hardanger area.

Photo: Mittet.

Finnmark is sprinkled with lakes and criss-crossed with rivers. Facilities for anglers are probably more varied here than anywhere else in Western Europe. But there are few roads in this enormous wilderness. Sportsmen must be prepared for long walks and exciting trips by river boat. This photo is from Skoganvarre on Highway 96 between Lakselv and Karasjok.

Photo: Røstad.

The Skaitielv river is a tributary of the Junkerelv which joins the Lønselv to form the mighty Saltdal river. All this happens in North Norway, just north of the Arctic Circle. The Junkerdal is known for its luxurious vegetation and wild beauty. This guide-book contains no description of the Skaitielv, but it looks worth trying.

Photo: Svendsen.

The Engerdal and lake Femund regions attract anglers. Most of the waters are situated in State common ground and are covered by one ticket. Our picture shows the Isterfoss rapids, where both trout and grayling, gwyniad and pike may be landed.

Photo: Johan Berge.

on foot or by bicycle from Sørkedalen (Skansebakken). South Heggelivatn, for instance, is reached in about 2 hours from Skansebakken. Map: Oslo Nordmark.

Fishing in Nibbitjern and Nibbitjernsløken east of the lodge, and in more distant lakes such as Aurtjern, Flåtan, Gobergtjern and South Heggelivatn. North Heggelivatn is private.

Centres: Løvlia (forest lodge) or Oslo. Booking for Løvlia at Skiforeningen, Skippergt. 40, Oslo.

Fishing permits: Krokskogen also is covered by Oslomarkas Fiskeadministrasjon's seasonal ticket, available at Løvlia and sports shops in Oslo, kr. 30 per season.

HEDMARK

Hedmark — the forest county of Norway — is enriched with great rivers: The Glomma, the Trysilelv (Klara) and the Rena. Between Os and Tolga you will probably find the best grayling fishing in Europe in the Glomma river. Good fishing may be had in these rivers, especially in the Trysilelv, and also in big lakes like Femund, Isteren, Sølensjøen, Ossjøen and Isteren. But the best sport is offered by smaller waters in the north-eastern mountain parishes. The best waters here are found in the north-eastern parts, and they contain red char, grayling, gwyniad and trout.

ENGERDAL

Highly valued by Norwegian anglers this district comprises both large and small lakes and a variety of rivers. Most of the systems within Engerdal are state common ground and are covered by one fishing permit. Fishing is not allowed between Sept. 1 and Oct. 10, but this may change. The fishing permit contains valid information on closed season, minimum sizes, etc.

SØMÅA-ISTEREN-GLØTA area (C/D 10). Travel by train from Oslo to Rena in 3 hours and then by bus to Femundsenden in 3 1/2 hours. Road distance from Oslo 190 miles. Highroad 26 runs along Gløta river, lake Isteren and Sømåa river. The distance from Femundsenden to Sømådal is approx. 20 miles. Map: 2018 IV (Isteren).

The Sømåa river runs between lake Langsjøen and lake Isteren. The width of the river is from 10 to 80 yards and the water is rather deep. The difference in height between lake Langsjøen and lake Isteren (1,900 ft. above sea level) is approx. 230 ft. Long quiet stretches where the river bed may be sandy, are interrupted by short rapids as Sømåa flows through boggy country and sparsely forested mountain moors. The river holds trout and

grayling; pike and gwyniad where the river flows slowly. Chances of big trout exist. The average fish is small but of good quality. In certain places grayling are plentiful and whereas trout fishing is best in the rapids, char are found in quiter water. Lake Isteren is a large, shallow lake west of lake Femund. It holds trout, gwyniad, grayling, pike, perch and some less exciting species. Gwyniad are numerous and of good quality and size. 4-pounders are not at all unusal. Perch and pike are fairly plentiful and the lake has yielded pike in the 20-pound class. Trout are becoming more numerous as a result of intensive cultivation. Trolling from a boat is probably the most rewarding fishing method. The Gløta river is a 1 1/2 miles long river between lake Femund and lake Isteren. The river is rapid — the difference in height between the lake is 60 ft. — and forms only a few pools. In some parts the river bed is filled with heavy boulders, and access to the river is everywhere difficult. Some time ago grayling and especially trout abounded in the Gløta river. Due to overfishing possibilities are reduced, and today it is not easy to bag a big catch, if one is not very lucky with the time and water level.

The upper reaches of the Femund river also belong to this area, and especially the Isterfoss rapids offers some good angling, mostly trout and grayling. But also here fishing is reduced, thanks to overfishing and also because some anglers do not respect the size-regulations. At the present time there is little trout, but fishing seems to be improving. Other waters are the upper and lower Galtsjø lakes. June to Aug. is the best season in the Sømåa-Isteren-Gløta area.

Centre: Femundsenden.

Fishing permits: Engerdal state common ground permits are reasonably priced and available at hotels, camping sites, shops and a number of farms.

LAKE FEMUND (C/D 10). Travel: See Sømå-Isteren-Gløta area. Maps: N. Femund and S. Femund.

Lake Femund, the third largest lake in Norway, covers an area of 80 sq. miles (202 sq. km) and lies 2,175 ft. above sea level in the desolate, vast and beautiful Femundsmarka region. The sparsely pine-clad moorland and conical mountains around the lake are covered by reindeer moss which gives the whole district a strange yellow-grey colour. Lake Femund holds trout, red char, grayling, perch, pike and some other species. Gwyniad and red char are quite numerous. The big lake is fairly well stocked with trout, pike and grayling also. Quality and size of all species vary greatly. 16-pounders have been caught, but average size would be around one pound for trout, red char, grayling and gwyniad. Trolling from a boat is likely to give the best results, and boats can be hired from hotels, guest houses and some farms along the lake. Season: June to August and fishing through the ice in March—April.

Centres: Femundsenden and Elgå.

Fishing permits: Engerdal state common ground, available from hotels, shops, farms etc.

STAUPÅ—JYLTINGEN area (D 10). Travel: See Sømåa—Isteren—Gløta area. Jyltingen farm lies 11 miles by car from Femundsenden. Map: S. Femund or 2018 I (Engerdal).

Staupåa river drains the lakes Storjyltingen (2,240 ft. above sea level), Glen, Bursjøen, Ånstjerna and Skjeftsjøen and flows into Sweden. On its way towards the border deep, still pools are followed by shallow rapids. Pike and perch are numerous, not so many trout and grayling. There are few trout in the lakes but plenty of grayling, pike, perch and some gwyniad. June and July are the best months.

Centre: Femundsenden.

Fishing permit: Engerdal state commond ground covers this area also. Available from hotels, shops, farms etc.

ELGÅDAL area (D 10). Travel by train from Oslo to Rena in 3 hours and then by bus to Femundsenden in 3 1/2 hours. Go by taxi to Elgå or next day by bus in 1 hour. The distance by road from Oslo is 210 miles. Maps: N. Femund and S. Femund.

The Elgådal is a beautiful valley east of lake Femund. Highroad 221 goes through the valley, and none of the waters are more than 1 1/2 hours walk from the nearest road. There are two river systems in this area. The Elgå river drains lake Djupsjøen and lake Elgåsjøen and runs into lake Femund south of Elgå. It is quite a turbulent river with several rapids and waterfalls, and it holds some pike, grayling and trout. During spawning trout up to 17 pounds have been caught, but the average fish is small and of medium quality. Lake Elgåsjøen holds few trout, but there are some red char of good quality. Lake Djupsjøen has some trout, red char and perch. The trout and the char are reported to be of quality. The Gutua river connects several big lakes in the Elgådal valley with lake Gutulisjøen and flows into Sweden. Between lake Gutulisjøen and the Swedish border both trout and grayling are quite numerous, but of fairly small size. Fjellgutusjøen (2, 378 ft. above sea level) belongs to the Gutua system. Before 1958 there were few trout, but it has been stocked since, and though not numerous yet trout are said to be

of good quality. There are plenty of perch in this lake. Lake Gutulisjøen (2,224 ft. above sea level) holds trout, grayling, gwyniad, perch and pike. Perch are numerous, especially in the northern parts. Other lakes in the Elgådal valley are Volsjøen, Båthussjøen, Storsjøen and Hammersjøen. Season: June—Aug.

Centre: Elgå.

Fishing permit: Engerdal state common ground available from Elgå Gjestgiveri, shops and farms in the area.

RØA—GRØTÅA area (C 10). This famous fishing district is off the beaten track east of lake Femund. Travel: See Elgådal area. Local steamer from Elgå to the mouth of Røa river. Map: N. Femund.

The Røa river runs between lake Rogen (2,483 ft.) and lake Femund (2,175 ft.). The length of the river is 18 km and consists of a number of small lakes connected by short river stretches. The river bed is stony, but the lakes tend to be muddy. Approx. halfway the Røa drains two bigger lakes, Upper and Lower Roasten. The river holds trout, grayling, red char, perch and some pike. Trout fishing is best in the rapids, red char dominates the Roasten lakes and Rogen, whereas grayling are numerous in the small lakes and quiet parts of the river. Best fishing in July and Aug. Fishing is prohibited between Sept. 1 and Oct. 31.

Grøtåa is a tributary to the Røa river. The confluence is just east of Upper Roasten. The river runs through a couple of tarns that used to be some of the best trout waters in Norway. Due to extensive fishing big fish are rare today.

Centre: The only accommodation in the area is the Norwegian Mountain Touring Club's unstaffed hut Røvollen, which has been built for hikers. Anglers must rely on camping.

Fishing permit: Engerdal state common ground ticket, kr. 12 per week, covers this area also. Available at Elgå, Svukuriset, Buvika and onboard the Femund steamer.

ENGERDAL area (D 10). This area consists both of the main valley and the Rødal valley east of lake Engeren. Travel: By train from Oslo to Rena in 3 hours and bus to Engerdal in 3 hours. Maps: 2018 I (Engerdal) and 2018 II (Engeren).

The Engeråa river runs along Highway 26 between Engerdal village and lake Engeren (1,450 ft). There are a fair number of trout and grayling in the river. The fish tend to be small but of good quality. Lake Engeren is a long and narrow lake and Highway 26 runs alongs its eastern side. Gwyniad, red char and grayling dominate the lake, but trout are becoming more numerous thanks to stocking.

12-pounders have been caught in the lake. The Rødalen area consists of the Røa river and a number of lakes approx. 2,500 ft. above sea level. There is a local toll road from Hylleråsen on lake Engeren to Lillerøåsen, 4 miles. From there about 2 miles on foot to the fishing area. Trout and red char in reasonable quantities. The trout may go up to 5 pounds. The river and the lakes are stocked annually by the local angling club. The best fishing is in July.

Centre: Engerdal.

Fishing permits: Reasonable tickets to Engeråa and Engeren, available from Erling Sand, Heggeriset. Part of lake Engeren is covered by the Engerdal state common ground ticket. Reasonable tickets to the Rødal area are also available locally.

FEMUNDSELV (D 10—11) is what the Trysilelv river is called in Engerdal. It is one of the best angling waters in Norway. Maps: 2018 II (Engeren), 2018 III (Elvdal) and 2018 IV (Isteren).

Trysil river, or Klara as it is also called, runs approx. 40 km through Engerdal, from lake Isteren (2,126 ft.) to the Trysil border (1,686 ft.). Its a sporting river between the Isterfossen falls and Husfloen, especially the upper stretches where the river is rapid and the river bed stony. After the confluence with the Sølna river the Trysilelv is less rapid and meanders its way through woodland, farmland and marshland. There are a fair number of fish, mainly trout and grayling, though the river is heavily fished. In some parts of the river grayling dominates, especially below the Isterfoss falls and at the outlet from lake Galtsjø. There are signs that the stock of trout is improving. The average weight of grayling and trout is approx. 12 to 16 ounces. A few years ago it was 1—2 lbs or more. In the upper part of Trysilelv big gwyniad is caught, but is not easy to say when, and where, they will rise to flies. Good catches are altoghether dependent on summer weather and water level. Best season should be June to Aug.

Centres: Femundsenden and Engerdal.

Fishing permits: The Engerdal state common ground ticket is available at Femundsenden, Engerdal and several places along the river (look for posters).

RENDALEN

Within the borders of Rendalen are found some very interesting waters. Moreover the lakes and rivers have been cultivated for years and should normally offer quite good fishing.

ØVRE RENDAL area (C 10). Travel by train from Oslo to Hanestad in 5 hours and then 1/2 hour by bus to Øvre Rendal. Distance by car from Oslo 186 miles. Map: 1918 I (Rendalen).

The Unsetåa and Tysla rivers join to form the Rena river in Øvre Rendal, which lies approx. 1,000 ft. above sea level. Both trout and grayling are fairly numerous in the main river. The tributaries hold trout mainly. The rivers are easily fished and have a number of fine pools. The average fish is small, but big trout do run up the rivers from lake Storsjøen.

Centre: Øvre Rendal.

Fishing permits: Reasonably priced day and week tickets are available from general stores in Øvre Rendal.

SØLENDAL area (C 10). In lake Sølensjøen tons of red char have been caught yearly since times immemorial. The lake has been properly harvested by the farmers of Rendal, and a village of fishing huts grew up at Fiskevollen. Around 1900 gwyniad were introduced into the lake and have become very numerous. The lake is very productive and is hardly fished sufficiently these days. There is a local toll road from Øvre Rendal to Fiskevollen, 23 miles. Another local toll road leads from Unset to the Sølendal valley. Map: 2018 IV (Isteren).

Lake Sølen, as has been said above, holds plenty of red char and gwyniad but there are not many trout. The average char is less than 1 pound, the average gwyniad almost 2 pounds and 9-pounders have been caught. Grayling are more numerous than trout, and are more easily caught on sporting gear than red char and gwyniad. There are also some grayling and trout in the Sølna river above the lake.

Centre: Øvre Rendalen (not listed in «Hotels in Norway») or camping in the fishing area.

Fishing permits: Tickets at reasonable prices to the Sølna river, available from Magne Finstad, Øvre Rendal. Tickets for Lake Sølensjøen, also reasonable priced, from Hågen Hangård, Øvre Rendal.

YTRE RENDAL area (C 10). Travel by train from Oslo to Koppang in 4 hours and then 1/2 hour by bus to Ytre Rendal. Distance by car from Oslo 168 miles. Maps: 1918 I (Rendalen) and 1918 II (Storsjøen).

In this area there is fishing in lake Lomnessjøen (840 ft.) and Rena river with its tributaries. Lake Lomnessjøen is a shallow lake, max. depth 95 ft., and holds trout, perch and gwyniad. Very good gwyniad fishing in the autumn and ice-fishing (perch) in early spring. Trout are numerous in the Rena river and there are also a fair amount of big grayling. Trout average 1/2 pound. Grayling fishing is best from the middle of May to the middle of June, trout fishing most rewarding from the middle of June. The season is closed from Sept. 1 to May 1, except for gwyniad, perch and pike. Highway 3 and local roads along the lake and the river.

Centres: Rendal (Ytre).

Fishing permits: Ytre Rendal fishing card, approx. kr. 10 per day, kr. 35 per week or kr. 50 per season, available from hotels and local shops.

STORSJØEN area (C 10—11). Travel: See Ytre Rendal. Map: 1918 II (Storsjøen).

Lake Storsjøen is 40 km long and 2 km wide lake and lies 820 ft. above sea level. Very deep, max. depth 1,020 ft. It contains trout, Vänern salmon, grayling, gwyniad, perch and pike. Trout are fairly numerous, average size about 5 pounds, fish up to 15 pounds are a possibility. In Storsjøen fishing is usually done from boats and trolling will produce the best results. Åsheim Hotel provides rowing boats. Åkrestrømmen is the name of the rapids in the Rena river where it enters lake Storsjøen. These 2 km long rapids are famous as fisheries. Trout and grayling play in the rapids and thousands are hooked every summer by hundreds of anglers. Åkrestrømmen often yields 13 and 15-pound trout. Grayling fishing is best from the middle of May, trout from the end of May, fishing is generally best when the flood is just over. In the autumn gwyniad run from lake Storsjøen up the rapid and are caught in great quantities in scoop nets.

The Flena river enters the east side of lake Storsjøen near the north end. Before it runs into the lake it is joined by the Renåa river which drains the Rensjøen lakes (approx. 2,650 ft. above sea level). Both these rivers hold trout, but they are reported to be «overpopulated» and the fish are small.

Highway 3 runs along the upper part of lake Storsjøen. There is a secondary road along the east bank of the lake and a local toll road follows the Flena river into the mountains. The season is closed in this area from Sept. 1 to May 1 except for gwyniad, perch and pike.

Centre: Rendal (Ytre).

Fishing permits: Ytre Rendal fishing card, see Ytre Rendal above, covers the area.

MISTRA area (C/D 10). Travel: See Ytre Rendal. Maps: 1918 II (Storsjøen) and 1918 I (Rendalen).

The Mistra river runs between lake Missjøen (2,250 ft.) and lake Storsjøen. Approx. halfway it is joined by the Grøna river and further down by the Renåa river (not the Renåa mentioned above). The lower 3 km of the Mistra is easily accessible from Highway 217, but fine trout lurks in the big pools. Some big ones also enter the lower reaches from lake Storsjøen, but they are difficult to catch. Trout of almost 20 pounds may be taken though. The average trout in the Mistra is small, and so are the fish in the Renåa. There is a toll road along Renåa from Renåvangen. The Grøna tributary holds a fair amount of medium-sized trout. Highway 217 touches the river at Holla seter. The lower stretches are accessible from the local road to Jotseter. Fishing is reported to be best from June 1 to Aug. 15. Closed season from Sept. 1 to May 1.

Centre: Rendal (Ytre).

Fishing permits: Ytre Rendal fishing, see Ytre Rendal above, covers the area.

OS—TOLGA

This is a composite district made up of stretches of Norway's longest river Glomma and its tributaries, as well as waters which empty themselves into lake Femund and the Trysilelv system. Moreover there are number of «independent» lakes and tarns on both sides of the Østerdal valley.

GLOMMA river (C 10) provides some fishing in OS—TOLGA. Travel by train from Oslo to Tolga or Os in approx. 6 hours. Distance by road from Oslo to Tolga 229 miles, Os 242 miles. Maps: Røros and Tynset.

From the Røstfoss falls north of Os station the Glomma river runs fairly fast but is easily fished. After Os station the flow becomes more gentle and the river here holds some trout and pike are numerous. Between Os and Tolga the river is probably the best grayling water in Europe. After Hummelvoll the river acquires more speed and trout tends to dominate. Between here and Tolga station Glomma forms 3 rapids. Here in the early spring grayling are easy to get whereas trout are more numerous later on. Trout up to 6 pounds have been hooked. After Tolga station there is a quiet stretch before the Eidsfoss rapids where grayling abound in May. At Kvennan there are some good grayling pools as well.

Centres: Os and Tolga (not listed in «Hotels in Norway»).

Fishing permits: Day tickets for the Os stretches at Os Park Hotel and local shops. Day tickets for the Tolga area, also at reasonable prices, are available at Malmplassen Gjestegård and Kvennan Camping.

TOLGA area (C 10). Travel: See Glomma river. Maps: 1614 I (Tynset), 1719 III (Holøydal), 1719 IV (Narbuvoll) and 1620 II (Dalsbygda). Lake Langen lies 2,375 ft. above sea level in the mountains north of Tolga. It is reached by car via Os. Trout fishing is reported to be quite good. Fishing is best in the latter half of July and in Aug. Fishing cards can be bought locally at reasonable prices.

The Tallsjøen lakes are situated in the mountains west of Tolga 2,191 ft. above sea level. The upper lake is fed by the Olaå river from Åssårtjern and Letjern tarns. There are big trout in these tarns and also in the Upper Tallsjø. The Tolga river drains this lake and falls into the Lower or Store (big) Tallsjø which is reached by car from Tolga station. This lakes hold some trout too.

Lake Telsjøen (3,464 ft.) lies in the mountains south of Tolga and 2 miles from the nearest road. This lake has been dammed by the local angling club and increased to twice its original size. It has also been stocked with trout. It yields fairly good sport in late July and August.

The Hodal lakes are a string of interconnected lakes in the Hodalen valley east of Tolga station. The biggest, lake Storsjø (2,480 ft.), holds gwyniad, perch, pike, grayling and trout, in that order. Trout up to 17 pounds have been caught, the record pike is said to have weighed 25 pounds. The usual trout will hardly scale 1 pound. Fishing is probably best in Aug. There is motoring road along the east side of the lakes.

Centres: Os and Tolga.

Fishing permits: Day tickets are available to lake Langen from Langen farm; to lake Telsjøen from Tolga Samvirkelag (Co-op); and to the Hodal lakes from Hodalen Tourist station. Everywhere at reasonable prices.

HOLØYDAL area (C 10). Travel by train to Tolga in 6 hours and then 1 hour by bus to Holøydal. The distance by car from Oslo is 254 miles. Maps: 1719 III (Holøydal) and 1719 IV (Narbuvoll).

This area affords fishing in the Hola river, its tributaries and lake Langsjøen (2,340 ft.). There is a motoring road along the main river and lake Langsjøen and also along the Øversjøåa tributary. The Hola river drains lake Storsjøen and is fairly streamy the first 3—4 km. After the confluence with Galåa the river becomes more quiet. Further down long glides are interrupted by small rapids and the river receives several tributaries. Between Storsjøen and Galåa the river holds trout mainly, further down pike and perch occur too. Trout here will average 1 pound. Langsjøen is an 11 km long, 1,2 km wide lake, boats can be rented. It is dominated by gwyniad, but big trout are a possibility. There are also grayling, perch and pike. July and Aug. will provide the best trout fishing.

Centres: Holøydal, Hodalen (not listed) and Narbuvoll (listed under Os in the hotel price list).

Fishing permits: Available from Olaf

Røstbakken, Øversjødalen and Jon Holøyen, Holøydal for two days at reasonable prices.

TUFSINGDAL area (C 10). Travel by train to Os in 6 hours and then 1/2 hour by bus to Narbuvoll. Road distance from Oslo: 256 miles. Maps: 1719 I (Røa), 1719 II (Elgå) and 1719 IV (Narbuvoll).

The Tufsingdal state common ground fishing permit covers the rivers Tufsinga and Flena, part of lake Femund, lake Flensjøen and several minor lakes. River Tufsinga drains lake Siksjøen and is joined by the Flena tributary and runs smoothly through the broad and sparsely forested Tufsingdal valley to empty itself into lake Femund. The river holds trout, char, grayling, pike, perch and gwyniad. The last three kinds dominate. Big trout may be caught when they run up the river from lake Femund. The usual trout is about 1 pound, big trout approx. 5 pounds. Highway 26 runs through the Tufsingdal and there is also a motoring road along most of the Flena.

Centre: Narbuvoll (see Os in «Hotels in Norway»).

Fishing permits: The state common ground ticket is available from Johs. Sæter and several other farmers in Tufsingdal.

TYNSET

The best trout fishing in the municipality of Tynset is provided by the Kvikne area. However, recent reports state that intensive cultivation schemes are yielding results in the Tynset area too, especially in the Aumdal valley.

TYNSET area (C 10). Travel by train from Oslo to Tynset in 5 1/2 hours. The distance by car is 215 miles. Maps: 1619 I (Tynset), 1619 II (Tylldal) and 1619 IV (Kvikneskogen).

The Tunna river drains a number of mountain tarns and receives the Såtta before entering lake Stugusjøen. The mountain tarns, the Tunna and lake Stugusjøen all hold trout and char of moderate size. Telneset on the Glomma provides good grayling fishing in May. The Glomma glides smoothly through Tynset, where it is fed by a number of tributaries. In spring fish will stick to the banks, during the summer the middle of the river provides the best chances. There are highways and local roads leading along both the Tunna and the Glomma. Lake Savalen (2,325 ft.) east of Tynset is also reached by car. This is a big lake (10 km long) which offers quite good trout and red char fishing in June—Aug., and fine char fishing through the ice in Nov.—Dec. and March—April. The season is closed after Aug. 15. Trout will average 1 pound. 11-pounders have been hooked in the lake.

The Speka river joins the Brya and falls into lake Finnstadsjøen (1,663 ft.). The lake and the rivers offer trout and red char fishing and are accessible from local roads. A toll road leads into the Aumdal where the Auma drains a string of small lakes approx. 2,300 ft. above sea level. These lakes have been stocked and good sport is anticipated.

Centre: Tynset.

Fishing permits: Glomma and Tunna available from Tynset Camping and petrol stations. Lake Savalen sold by Savalen Fjellstue. Day tickets to lake Finnstadsjøen from Olaf Aas, Brydalen and weekly tickets to the Brya and the Speka rivers from Martin Vestlie, Brydalen. The Aumdal fishing card is available from Tynset Tourist Office between June 15 and Aug. 15. All tickets are available at reasonable prices.

KVIKNE area (C 10). Travel by train from Oslo to Tynset in 5 1/2 hours and then 1 hour by bus to Kvikne. The distance by car from Oslo is 243 miles. Map: Kvikne.

There are a number of fine lakes and rivers in this area, and good sport may be expected. The following lakes belong to Kvikne state common ground: Øvre Stallitjern, Grønlitjerna, Gråbergstjerna, Storbekktjerna, Vartjern, Hanstjern, Sanfjelltjerna, Store Hiåsjø, Lille Hiasjø, Gåsengtjerna, Langvatnet, Nordyatjerna, Store Ensjøen. The lakes and the adjoining rivers hold trout and red char, average size 1—2 pounds, max. size 11 pounds. The quality is very good. Trout fishing is at its best in July and Aug. Closed season from Sept. 15 to Oct. 15. The mountain tarns and lakes are not accessible by car. Walking time to the fishing area is approx. 1 1/2 hours. It is possible to get accommodation in huts on the lakes, contact Kvikne Samvirkelag.

Centre. Kvikne.

Fishing permit: The state common ground fishing card is sold by Kvikne Samvirkelag (Co-op) at a very reasonable price.

STOR-ELVDAL

Here is a vast district dominated by the Glomma and its tributaries. The most rewarding trout fishing is found in the Sollia area.

GLOMMA area (C 10). Travel by train from Oslo to Koppang in 4 hours. Road distance: 157 miles. Map: 1918 III (Storelvdal).

The Glomma river in Stor-Elvdal offers good sport, especially the northern stretches where the river runs faster and the river bed is stony. Here grayling will take readily to flies during the summer months. At Koppang the river splits into 75 channels between low islands and forms a great number of enticing pools where trout and grayling rise to the fly. Glomma is stocked every year, and local anglers state that trout have become more numerous lately.

Centre: Koppang.

Fishing permit: Sold locally.

SOLLIA area (C 10—11). Travel by train from Oslo to Atna in 4 1/2 hours and then 1 hour by bus to Enden. Road distance from Oslo: 180 miles. Maps: 1818 I (Sollia) and 1818 IV (Atnsjøen).

Fishing in the Atna river with lake Atnsjø (2,300 ft.) and the tributaries Setninga and Vulua with the lakes Setningen, Rundtjern, Langtjern, Hamntjern and others. This area is covered by a state common ground ticket. In the rivers the average size is moderate, in the lakes there are chances of big fish (trout and red char). Best season July and Aug. Closed season Sept. 1 — Dec. 1.

Centres: Enden, Vollum, Atnbru, Neset and Straumbu, none of them listed in «Hotels in Norway».

Fishing permit: The state common ground ticket, approx. kr. 20 per week, is available at pensions and mountain inns in the area.

TRYSIL

This vast forest province contains several interesting angling areas.

TRYSILELV river (D 10—11) is quite good between lake Sensjøen and Trysil Innbygd and between Kolos and the Swedish border. Travel by train from Oslo to Elverum in 2 1/2 hours and then 2 hours by bus to Innbygda. Road distance from Oslo 147 miles. Maps: 2018 II (Engeren), 2017 I (Jordet), 2117 IV (Trysil) and 2117 III (Plassen).

The Trysilelv holds mainly trout and grayling, but there are also salmon of the Vänern (inland) variety. In the lower parts of the river there are pike (22-pounders). Fishing is best in June and Aug. Closed season from Sept. 1 to Oct. 10 and grayling hatching areas in May. Highway 26 and local roads along the river.

Centres: Nybergsund and Innbygd and Jordet, none of them listed.

Fishing permits: From Trysil Tourist Office, Trysil at a modest price indeed.

FLENA area (C 10). Travel: See Trysilelv river. Map: 2117 IV (Trysil).

The Flena is a tributary to the Trysilelv. It joins the Skjetflena, which drains the Flensjøene lakes, at Flenenga. Both the Flena and Skjetflena are typical forest rivers. They both hold trout of moderate size. In the lakes perch dominate, but there are some trout as well.

There is a local road along the Flena to Elshø followed by a forest toll road to Rømonyseter. Huts can be rented in the fishing area, contact Trysil Tourist Office.
Centre: Trysil Innbygd, not listed.
Fishing permit: Tickets available from Trysil Tourist Office, Trysil at a very reasonable price.

OSENSJØEN area (D 11). Travel by train from Oslo to Rena in 3 hours and then by bus 1 hour to Nordre Osen. Road distance from Oslo 142 miles. Maps: 2017 IV (Nordre Osen) and 2117 III (Julussa).
Lake Osensjøen (1,430 ft.) is a big lake, 28 km long, max. width 2,8 km, max. depth 108 m. There are trout, gwyniad, grayling, perch and pike. Gwyniad are very numerous. Chances of big trout (up to 15 pounds) and pike. The lake has been stocked with trout for a number of years. Trout fishing is best from midsummer to the end of July. Closed season Sept. 1 to Oct. 15. Søndre Osa river flows between lake Osensjøen and the Rena river, dropping 189 metres in the course of a 17 km run. It is a broad river, 40 to 60 metres across, with large pools interrupted by several rapids. Trout up to 1/2 pound are numerous (minimum size 10 in.) and 4 to 8-pounders may be taken. Best season from mid-summer to end of July. Closed season Sept. 1 to May 20. Highway 215 runs along Søndre Osa and there are motoring road on both sides of lake Osensjøen.
Centre: No pensions or inns in the area, but camping huts can be rented on several camping sites.
Fishing permits: Tickets available at shops and camping sites at very reasonable prices.

LJØRA area (D 11). Travel by train from Oslo to Elverum in 2 1/2 hours and 3 hours by bus to Østby. Road distance from Oslo to Østby is 150 miles. The distance from Østby to the upper reaches of the Ljøra is approx. 40 miles. Maps: 2117 I (Ljørdal) and 2117 IV (Trysil).
The Ljøra with its tributaries is a 95 km system and there are local roads along most of these rivers. The average height of the fishing area is 1,600 ft. above sea level. Ljøra rises in Sweden, flows through the Ljørdal valley into Sweden where it becomes Västre Dalelv. The upper parts are streamy with some fine pools. However, the bigger fish are hooked below Ljørdalen village where the river becomes deeper and wider (40 to 60 metres across). The river holds trout and grayling. Trout are more numerous and practically dominates all the tributaries. Average size 1/2 pound, max. size 5 pounds. The river system is well kept and stocked. The trout fishing is best in June and July.

Centre: Østby (nearest guest house), see Trysil in «Hotels in Norway».
Fishing permits: The Ljørdalen fishing card, inexpensive, is sold by Ljørdalen Samvirkelag (Co-op), Kjøpmann (storekeeper) Bakken and Ingeborg Torgals, Ljørdalen.

OPPLAND
The main water courses, Lågen and Begna, to-day provide only second-rate sport. The same is true of most of the big lakes in the southern parts of the county, whereas fine trout may be caught in some of the great mountain lakes. The best sport is probably found in the classical angling areas of the high mountains. Many waters have been affected by damming, but there are still good trout to be caught in the mountain parishes.

DOVRE
This used to be a classic angling area, but the good old days are gone. Yet a lot is done to improve the situation, and there are some promising "pockets ", for instance the Fokstu moors, which are worth investigating. Good fishing may also be enjoyed in some reservoirs, most of which are found south of the Grimsdalen valley.

FOKSTUEN area (C 10). Travel by train to Dombås from Oslo in 4 hours. Road distance from Oslo is 219 miles. Map: Dovrefjell.
The Fokstumyrene bogs on the Dovre plateau (approx. 3,300 ft.) with its rich bird life became a natural preserve in 1923. No traffic is allowed on the moors, and consequently no fishing, before July 8. The season closes Aug. 20. There are some small lakes or tarns on these moors which hold grayling and trout of good quality. The Fokseåa river drains the moor and forms some fine pools and long glides where some big trout lurk. Angling is allowed between June 1 and Aug. 20, fishing is best in July. E 6 leads across the Dovre plateau and short walks will bring anglers to the waters.
Centres: Dombås and Vålåsjø.
Fishing permit: The Dovre fishing card covers this area and is available in all hotels and persions, Grimsdalshytta, Dårølseter, Hjerkinn station, NOROL petrol station at Dovre and in the sports shop and tourist information at Dombås.

FRON
There is some fishing in the Lågen river in the Gudbrandsdalen, mainly for trout and grayling of moderate size, and also in the mountains east of the main valley, where tarns are reported to be overpopulated and in

dire need of fishing. Angling is also possible along the Peer Gynt Road. The Vinstra Tourist Office will inform visitors as to these possibilities. Here we will deal with the mountain areas west of the Gudbrandsdalen, where good sport can still be had in spite of the dams built in connection with the Vinstra power stations.

ESPEDAL area (C 11). Travel by train from Oslo to Lillehammer in 2 1/2 hours and then by bus to Espedal 2 1/2 hours. The distance by road is 152 miles. Maps: 1718 II (Vinstra), 1718 III (Skåbu) and 1717 IV (Espedal).
Espedal lies approx. 2,300 ft. above sea level in a fairly narrow valley with open pine woods. On both sides of the valley the terrain is hilly mountain country, mostly treeless. Fishing can be had in the big lakes in the main watercourse — the Espedal and Breisjøen lakes — and in smaller lakes on both sides of the valley. In Lake Espedal there are large stocks of fish, but the average size is small, 5 to 10 ounces, even though fish as big as 12 pounds can be caught. On the northern side of the Espedal Valley lie Bingtjønn, Sprengtjønn, Svarttjønn and Børkedal lakes, on the southern side the Agn lakes. Fish are generally plentiful in these waters, sometimes too plentiful, but some of the lakes have very good fish. Fishing is usually best in July and Aug. Highway 255 runs through the valley. Walking time to the mountain lakes is between 2 and 4 hours. In the valley most of the fishing is done from boats—hotels and mountain lodges have rowing boats — in the smaller mountain lakes and tarns from the banks.
Centre: Espedal.
Fishing permits: Some of the lakes belong to Fron state common ground, other to Espedal common ground, lake Espedal is private (Espedal Angling Ass.) Fishing cards, inexpensive, from Skåbu petrol station or hotels and lodges.

SIKILSDAL area (C 11). Travel by train from Oslo to Vinstra in 4 hours and by bus and car to Sikilsdal in 2 hours. Distance by road from Oslo is 206 miles. Map: Sjodalen. Sikilsdal is a wild and beautiful valley at the entrance to the Jotunheimen mointains. The two Sikilsdalsvatn lakes, the Sikildalselv river and Skåltjern approx. 3,300 ft. above sea level, offer good sport. Fine trout, average weight 1/2 pound, max. size 5 pounds. Fishing is best in July and Aug., closed season Sept. 5 to Oct. 31. There is a toll road along the river, walking time to the lakes 15 mins to 1 hour.
Centre: Sikilsdalseter, see Vinstra in «Hotels in Norway».
Fishing permit: Fishing is reserved for guests

at the lodge and free, but the catch must be delivered to the lodge.

SKÅBU area (C 11). Travel by train from Oslo to Vinstra in 4 hours and then 1 hour by bus to Skåbu. Distance by road from Oslo 187 miles. Map: Sjodalen, 1718 III (Skåbu) and 1718 II (Vinstra).
This area lies 2,400 to 3,300 ft. above sea level. There is fishing in big lakes like Slangen and Olstappen, some rivers and several smaller lakes. The water courses are somewhat affected by damming. In the big lakes fishing is best from a boat. The hotels have boats available.
The area is often subdivided as follows:
Slangen including lake Slangen, the Slangselv river, lake Olstappen, Vinstra river, Espa and Muru. The whole of this watercourse is accessible by car. The waters hold trout gwyniad and perch, average size 4 to 6 ounces max. size (in the big lakes) 6 pounds.
Åkre consist of the 3 Åkrevatn lakes, Stubben river and Hinøgla river, all accessible by car. Trout only, average size 1/4 pound, max. size 4 pounds.
Flekka includes the rivers Flekka, Gryta, Skinnrevo and Stråla and the lakes Flekkvatn and Strålvatn. All lakes are reached in 1/2 hour's walk. Trout only, max. size 1 pound.
Vinstra river above lake Olstappen with the Kroklonene and Vinsterlonene glides and the lakes Langvatn, Vesle Øyangen, Lomtjern and the Hølsa tributary. The Jotunheimen toll road runs at some distance from the system, walking time varies from a couple of minutes to several hours. Trout and a few perch and gwyniad. Generally small fish, but 6-pounders have been caught.
Vinstervatna is the common name for big lakes Sandvatn. Kaldfjorden, Øyvatn, Øvre and Nedre Hersjøen which are all reservoirs for the Vinstra power stations. All are accessible by car along the Jotunheimen toll road. Fairly big trout and gwyniad.
Centre: Skåbu, see Vinstra.
Fishing permits: Some of the waters are situated in Fron state common ground, others in Espedalen common ground. Tickets for Espedalen and Fron are available at Skåbu petrol station and in hotels and pensions at reasonable prices.

LILLEHAMMER

We should like to point out to you some of the possibilities that exist in the mountains on both sides of the Gudbrandsdal valley. Among trout waters east of Lillehammer there are Nevervatn (2,939 ft.), Melsjø (2,929 ft.) and Kroksjø (2,892 ft.), where fishing is permitted from June 10 to Sept. 1. The Mesna river may be fished from June 20. The Lågen river and lake Mjøsa may be fished all year round, but the chances are best in May — June, after the ice is gone.

The best fishing is probably in the Gausa river, where big trout run in the summer. But if you are going to get them, you must seek the advice of the locals. Between June 15 and Aug. 15, 12-pounders have been landed and the river is running fast, so you lead should not be less than 0 30. In the Øyer mountains there are a number of small lakes, accessible by car from Lillehammer in 3/4 hours. The Hornsjø (by the hotel) and Lyngen (2 hours' walk), as well as the Åsta river and its tributaries, Gjæsa and Hymna, are well known both to locals and hotel guests.

The Sjusjøen waters are heavily fished, but there is still some fishing to be had in the Sjusjøen lakes and the river between them. In addition to trout, there is also perch and gwyniad in the area, and fishing is permitted from June 1 to Sept. 1. Fishing cards for all waters in the Lillehammer district are sold by sports shops in Lillehammer, as well as in some other shops, hotels and pensions.

GAUSDAL

This romantic farm- and woodland valley west of Lillehammer also include vast mountains moors with some good fishing waters. Most of the area belong to the State and is usually referred as Gausdal West Mountains.

GAUSDAL WEST MOUNTAINS area (C 11). Travel by train to Lillehammer in 2 1/2 hours and then by bus in 2 hours to the area. Distance by road from Oslo approx. 140 miles. Maps: Synnfjell and N. Etnedal or 1717 II(Synnfjell) and 1717 III(Fulsenn).

The central watercourse of the area is the Dokka river which is called Fjelldokka (Mountain Dokka) above lake Dokkvatn. It is a sporting fishing water with stony bed and fine pools, and holds trout of good quality. 1/2-pounders are numerous, bigger fish a definite possibility. There is a toll road along the river to Liomseter lodge (2,550 ft.), which is the best place from which to tackle Fjelldokka. In this area there are numerous small waters such as the Roppa tarns and Ognsjø lakes. The Roppa tarns and lake Hornsjø is reached on a 9-mile toll road from Bødal in Vestre Gausdal. Altogether there must be 100 big and small lakes in this area, as well as numerous brooks and rivers. Apart from some private lakes, this area belongs to the State and the general Gausdal ticket permits you to fish in practically all lakes. In the last years efforts have been made to improve fishing. The best season is in July and Aug. Trout dominates, but in some lakes there are also perch, red char and gwyniad.

Centre: Liomseter (Norwegian Touring Club lodge), not listed.
Fishing permit: The Gausdal State Common Ground ticket is sold by toll gate keepers, hotels and pensions, petrol stations and shops in the area as well as by sports shops in Lillehammer.

LESJA

This is the uppermost parish in the Gudbrandsdal valley, surrounded by mountains and mountain moors. The lakes and rivers of this district have been well kept, regularly stocked and good sport can be excepted.

DALSIDA area (B 10). Travel by train to Dombås from Oslo in 5 hours or Lesja in 6 hours. The distance by road is 230 miles. Maps: 1419 I (Storskrymten), 1419 II (Dombås) and 1419 IV Aursjøen.

The dominant water of this state common ground is a huge reservoir. When the water is low it consists of the 3 original lakes Aursjøen, Grynningen and Gautsjøen, but when the water is high they form one 30 km long lake, situated 2,800 ft. above sea level. This reservoir is yearly stocked with some 40 000 trout fry and is a reported to hold trout and grayling in reasonable quantities and of good quality, average size 3/4 pound, max. size 5 pounds. Better sport can be expected from rivers which empties themselves into this reservoir. Trout are numerous but somewhat smallish in the Merrå, Yelsåna and Grøna rivers. There are also exciting possibilities in lake Vangsvatnet still further away (4 hours walk from the nearest road). Perhaps the best sport can be enjoyed in the Jora, east of the huge Aursjø reservoir, and its tributaries Grøna and Reinåa. Trout are of moderate size in the tributaries, but the Jora has some sporting big fish and the lakes Sjungsjøen and Tandsetervatn hold a fair number of 1-pound trout and red char of excellent quality. Fishing in Dalsida area is best in July and Aug., closed season Sept. 2 to June 1. There are motoring roads along the Jora and the Aursjø.
Centres: Dombås and Lesja.
Fishing permits: Dalsida state common ground ticket can be bought in shops and at the turn-pikes on the toll roads. This inexpensive fishing permit also cover Lordalen state common ground south of the main valley where small trout is numerous in Lora river and some small lakes.

LESJASKOG area (B 10—11). Travel by train from Oslo to Lesjaskog in 6 1/2 hours. The distance by road is 243 miles. Map: 1419 III (Lesjaskog).
Lake Lesjaskogsvatn (2,010 ft.) forms the

60

watershed between the Gudbrandsdal and the Romsdal. The Rauma river flows from its west end, and the Lågen river from the east end of the lake. 11 km long lake Lesjaskogsvatn holds plenty of trout and grayling, average size 1/2 pound, of good quality. There is also some good trout fishing in mountain lakes east of lake Lesjaskogsvatn. The best season for lake Lesjaskogsvatn is said to be July 1 to Aug. 10. The season is closed from Sept. 10 to May 15. E 69 runs along the north side of lake Lesjaskogsvatn. Boats can be hired from hotels and camping sites.

Centres: Lesjaskog, Bjorli and Lesjaverk.

Fishing permits: Reasonably priced tickets to lake Lesjaskogsvatnet are available at hotels, camping sites and shops, approx. kr. 10 per day or kr. 30 per week. Mountain fishing may be obtained through O. Berget, O. Steine or H. Sandgro, Lesjaverk. There is a toll road from Lykkjom to Viggebakken in the mountains north of lake Lesjaskogsvatn.

SEL

This mountain parish has trout fishing both in the Heidal and Rondane areas.

HEIDAL area (C 11). Travel by train to Otta in 4 1/2 hours and by bus from there to Heidal in 1 hour. The distance by road from Oslo is 194 miles. Maps: Sjodalen and Vinstra.

The Murua river drains lake Muvatn (2,845 ft.) and falls into lake Mæringsdalsvatn (2,057 ft.). There is also fishing in the Ståltjern tarns (2,952 ft.). Muvatn, which lies south of prominent Mount Heidalsmuen, is accessible by car from Leirflata on Highroad 257. There are trout of good quality and size (approx. 1 pound) in this 4 km long lake and in the small rivers which feed it. Fishing is best in June and the first weeks of July. Lake Mæringsdalsvatnet is reached by the same road from Leirflata. This shallow lake surrounded by forest holds plenty of small trout. The Ståltjern tarns are red char waters.

Centre: Heidal, see Sjoa.

Fishing permit: Fishing cards can be bought at Leirbu Handel (local shop), Leirflata, Johs. Garmo, Bjølstadmo or A.E. Bilben, Faukstad.

RONDANE area (C 11). Travel by train from Oslo to Otta in 4 1/2 hours and from there by bus or car to Høvringen or Mysuseter or Rapham in approx. 1 hours. The distance by car from Oslo to Otta is 190 miles. Map: Rondane.

In Sel and N. Kolloen state common ground there is fishing in some 46 small and big lakes in the Rondane mountains. The biggest lakes are Furusjøen (2,764 ft.), Vålåsjøen (2,764 ft.) and Rondvatn (3,815 ft.). Lake Furusjøen

and lake Vålåsjøen are reached by car from Mysuseter. Lake Rondvatnet lies in the heart of the Rondane National Park, 2—3 hours walk from Mysuseter. Lake Furusjøen holds some trout, red char and some grayling. Trout also occur in lake Vålåsjøen where there are also red char, grayling and even perch. Fishing in these lakes will not yield great result. Red char are found in lake Rondvatn, and some trout too, boats are available from the Rondvassbu lodge. The Illmanntjern tarns form a string of small lakes east of Rondvassbu. The first is reached in 10 mins. on foot. These tarns used to abound in red char. Store Ula drains lake Rondvatn and flows through the National Parl towards Mysuseter. The river holds red char and trout. The higher lakes should be fished in Aug., the lower lakes in July as well. Some private waters in the Rondane area are also worth trying. These are the Rapham tarns (2,985 ft.), the Bergetjern (3,510 ft.) and Ula river below the forest line. The Rapham tarns are reached by car. Bergetjern is only 15 mins. walk from Mysuseter, and a toll roads runs along the Ula river.

Centres: Høvringen, Mysuseter and Rapham, see Otta. Rondvassbu (Norwegian Touring Club) is not listed in «Hotels in Norway».

Fishing permits: The Sel and N. Kolloen state common ground ticket can be bought at most hotels and lodges in the mountains and at Otta Sykkel & Sport, Otta. The ticket to the private waters, is available at the Mysuseter shops and Otta Sykkel & Sport, also at a reasonable price.

SKJÅK

Skjåk is the name of the district on both sides of the Ottadal. There is fishing both in the forest-clad valley and on the mountain moors.

GROTLI area (B 11). Travel by train to Otta from Oslo in 4 1/2 hours and then by bus to Grotli in 3 1/2 hours. Distance by road from Oslo is 266 miles. Maps: Skjåk, Lom and Ålesund (M 515).

The area consists of mountain moors 2,700 to 3,600 ft. above sea level, treeless and in some places steep, but generally easy to walk. The Otta river is open for fishing and also a number of lakes, both those along Highroad 15 and further in across the moors. At times the lakes along the road are heavily fished, and the catch may be small. Some lakes in the mountains offer good sport with fish of good average size (1 pound). Grotli Hotel will advise anglers on when and where to fish in this area which is dependent on warm weather. Usually the best season is from early

July to about Aug. 20. Closed season Sept. 20 to Oct. 31.
Centre: Grotli.
Fishing permit: Inexpensive Skjåk common ground ticket, available at Grotli Hotel.

LOM

This is a wild beautiful parish which includes the highest peaks in Norway. There is fishing in the big lakes, Vågåvatn and Ottavatn, from Lom centre but chiefly in the Bøverdal area.

BØVERDAL area (B 11). Travel by train from Oslo to Otta in 4 1/2 hours and then 2—3 hours by bus. The distance by car from Oslo is approx. 250 miles. Maps: Lom, Skjåk and Sygnefjell.

The Bøverdal is a steep valley running southwest from Lom centre into the Jotumheimen mountains. Fishing in the Bøvra river, its tributaries, and several lakes along the water course, which falls rapidly. The fish are fairly small, particularly in the river itself. In the lakes one may catch bigger fish of good quality, but stocks are not large. The lakes include lake Bøvertunvatn (2,850 ft.), the Bøvertjern tarns and lake Høydalsvatn (2,973 ft.) and several others. Fishing is probably most rewarding from Høydalsseter lodge. All waters are accessible by car, and the tourist lodges will provide boats on the lakes. Best fishing in July and Aug.
Centres: Røysheim, Elveseter, Høydalsseter and Bøvertun, see Bøverdal.
Fishing permits: Available from hotels and lodges in the area.

VÅGÅ

This is another wildly romantic parish with vast angling interest in the beautiful Sjodalen in the heart of Jotunheimen.

SJODALEN area (C 11). Travel by train from Oslo to Otta in 4 1/2 hours and then 3 hours by bus. The distance by road is approx. 170 miles. Maps: Sjodalen and Gjende.
Consists of the Sjoa river with adjoining lakes and tributaries. Lake Gjende from where the Sjoa river rises is the biggest of these lakes. It lies 3,000 ft. above sea level, surrounded by steep mountains. This 18 km long and 1,3 km wide lake has a stock of fine mountain trout, average size 1 pound. Fish are, however, not plentiful, and the outlet is heavily fished. The best time for anglers is towards the middle of Aug. Boats may be rented at the Gjendesheim lodge and at the Gjendeosen parking lot. Also at most hotels, pensions and camping sites situated by lakes in this area. Other lakes in this area includes lake Bessvatn (3,500 ft.), the Sjodalsvatn lakes (approx. 2,800 ft.) and the Leirungen lakes (approx. 3,300 ft.). The

lakes hold moderate stocks of fine mountain trout, usually up to one pound, but there are fish of more than 2 pounds to be caught. The lakes along the main water course have been too heavily fished. Yet fish is of good quality. If you are prepared to walk a distance, the higher situated lakes, for instance the Brudskard tarn, promise better angling. August is the best season in these altitudes. The Sjoa river must not be overlooked. It is a good trout river with enticing glides, pools and rapids. There are chances of big fish between lake Gjende and lake Øvre (Upper) Sjodalsvatn especially in the Kråkåhølen pool. There is also an interesting stretch of river between the two Sjodalsvatn lakes. Fishing is probably most rewarding in Aug. and the first two weeks of Sept. Highway 51 runs along the main watercourse. The east end of lake Gjende is accessible by car. Lakes like Bessvatn and Leirungen require 1—2 hours' walk.
Centres: Gjendesheim (touring club lodge), Bessheim and Hindseter (see Vågåmo).
Fishing permits: Lakes and rivers in the Vågå and Langmorkje areas are covered by one card. This, and a special hunting- and fishing map, is available in hotels, pensions, etc.

VÅGÅ area (C 11). Travel by train from Oslo to Otta in 4 1/2 hours and then 45 mins. by bus to Vågå. The distance by road from Oslo 209 miles. Map: Vågå.
Fishing in lake Vågåvatn (1,187 ft.) and in mountain lakes and rivers south of the main valley. There is also some trout in the Finna river and the Skjerva tributary north of the valley. Lake Vågåvatn holds trout, red char and grayling. Size and quality vary. Rowing boats are available from hotels and pensions, but there is also bank fishing at the outlet near Vågåmo. The mountain lakes lie approx. 2,600 ft. above sea level and most of them are accessible by car. Lake Flatningen holds plenty of trout and red char of good quality, and chances of catching big red char are there. Lake Lemonsjø on Highroad 51 is reported to have trout up to 5 pounds of good quality. Smaller lakes in the area are Kvitingen and Melingen. Fishing in Kvitingen requires half an hour's walk across the mountain moors. Trout in Kvitingen are reported to be in sporting condition, averaging around 1 pound. The Melingen and Surtningen lakes have been cultivated lately, and the quality of fish has improved. In the Heimfjellet («home mountains») lakes fishing is best in June — Aug.
Centres: Vågåmo and Lemonsjø, see Vågåmo.
Fishing permits: The Sjodalen fishing permits cover this area as well. See Sjodalen above.

ETNEDAL

Etnedal provides trout fishing in the Etna system and some mountain lakes.

ETNA area (C 11). Travel by train from Oslo to Tonsåsen or Fagernes in 4 hours. The distance by car from Oslo to Fagernes is 118 miles. Maps: N. Etnedal and Aurdal or 1816 IV (Dokka), 1716 I (Bruflat) and 1716 IV (Aurdal)

The amount of trout that the Etna river yields depends upon the season and the water level. There is little water in the upper reaches, yet there is no lack of trout above lake Etsenn. Conditions further down are much the same down to the Høljarast waterfalls. From here down to lake Randsfjorden there are also perch, gwyniad and pike. Near the outlet into lake Randsfjorden, after the confluence with the Dokka, extremely good gwyniad fishing takes place from the middle of Sept. to the middle of Oct. The fish is caught in scoop nets attached to long poles. If you do not regard this as sport, make a note of the fact that quite a few big trout are killed in the lower parts of Dokka and Etna.

Of the Etna tributaries perhaps the Dalselv is the most promising, especially the upper reaches with its long glides and inviting pools when the water is high. Further down Dalselv gets more streamy, and both the pools and the fish are smaller. The Rotvolla is another Etna tributary. The first half of this 7 km long river provides good sport in small rapids, pools and glides. The trout are on the small side. The Dalselv drains lake Steinsetfjorden, which holds a middling amount of trout in the half-a-pound class. Perch are numerous in this lake which lies 2,290 ft. above sea level. Rotvolla drains lake Rotvollfjorden (2,290 ft.) where trout and perch of fine quality can be hooked. The same applies to lake Garden (2,594 ft.) in the mountains east of Flatøydegard. All the waters mentioned above are accessible by car. Fishing is best in July in the upper reaches of the Etna system and the mountain lakes and after July 25 in the lower reaches. The season is closed in lower Etna (gwynaid excepted) from Sept. 1 to Sept. 25. These water belongs to the Nordre Land municipality. The closed season the Etnedal fisheries — or the middle parts of the system — is Sept. 1 to May 25. In the upper reaches the season is closed between Sept. 10 and

June 10. The upper reaches of the Dalselv are closed Sept. 15 — June 5 and also July 1 — Aug. 15, the lower waters are closed Sept. 15 — May 25.

Centres: Dokka and Fagernes. Smaller pensions and mountain lodges closer to the waters at Bruflat, Steinsetbygda and Kruk.

Fishing permits: Fishing cards to all above-mentioned waters are sold locally.

NORD-AURDAL

This district offers fishing both in the main valley and on the mountain moors north and south of Fagernes.

FAGERNES area (C 11). Travel by train from Oslo to Fagernes in 4 hours. The distance by road is 118 miles. Maps: Gol, Aurdal and 1716 IV (Aurdal).

Fishing in lake Strondafjorden, lake Aurdalsfjorden and the Begna river between the lakes, 1,000 to 1,150 ft. above sea level. Lake Strondafjorden is almost 9 km long and holds trout, perch and gwyniad. Best fishing is June and parts of Aug. Closed season Sept. 10 — Oct. 10, in the mountains Sept. 10 — June 15. In lake Aurdalsfjorden trout, perch and gwyniad are too numerous and size and quality has suffered accordingly. Fishing is probably best in June. Closed season Sept. 10 — Oct. 10. There is no fishing in privately owned lake Fløafjorden, but the river stretch between lake Fløafjorden and lake Strondafjorden provides excellent rod fishing in the Fjøshølen pool below the Faslefoss. Lake Sæbufjorden north of Fagernes holds trout and perch and is reported to be «overpopulated.»

Centres: Fagernes, Leira and Aurdal. The small pensions in the last-mentioned villages are listed under Fagernes.

Fishing permits: Tickets to lake Strondafjord, Begna river and Neselv river are available at reasonable prices from sports shops in Fagernes and Aurdal and the Fagernes Tourist Office. Tickets to lake Aurdalsfjorden, also reasonably priced, can be bought in the same places. Tickets to lake Sæbøsjøen are only available at the camping site near the outlet.

SVARTHAMAR area (C 11). Travel: See Fagernes above. From there a county road to Skinnarløk 10 miles north of Fagernes followed by a local toll road to Svarthamar. Maps: N. Etnedal and Slidre.

Lake Fullsen (2,972 ft.) lake Etnsenn (2,627 ft.) and the Folda river between them are the main waters. 3 km long and 2 km wide lake Fullsenn holds a moderate amount of trout, average size 10 ounces, good quality. Closed season Sept. 10 — June 1. In lake Etnsenn trout are more numerous and the quality is good. Closed season Sept. 10. — June 1. The Folda river forms long glides and drains lake Fullsjøen. After the confluence with Svarthamarbekken the river runs faster and becomes more difficult to fish. There is a fair amount of trout in the river (up to 10 ounces in lake Fullsjøen), especially in the upper reaches. Fishing is best immediately after the spring

flood around Midsummer. Closed seasons Sept. 10 — June 15.
Centres: See Fagernes in «Hotels in Norway».
Fishing permit: The Skrautvål common ground tickets covers the water, available locally.

SANDERSTØLEN area (C 11). Travel by train from Oslo to Leira in 4 hours and then 1/2 hour by bus to Sanderstølen. The distance by road from Oslo is 130 miles. Maps: Aurdal and Gol.
The Tisleia river flows between lake Tisleifjorden (2,690 ft.) and lake Ølsjøen (2,460 ft.). Both lakes are reservoirs for the Åbjøra power station. Lake Tisleifjorden (11 km long, max. width 1,8 km) holds few trout but plenty of perch. In lake Ølsjøen there are gwyniad as well. The best sport is found in the 12 km long Tisleia river. It is heavily fished, but the many fine pools still yield fine catches. Fishing is best in June and July. All waters are closed from Sept. 10 to June 15.
Centres: Sanderstølen and Hovda (see Fagernes in «Hotels in Norway»).
Fishing permits: Tisleia river is covered by 3 permits, available locally. Tickets are also sold to the lakes by the local owners.

SØR-AURDAL

The southernmost district of the fair Valdres province provides fishing on the mountain moors west of the main valley.

HEDALEN — VASSFARET area (C 11). Travel by bus from Oslo to Hedalen in 3 hours. The distance by car from Oslo to Sørbekkseter is 92 miles. Maps: 1716 II (Hedalen), 1716 III (Vassfaret) and 1716 IV (Aurdal).
Gently rolling mountain moors with brushwood vegetation and marshes, easy to traverse. Fishing in several smaller lakes in Hedalen and in larger lakes in Vassfaret, 15 mins. to 3 hours walk from Sørbekkseter lodge. The lakes in the mountains contain pretty good stocks of trout, generally of average size and good quality, well suited for fly fishing in warm weather. The lakes in Vassfaret have more uneven stocks of trout, gwyniad and some char. Trout are more numerous than other fish. Chances of big fish, also in the rapids between the lakes. Season from approx. June 20 to end of Aug. Closed season from Sept. 1 to Oct. 15 in Hedalen and to Oct. 10 in Vassfaret.
Centre: Hedalen (not listed).
Fishing permits: Hedalen common ground ticket covers the area, available from the Post Office, local shops and lodges.

REINLI area (C 10). Travel by bus from Oslo to Bagn in 3 1/2 hours. Taxi from there to Fjellstølen. Distance by road from Oslo to Fjellstølen is 106 miles. Maps: 1716 IV (Aurdal).
Trout fishing in a number of lakes approx. 2,800 ft. above sea level. The fishing varies, and the stock consists of trout and/or gwyniad and perch, in fairly good supply. Trout are of moderate size, but of good quality.
Centre: Fjellstølen (see Fagernes in «Hotels in Norway»).
Fishing permit: Tickets, at reasonable prices, available from shops in Bagn or Fjellstølen lodge.

VANG

This district includes the wildest tracts of Valdres and fishing both in the Jotunheimen mountains and on the Filefjell.

EIDSBUGAREN area (C 11). Travel by train from Oslo to Fagernes in 4 hours and then by bus to Eidsbugaren in 3 hours. The distance by road from Oslo is 164 miles. Map: Gjende.
Eidsbugaren lies at west end of lake Bygdin (3,180 ft.). The hotel owns the fishing rights in half of that 25 km long lake and in some smaller lakes approx, one hour's walking distance away. In the lakes there are mountain trout, from 6 ounces to 6 pounds, of excellent quality, but stocks are rather small, and lake Bygdin — a water power reservoir only full in rainy years — is difficult to fish. Season is approx. July 10 to Aug. 20. Closed season Oct. 1 — Dec. 31. Boats available at Eidsbugaren.
Centre: Eidsbugaren, see Vang.
Fishing permit: Fishing is free to guests staying at the Eidsbugaren.

TYIN area (C 11). Travel by train from Oslo to Fagernes in 4 hours and then 2 1/2 hours by bus to Tyin and 3 hours to Tyinholmen. The distance by road from Oslo to Tyin is 167 miles. Maps: Vangsmjøsi and Filefjell. Tyinholmen lies at the north end of lake Tyin (3,240 ft.), Tyin at the south end, both well above the timber line. The proprietor of Tyinholmen Hotel owns the fishing rights in lake Tyin which has a moderate stock of trout of fine quality, average size 2 pounds. The lake is to large for rod fishing from the banks. Boats are available at Tyinholmen and Tyin. There are also facilities for fishing in smaller lakes further away. Lake Steinbusjøen (3,968 ft.). reached on foot from Highroad 252 in one hour, holds very fine trout. Trout fishing in all lakes is best in July. Closed season Oct. 10 — May 15.
Centres: Tyin and Tyinholmen (listed under Vang).
Fishing permits: Tickets to lake Tyin at

Tyinholmen. Tickets to Steinbusjøen are available Grimhamarstølen.

NYSTOVA area (C 11). Travel by train to Fagernes in 4 hours and bus 2 1/2 hours to Nystova. Distance by road from Oslo 170 miles. Map: Filefjell.
The nearest lake, Otrøvatn (2,950 ft.) is just by the hotel which also owns a large area containing numerous lakes and rivers. The fishing is typical mountain fishing, medium stocks of good quality fish. Usual size 10 ounces, max. size 10 to 12 pounds in the larger lakes. Season July — Aug. Closed season Oct. 1 — Dec. 31. Boats for hire in several lakes.
Centres: Nystova (listed) and Tyinkrysset are listed under Vang in «Hotels in Norway».
Fishing permits: Tickets for lake Utrovatn, kr. 10 pr day, available at Nystuen Hotel. Tickets for Vesleskartjern kr. 20 per week.

VESTRE SLIDRE
Vestre Slidre, the most typical of all Valdres districts with its string of lakes connected by the Begna, its farmland and wooded hills, offers fishing both in the valley and on the mountain moors.

NØSEN area (C 11). Travel by train to Fagernes in 4 hours and by taxi or hotel car to Nøsen in 1 hour. Distance by road from Oslo is 135 miles. Maps: Gol and Slidre.
The Panarama (toll) Road runs across the mountain moors and provides (with its side roads) easy access to most of the waters. The lakes are situated approx. 3,000 ft. above sea level. Lake Flyvatn (Storefjord) holds trout and perch, lake Grønsennvatn trout only, lake Movatn has stocks of trout and perch. Lake Nesvatn is a typical trout lake and in lake Rensennvatn anglers will find both trout and perch. There are trout and perch also in lake Veslevatn which is drained by the Flya river on its way to the Tisleifjord. Trout are of moderate size and good quality in all these waters which are heavily fished. Whereas the above mentioned lakes are moderately stocked lake Vasetvatn is «overpopulated» and size and quality of trout is below average. Perhaps the best sport is to be had in the Flya river where 4-pounders have been killed on several occasions. Boats are available to guest staying at Nøsen in lake Flyvatn. Fishing is best in June and July. Closed season Sept. 1. — May 31.
Centres: Nøsen, Gomubu and Vaset are listed under Fagernes.
Fishing permits: A general ticket covering most of the lakes is available at Nøsen Hotel and shops at Røn and Lomen, at a reasonable price. Day tickets to lake Vasetvatn cost

approx. kr. 10 (or kr. 30 per week), available at Vasetseter and sports shops in Fagernes.

RYFOSS area (C 11). Travel by train to Fagernes in 4 hours and then by bus to Ryfoss in 1 hour. Distance by road from Oslo is 142 miles. Map: Slidre.
The village of Ryfoss lies in the Vestre Slidre valley 1,400 ft. above sea level. In the valley there is fishing in the Begna river with pools and streams and lake Slidrefjorden. E 68 runs north of the river and the lake and a county road along the south banks. Begna has moderate stocks of trout and some scattered perch. Average weight of trout 6 to 8 ounces. Fish weighing several pounds have been caught. The quality is good and stock is kept up. Season June to September.
Lake Slidrefjorden (15 km long, max. width 1,3 km) has stocks of mediumsized trout and perch. Fishing is best in June. The season is closed both for the lake and the river between Sept. 25 and Dec. 31.
There is fishing also in the Syndin lakes (approx. 3,000 ft. above sea level) on the mountain moors south of the village. The lakes are accessible by car on local toll roads. These shallow lakes are moderately stocked with good quality trout and fishing is best in June — July. Closed season Sept. 25 to Dec. 31.
Centres: Ryfoss (see Vang) and Vestre Slidre (see Fagernes in «Hotels in Norway»).
Fishing permits: Tickets, at reasonable prices, both to valley and mountain fisheries are sold by local shops.

ØYSTRE SLIDRE
Øystre Slidre is another doorway to the Jotunheimen mountains. Bygdin area is part of Vang municipality, but as it is reached via Øystre Slidre it is also natural to describe it under this heading.

BYGDIN area (C 11). Travel by train from Oslo to Fagernes in 4 hours and then 2 hours by bus to Bygdin. The distance by road from Oslo is 150 miles. Maps: Gjende, Sjodalen, Vangsmjøsi and Slidre.
Fishing in Øystre Slidre state common ground (mainly lake Bygdin and the Vinstra water course) and for guests staying at Bygdin Hotel also in several smaller lakes south and north of Bygdin. These lakes are well stocked and looked after. In lake Bygdin (3,150 ft.) there are meagre stocks of trout, but chances of big fish exist. The Vinstra water course has been reduced by damming, but still offers good sport. Quality is good everywhere. Bygdin Hotel has rowing boats on the lakes which are reached by car and/or by foot. Season from approx. July 10 to Aug.

20. In the higher lakes good fishing in dependent on warm weather. Closed season Sept. 10 — Oct. 20.
Centre: Bygdin (see Vang).
Fishing permits: The common ground ticket is available from Bygdin Hotel or Valdresflya Yout Hotel at a reasonable price.

BEITOSTØLEN area (C 11). Travel by train to Fagernes in 4 hours and then 1 hour by bus to Beitostølen. The distance by car from Oslo is 142 miles.
Map: Slidre.
Fishing in the valley of Øystre Slidre and on the mountain moors. The Storå/Dalselv/Vollbuelv/Røså rivers flows through the valley draining a number of lakes 2,200 to 1,400 ft. above sea level. Some of these lakes, for instance lake Heggefjorden, are very well stocked with trout. The Røså river between lake Hovsfjorden and lake Vollbufjorden should also provide good sport. Fishing is best in June and July. Closed season: Sept. 10 to Oct. 20.
Mountain fishing is available in lake Javnin, the Kjølavatn lakes and adjoining rivers, 3,300 to 2,600 ft. above sea level. The waters are reached on local toll roads. Some of the lakes are well stocked with good quality trout. Javanåa river is reported to be good. Fishing is probably best in July. Closed season Sept. 10 — June 15.
Centres: Beito, Beitostølen and Heggenes, see Beitostølen.
Fishing permits: The Øystre Slidre common ground ticket, reasonably priced, is available from hotels, pensions and at the Fagernes tourist office. It covers some of the fisheries on the mountain moors. For others, and all available waters in the main valley, local fishing permits must be acquired.

GJØVIK
The town covers an area of 680 sq.km and affords fishing both within its limits and in the surrounding districts.

GJØVIK (C/D 11). Travel by train from Oslo in 2 1/2 hours. Distance by road is 78 miles. Maps: 1816 I (Gjøvik) and 1816 IV (Dokka).
Mjøsa is the largest lake in Norway and it holds some big trout (to be fished by special methods), red char, perch and gwyniad. Boats can be rented at Vikodden and Sveastrand camping sites. Lake Skumsjøen (1,417 ft.), 10 miles southwest of Gjøvik, is a 2-mile long woodland lake. It holds trout, red char, perch and gwyniad. The Kongelstad river, which drains the lake, can also be fished. Boats for rent at Osbakken Pension. The season starts in May, when the ice is gone, and lasts to the end of Sept. Lake Einavatn,

16 miles south of Gjøvik, is a big lake (1309 ft.), and surrounded by farms and forest. It is reported to be fairly well stocked with trout, red char. Lake Randsfjorden, Norway's fourth biggest lake is also worth investigating. It abounds in gwyniad, which are caught in nets and handnets in great quantities at the northern end of the lake, and in the rivers that flows into the lake there, in the late autumn. Lake Randsfjorden also holds some trout, perch, red char and big pike.
Centre: Gjøvik.
Fishing permits: Angling is free in lake Mjøsa and Randsfjorden. Inexpensive tickets to Skumsjøen at Osbakken pension and to lake Einavatn from Einastrand Samvirkelag (Co-op) and Stener Hveem's shop, both Eina, and Hans Eidstuen, Trevatn.

BUSKERUD
This county, which reaches from the Oslo fjord almost to the Jotunheimen mountain, features two main water courses, Hallingdalselva river and Numedalslågen river, both heavily exploited by hydro-electric power stations. However, some lakes and rivers in this vast district have escaped damming, and others afford good sport in spite of it.

GOL
Gol on the Bergen Railway has fishing both in the Hallingdalselva river in the main valley and on the mountain plateau.

GOL VALLEY area (C 12). Travel by train from Oslo in 3 1/2 hours or from Bergen in 5 hours. By road from Oslo 125 miles, from Bergen 190 miles plus one ferry. Maps: Gol and Tunnhovd.
Fishing in the Hallingdalselva river south of Gol, where the river receives the water from Heimsila through Heimsil II power station. North of Gol there is very little water in the river. Between Gol and Sjongshølen, where the river receives the water from Nes power station, trout dominates the water. Below Sjongshølen perch are more numerous than trout. There are also some tarns in the mountains north of Gol which contain trout and perch. They lie 3,000 to 3,300 ft. above sea level and are reached on foot in approx. 1 hour from the top of the chair lift. Trout both in the river and in these tarns will average 10 ounces, but almost every summer 15-pounders are hooked in Hallingdalselva. Fishing in the river is at its best in July and Aug., in the mountain tarns from approx. July 10 to Aug. 20. The season is closed from Sept. 10 to June 1.
Centre: Gol.
Fishing permits: Tickets, at reasonable prices, for the main river, the mountain tarns,

and a seasonal ticket covering all waters in the Gol area are available from the Tourist Office and hotels and pensions.

GOL MOUNTAIN area (C 11). Travel See Gol Valley area. From Gol village it is only 10—15 miles by car or bus to the mountain area. Map: Gol.
In the mountains there is trout fishing in lake Tisleifjorden (2,690 ft.) and the Tisleia river. Lake Tisleifjorden (11 km long, max. width 1,8 km) holds few trout but plenty of perch. The best sport is offered by the heavily fished Tisleia river. There is also fishing in lake Fjellheimsvatn and several smaller lakes. Trout will average 10 ounces. The best season for trout fishing is July and Aug. and the season is closed in all Gol waters from Sept. 10 to June 1.
Centres: Oset, Storefjell, Ørterstølen and Kamben (see Gol in «Hotels in Norway»).
Fishing permits: Fishing cards are available locally from hotels and camping sites.

HEMSEDAL
This is a beautiful valley north of Gol flanked by almost perpendicular mountains. Hemsedal offers both river and lake fishing.

HEMSEDAL area (C 11—12). Travel: See Gol. The village of Hemsedal lies 20 miles north of Gol and is reached by bus in 1 hour. Map: Hemsedal.
Below the Eikre dam the Hemsila river is dry. Above this dam there is trout fishing, very good at times, both in the main river and in the Grøndøla, Mørkdøla and Buliåna tributaries all of which are accessible by car. Trout will average 10 ounces, but 4 to 6-pounders are caught every season. The fishing is usually best from the middle of July (the area lies 2,000 to 3,000 ft. above sea level) to the end of Aug. Closed season from Sept. 15 to June 1.
Centre: Hemsedal.
Fishing permits: Reasonably priced daily and weekly tickets from hotels, pensions, shops and the tourist office.

HOLDESKARET area (C 11). This area is reached by the Fanitull Road, which crosses the mountain moors between Hemsedal and Hol, or by the chair lift from the valley. Map: Hemsedal.
Trout fishing in the Tottentjern tarns (approx. 3,500 ft.) 1/2 hour's walk from the chair lift. Trout are reported to scale 15 to 20 ounces, max. size 4 1/2 pounds. Trout fishing also in the Kjelltjern and Øvretjern tarns, where trout are somewhat smaller apparently, both accessible by car. These tarns lie 3,400 ft. above sea level. Fishing in these

waters is reported to be at its best between July 20, and Aug. 20, and the season is closed from Sept. 15 to June 1.
Centre: Hemsedal.
Fishing permits: Fishing is free for chair lift passengers in the Totten tarns. Tickets to the other tarns, approx. kr. 10 per week, are sold at Holdeseter.

HYDALEN area. (C 11). Travel: See Hemsedal. Map: Hemsedal and Vangsmjøsi.
Lake Søndre Hydalsvatn (2,975 ft.) lies 2 hours' walk from the Vavatn toll road on the mountain trail between Hemsedal and Vang (in Valdres). Trout are numerous, if somewhat small, in this lake where fishing is said to be best in late July and the first half of Aug. Closed season Sept. 15 to June 1.
Centre: Hemsedal.
Fishing permit: Available at Hemsedal tourist office.

HOL
This mountain parish includes part of the unspoilt Hardangervidda mountain plateau as well as the almost cosmopolitan Geilo resort.

GEILO area (C 12). Travel by train from Oslo or Bergen in 4 hours. By road from Oslo 148 miles, from Bergen 156 miles and one ferry. Maps: Dagali and Hallingskarvet as well as 1515 I (Skurdalen).
The charming village of Geilo lies 2,620 ft. above sea level on the Bergen Railway. The fishing in the immediate neighbourhood will hardly result in big catches, but there are some trout in lake Ustedalsfjord and more in a string of tarns on the Skurdalsåsen (Geilotjønn, Hovdetjønn, Svartesteinstjønn, Yngletjønn, Store Hakkeset, Vesle Hakkeset, the Grøndalstjønn tarns) accessible on foot in 10 to 45 mins. from Highway 7 south of Geilo. There are also trout in the Vedal lakes.
Centre: Geilo.
Fishing permits: Reasonably priced day and week tickets available from the Tourist Office, A.E. Tufte, N.J. Furuseth and Sandven Kafé.

DAGALI area (C 12). Travel: See Geilo area. From Geilo Highway 8 leads to Dagali 15 miles away. The bus journey takes a little more than 1 hour. Map: Dagali.
The mountain hamlet of Dagali is situated 2,550 ft. above sea level. Fishing in a 15 to 18 mile stretch of the Numedalslågen river, including lake Ossjøen, tributaries and part of Heinelva river, which is half an hour's walk from the upper end of Ossjøen. The stretch comprises the Lågen river from lake Pålsbu-

fjorden to Skriubekken. There is a local road down the river towards Pålsbufjorden and a local toll road up the river to lake Ossjøen. The water course follows a gently sloping valley. The stock contains trout and char of uneven quantity, mostly medium size 6—10 ounces to 2 pounds and óf good quality.

Centres: Geilo or Dagali.

Fishing permits: Available in shops and pensions at Dagali and from Geilo Tourist Office.

HOL area (C 12). Travel by train from Oslo i 4 hours or Bergen in 4 1/2 hours. There is a bus service up the valley to Hovet 1/2 hour and Sudndal 3/4 hour. The distance by car from Oslo to Hovet is 147 miles, from Bergen 170 miles. Map: Hallingskarvet.

Fishing in lake Holsfjorden (1,780 ft.), lake Sudndalsfjorden (2,400 ft.), lake Hovsfjorden (1,935 ft.) and lake Strandavatn (3,116 ft.). Lake Holsfjorden holds trout of good quality and medium size (12 ounces). In Hovsfjorden there are trout and a few red char. This shallow lake is said to provide good fly fishing from boats. Lake Strandavatn is a vast mountain lake with some trout. All these lakes are water power reservoirs with fluctuating water levels.

Centres: Hovet, Sudndalen and Raggsteindalen, see Ål.

Fishing permits: Raggsteindalen chalet provides fishing in lake Strandavatn for guests and Hallingskarvet Hotel in lake Sudndalsfjorden. Tickets to Holsfjorden and Hovsfjorden are sold by E.S. Tufte and Thingstad Kafé.

NESBYEN

This municipality on the Bergen Railway provides fishing in several areas both east and west of the Hallingdal valley. There is also some fishing to be had in Hallingdalselva river. The areas are called Nes Sørmark (Southern Moors), Nes Nordmark (Northern Moors), Nes Østmark (Eastern Moors), Limarka, Bøgasetmarka, Garnåsmarka and Børtnesmarka and they are situated from 2,600 to 3,700 ft. above sea level. In the various waters trout will average 10 ounces with 6 to 16-pounders as rather vague possibilities. Fishing in all areas seems best in July and the closed season extends from Sept. 20 and June 15. Nes Sørmark probably provides the most interesting fishing and is dealt with below.

NES SØRMARK (C 12). Travel by train from Oslo to Nesbyen in 3 hours or from Bergen in 5 1/2 hours, and by taxi from Nesbyen to Fekjan in 20 mins. By car from Oslo 100 miles, from Bergen 202 miles. Map: Tunnhovd.

There is a toll road from Sanden on Highway 7 to Fekjan Seter and other summer farms on the mountain moors, where the waters are situated approx. 3,200 ft. above sea level. The Fekjaelva river follows the toll road to Fekjan. During its 14 km course this river drops almost 3,000 ft. The lower parts of the river lie in rugged terrain and are very difficult to fish, whereas the upper stretches offer good rod fishing and trout are big, average size is said to be 3 pounds. The river drains lake Brynhilstjern, where trout are more numerous than in the river but much smaller. This lake is fairly well stocked with gwyniad, scaling from 10 ounces to 2 pounds. Trout are also numerous and of medium size (12 to 16 ounces) in lake Forkétjønn. There are plenty of trout too in lake Kringletjønn, but the fish are on the small side (8 ounces). The same applies to lake Mortenstjern. The Ormevatna and Småvatna lakes have somewhat bigger trout (10 ounces) but they are fewer. There are also some trout in Skurvåstjern, Øyvatnet and Ålsvatnet. All these small lakes are reached on foot from the Fekjan road in 1—2 hours. Fishing is best in June—Aug. Closed season from Sept. 20. to Nov. 1 and from May 10 to June 15.

Centre: Fekjan (not listed) and Nesbyen.

Fishing permits: Available from Fekjan Kafé.

Notes to the other Nes areas: Visitors desiring to try the Nes Nordmark may stay at Myking where tickets may be bought at the turn-pike, from the Post Office or the pensions. In Bøgasetmarka tickets are available from Bøgaseth Kafé, stay at Nesbyen. Nes Østmark should be fished from Buvatn mountain lodge, where fishing permits are sold. Tickets to Bergsmarka are available from Bjarne Li (shopkeeper) at Liodden, visitors should stay at Nesbyen. Limarka anglers will get their permits from shopkeeper Knut Li at Liodden and find their lodgings at Nesbyen. In most of these areas comfortable private chalets can be rented for a week or more through the Nesbyen Tourist Office. All tickets mentioned are inexpensive.

NORE AND UVDAL

This municipality, comprising the parishes of Nore and Uvdal with venerable stave churches, used to be one of Norway's finest angling districts. Extensive damming has destroyed much of the trout fishing but red char seem to thrive in the huge reservoirs.

RAUHELLEREN area (C 12). Travel by train from Oslo to Rødberg in 4 hours and by bus and taxi to Solheimstulen in 1 1/2 hours. From there along cairned path to Rauhelleren in about 7 hours. The distance by road from Oslo to Solheimsstulen is approx. 140 miles. Map: Hardangervidda.

Rauhelleren Turisthytte (mountain chalet) lies on lake Langesjøen 3,630 ft. above sea level in treeless and fairly flat mountain country. Fishing in lakes and rivers owned by the Uvdal State Common Ground. Most of the waters are privately owned and well kept. These lakes contain trout, the stock is generally fair and quality good, usually up to 1 pound, with chances of larger fish. Permission to fish must be acquired from the owners (among others Sønstebø in Uvdal). Fishing in this area is allowed from Aug. 1 to Sept. 25.
Centre: Rauhelleren (not listed).
Fishing permits: Available at the mountain chalet. If you should spend the night at Solheimstulen, you might try the Jønndalsåa river where fishing is free for guests.

TUNNHOVD area (C 12). Travel by train from Oslo to Nesbyen in 3 hours or Bergen in 5 1/2 hours, and then by bus to Tunnhovd in 1 hour. The distance by car from Oslo is 116 miles, from Bergen 218 miles and one ferry. Map: Tunnhovd.

Trout but mainly red char fishing in the huge reservoirs lake Pålsbufjorden and lake Tunnhovd 2,465 ft. above sea level. There are some huge trout in these waters, every 7th specimen caught scales more than 2 pounds, the biggest fish on record weighed 27 pounds. Trout are mostly netted, some are caught on spoons from boats. When water is low in the Tunnhovd reservoir the original 3 lakes reappear and with them such fishermen's haunts as Sagodden, Bustrøm, Gravikstrøm and Turrsnippen and above all the Torkelsstryket rapids between lake Pålsbufjorden and lake Tunnhovd where red char fishing is extremely good in spring.
Centres: Tunnhovd and Øygardsgrend, not listed in «Hotels in Norway».
Fishing permits: Fishing cards are available to the Torkelbustryket rapids. Guests staying at Tunnhovd or Øygardsgrend may obtain permission to fish additional waters.

SIGDAL

Sigdal is made up of the parishes of Eggedal and Sigdal. The Simoa river runs trough the valley draining in its way to Åmot beautiful lake Soneren.

SIMOA — SONEREN area (C 12). Travel by train from Oslo to Åmot in 1 1/2 hours and then by bus in 45 mins. to Sigdal or 2 hours to Eggedal. Road distance from Oslo to Sigdal is 65 miles, Eggedal 86 miles. Map: Sigdal or 1715 II (Krøderen), 1715 III (Eggedal) and 1714 I (Hokksund).

The Simoa river holds trout, perch, gwyniad and even eels. Trout are small and of inferior quality in the lower and middle reaches of the river. Higher up the river contains a fair amount of good quality trout and gwyniad. Where tributaries join the river good fishing may be expected when the water level is favourable. In the Owernbekken tributary, which joins Simoa below Haugsfoss, there is a fair amount of char. Lake Soneren (398 ft.) belongs to the Sigdal (Simoa) water course. In this 10 km long and 1 km wide lake trout, perch, gwyniad and eel are numerous, but small, average size 6—8 ounces. Boats can be rented from Blegeberg Gård (farmhouse pension), Båsheim. In the Simoa river fishing is best around Midsummer and in lake Soneren June and the late Aug. is reported to yield the best results. There are motoring roads along the Simoa system.
Centres: Eggedal and Sigdal.
Fishing permits: Tickets, approx. kr. 10 per day and kr. 20 per week, available at pensions, cafés and shops. This fishing permit also includes the Horgeelva tributary with Horgesetervatn and Gryteelva tributary.

ÅL

This mountain parish once offered fabulous fishing, but most of the big lakes have been turned into one vast reservoir. Yet there are still some «pockets» left where good sport awaits the eager angler.

BERGSJØ area (C 12). Travel by train from Oslo or Bergen to Ål in 4 hours and from there by hotel car or bus to Bergsjø or Rødungstøl. Road distance from Oslo 148 miles, from Bergen 193 miles and 1 ferry. Map: Djup.

Fishing takes place in rugged mountain terrain approx. 3,300 ft. above sea level. From Bergsjø there is fishing in two groups of lakes and tarns. The nothern group of lakes, which is drained by the Eitra river, includes Kroktjern, Dyrebotntjern and Lumreitjern. The southern group comprises Tulletjern, Lappetjern, Damptjern and Revtjern. There is also trout fishing in lake Bergsjø and Lille (little) Bergsjø. Several rowing boats are available free of charge to the guests staying at Bergsjø or Bergsjøstølen.

From Rødungstøl there is fishing both in the reservoirs and in a string of smaller lakes to the north, Eitretjerna, Lumreitjern, Dyrebotntjern, Kroktjern and in the streams between the tarns, and also in Julsentjern, 9 miles further to the north.

The stock of trout in the small lakes in reported to be good, average size about 1 pound and of good quality. Season from beginning of July to middle of Aug.
Centres: Bergsjø, Bergsjøstølen, Skarslia and

Rødungstøl — listed under Ål in «Hotels in Norway».
Fishing permits: All waters are private, but fishing is offered free of charge to visitors staying at hotels and pensions in the area.

IUNGSDALEN area (C 12). Travel by train from Oslo or Bergen to Ål in 4 hours and from there by bus to Djup, where a boat from Iungsdalshytta meets guests. The distance by car from Oslo to Djup is approx. 160 miles, from Bergen 205 miles. Toll road between Tvist and Djup and 3/4 hour's walk from the end of this road to Iungsdalshytta. Map: Djup.
The Iungsdalshytta lodge lies at the northern end of lake Djupsvatn (3,450 ft.). Fishing in the lakes Djupsvatn, Førdalsvatn, the river Fossebrekka between Førdalsvatn and Djupsvatn and in the river Iungsdøla. Also in the lakes Skorpetingsvatna approx. 6 miles south-east of the lodge. All waters are reached on foot. Lake Djupsvatn is part of the big reservoir mentioned under Bergsjø and not so well suited for rod fishing. Fishing in the rest of the area is known to be good. Season from beginning of July to approx. Aug. 20.
Centre: Iungdalshytta lodge. (Norw. Touring Club) not listed in «Hotels in Norway».
Fishing permits: Resident guests may fish gratis if the catch is handed over to the lodge.

TELEMARK
The lower part of this county, which stretches from the Skagerak to the Hardangervidda mountain plateau, abounds in «overpopulated» lakes where trout fishing is of little interest. In the middle districts, between 1,300 and 1,600 ft. above sea level, some good waters are found. In the north, on the outskirts of the Hardangervidda and on the plateau itself, there is still fine fishing, though angling in many lakes and rivers has deteriorated through extensive damming for hydro-electric power stations.

BIRTEDALEN area (C 13). Travel by train from Oslo and then by bus to Fyresdal in 3 hours. The distance by road from Oslo is 156 miles. Maps: Fyresdal and Nisser.
From Fyresdal village some of the waters are reached by car. Others imply walks of 1—2 hours from the nearest road. The fishery is situated in the mountains east of lake Fyresvatn 2,000 to 2,500 ft. above sea level. It comprises the following lakes: Grodvatn, Gjævarvatn, Ufstjønn, Langvatn, Sundbekk, the Lomtjønn and Tovslitjønn tarns, as well as parts of the lakes Øyarvatn, Birtevatn and Brutjønn. These lakes contain a moderate amount of trout, average 10 ounces with fair

chances of bigger fish (up to 2 pounds). Fishing is known to be best in July. Also fishing in lake Fyresvatn.
Centre: Fyresdal.
Fishing permits: Tickets at reasonable prices are available in Fyresdal, for instance at Fyresdal Hotel.

KILEGREND area (C 13). Travel by train from Oslo to Nelaug in 5 hours or from Kristiansand in 1 hour and then by bus to Tjønnefoss in 1 1/2 hours. Road distance from Oslo 156 miles, from Kristiansand 73 miles. Map: Nisser.
From Tjønnefoss (the nearest centre) the area is reached by car. The northernmost lakes of the area require a walk of several hours from the end of this road. Huts in the area may be rented. The fishery consists of a string of lakes drained by the Kileåna river. Some of these lakes are only sparsely stocked with trout, others moderately, but all are intensively cultivated and fair sport may be expected gradually. In the Kileåna river trout are not numerous. The uppermost lake (Rundemannstjern) lies 2,240 ft. above sea level. Eventually Kileåna flows into lake Drang (889 ft.) the biggest of all the lakes and conveniently fished from Highway 355. Lake Drang holds plenty of trout, char and gwyniad. The average trout here are small (6 ounces), but 6 to 8-pounders occur occasionally. The gwyniad are of fair quality and size (10 ounces). Char too are plentiful and accordingly of moderate size. Fishing in the area is best in June — July.
Centre: Tjønnefoss (not listed).
Fishing permits: Tickets, approx. kr. 5 per day and kr 20 per week, are available from the members of the local fishing co-operative.

NISSEDAL
This is the district on both sides of lake Nisser. Until recently you could fish in the mountains on both sides of the big lake, but fishing has deteriorated. Alle lakes are affected by pollution (sour downpour), and few trout and perch have survived. The best fishing can be expected in the lower lakes of this area.

TJØNNEFOSS — TREUNGEN area (C 13). Travel: See Kilegrend area above. Maps: Nisser and Åmli.
9 km long and 900 metres wide lake Kjørull lies 828 ft. above sea level in typical forest country. This lake used be «overpopulated». Now it holds a fair amount of trout, red char, gwyniad and perch. Trout are more numerous than other fish, but size varies greatly — from 4 ounces to 1/2 pound. Red char will scale around 8 ounces and gwyniad 10 ounces, perch are usually smaller. Boats are

available to guests at Tjørull Pension. Lake Nisser can be conveniently fished from Tjønnefoss or Treungen is best in the shallow water between Trontveit and Fjone along which a local road leads from Treungen. Fishing in lake Nisser has also deteriorated, probably because of the severely regulated water level. But there is still plenty of fish left: trout, gwyniad and red char. The char is small, trout also, but now and again 8 — 10-pounders are caught. Angling in lake Nisser is best when a light breeze is blowing. Rod fishing in the Nidelv river is still passable, especially between Haugsjåsund and Åmli.

Centres: Tjønnefoss (not listed) and Treungen.

Fishing permits: Fishing is free in lake Kjørull for guests staying at Tjørull Pension. There is no charge for fishing in lake Nisser either, but the lake is owned by the farmers along the shores and their permission should always be asked.

NOTODDEN

The industrial town of Notodden is just a speck in a vast district of hills and forests where the Tinnåa river is the most important water.

TINNÅA area (C 12). Travel by train from Oslo to Notodden in 3 hours. The distance by car from Oslo is 70 miles. Maps: 1714 III (Notodden) and Tinnsjø.

The Tinnåa river flows from lake Tinnsjøen (626 ft.) to lake Heddalsvatn (52 ft.) to lake Heddalsvatn (52 ft.). In the course of its 25 km long run it is harnessed by 4 power stations, yet it remains an exciting rod river especially between Tinnoset and Gransherad. Here are pools like Nisihølen, Mjellekåshølen, Flisehølen, Lihølen and Kjerketjønna and Mjellekåsstrykene, the best of all rapids along the river. Further down the upper end of the Grønnvollfoss reservoir provides good fishing in the Kleivhølen pool. Here, however, the river is difficult to fish and a boat should be hired. Below Grønnvollfoss sandy banks and eddies provide fine beats especially in late summer and autumn. The Folldøla tributary holds fine trout too. Below Stormo many a fine trout has been killed and similar chances for big fish exist below the Tinnfoss dam, where a 25-pounder has been landed. Fly fishing is best in July and Aug. and in fine weather, preferably in the evening.

Centres: Bolkesjø and Notodden.

Fishing permits: Day tickets (approx. kr. 10) are available from the Notodden Tourist Office.

SILJAN

Siljan is the name of the woodland parish east of Skien. The landowner has leased more than 50 lakes to the local angling club on the conditions that the waters are cultivated and tickets sold.

SILJAN area (D 12). Travel by train to Skien from Oslo in 3 hours and then by bus to Siljan in 30 mins. The distance by car from Oslo is 93 miles. Map 1713 I (Siljan).

The lakes in this area are situated from 1,500 to 2,500 ft. above sea level and most of them belong to the Siljanelv or Varnebuelv system. In the lower lakes there are few trout but plenty of perch and pike. This is reversed in the higher lakes where trout are quite numerous, averaging 10 ounces with chances of bigger fish, up to 2 pounds. In addition to trout these lakes are stocked with small-sized perch as well. Most of the waters are accessible by car, either along the country road or by means of local toll roads.

Centres: Siljan and Skien.

Fishing permits: These are sold locally, for instance at the turnpikes.

TINN

The centre of Tinn is industrial Rjukan. Here fishing is offered in several widely separated areas, three of which are described below.

RJUKAN area (C 12). Travel by train from Oslo to Kongsberg in 2 hours and from there by bus in 3 hours to Rjukan. The distance by car from Oslo 120 miles. Map: Rjukan.

Access to this area is by means of the cable railway to Gvepseborg or a motoring road via Kalhovd. The area includes the lakes Våervatn, Sandvatn and Vrangtjønn. Lake Våervatn holds a fair amount of good quality trout, averaging 10 ounces. Lake Sandvatn is moderately stocked with trout, average weight 10 ounces, but bigger fish are a definite possibility. Fishing is best in June and Aug. — Sept. There is a closed season in Oct. All lakes in this area are well kept by the local angling club.

Centre: Rjukan.

Fishing permits: Inexpensive tickets available from Rjukan Tourist Office.

SKINNARBU area (C 12). Travel, see Rjukan and add 1 hour's bus ride or 12 miles of serpentine road. Maps: Rjukan and Rauland. Skinnarbu lies on the Hardangervidda mountain plateau and there is fishing both in the large Møsvatn reservoir (3,000 fr.) as well as in private waters (Grasfjell) in rivers and lakes on Hardangervidda State Common Ground. The last mentioned waters are reached on foot. Lake Tinnsjø holds some big trout (6 to 11 pounds) and red char averaging 10 ounces are very numerous. The char,

however, are mostly caught in winter by fishing through the ice.
Centre: Skinnarbu (see «Hotels in Norway» under Rjukan).
Fishing permits: Fishing is free for guests staying at Skinnarbu in Møsvatn and at Grasfjell. Reasonably priced fishing permits for the Hardangervidda State Common Ground are available at Skinnarbu.

MOGEN area (C 12). Travel: See Skinnarbu area above. From Skinnarbu (Møsvassdammen) there is a motor boat service (3 hours) across lake Møsvatn to Mogen.
Maps: Rauland and Hardangervidda (large scale).
Mogen lies in an open valley approx. 2,700 ft. above sea level surrounded by bare mountains. Fishing in the lower reaches of the Kvenna river and in Rauland State Common Ground approx. 6 miles to the southwest. All waters are reached on foot from Mogen. In the Kvenna river there are uneven stocks of trout, average size 4 ounces with chances of bigger fish. In the State Common Ground there is good trout fishing in warm summer. Several lakes, however, are closed to fishing. Season for anglers approx. July 1 to Aug. 15.
Centre: Mogen lodge (Skien — Telemark Touring Club), not listed.
Fishing permits: Reasonably priced tickets for the Kvenna are available at Argehovd farm on the river. Fishing cards to the State Common Ground are sold at Mogen.

TOKKE

This municipality provides fishing in various waters which can be reached by car from Dalen.

DALEN area (C 13). Travel by train to Bø from Oslo in 3 hours and then by bus to Dalen in 3 hours, or if you want a romantic out-of-this-world journey take the train to Lunde in 3 1/2 hours, and go by canal and lake steamer to Dalen in 5 hours. The distance by car from Oslo is 143 miles. Map: Tokke.
Lake Bandak (230 ft.) at western end of which Dalen is situated is 27 km long an 1,7 km wide and very deep lake surrounded by steep, forest-clad mountains. The lake contains trout red char, gwyniad, perch and eel. Trout are fairly numerous and fairly big, and are most easily caught in the late autumn or at the mouth of the Tokke when there is plenty of water in the river. Lake Børtevatn (1,450 ft.) is reached by road from Dalen. The lake is dammed but holds both trout and gwyniad (average weight 12 ounces).
Centre: Dalen.
Fishing permits: Fishing is free in lake Ban-

dak. Inexpensive fishing permits to lake Børtevatn are available from Gunnar Slettveit or A.O. Håtveit, Mo on the road to the lake.

VINJE

Vinje consist of the parishes of Rauland and Vinje and comprises vast areas of the Hardangervidda mountain plateau.

EDLAND area (C 12). Travel by train to Bø in 3 hours and then by bus to Haukeligrend in 4 hours or Haukeliseter in 5 hours. The distance by road from Oslo is 392 miles, from Bergen 173 miles and one ferry. Maps: 1414 II (Sæsvatn), 1414 III (Breive) and 1414 IV (Haukeliseter).
The Kjela river has been «regulated» and is more or less dry, but the lakes along the water course still offer good trout fishing. These include Vågslidvatn, Arbuvatn and Eivindbuvatn situated approx. 2,500 ft. above sea level. There is also fishing in several smaller lakes outside the main water course. Boats are for hire in the lakes belonging to the Kjela system, ask at hotels and pensions along E 76. There are also facilities for renting cabins. The waters contain a fairly large stock of trout. The quality varies, and the average size is from moderate to small (6 ounces). Season from July 1 to Aug. 20. For energetic walkers lakes in Røldal State Common Ground are within reach from Haukeliseter. The terrain is treeless, alt. 3,000 ft. or higher, and the ground is firm and easy to walk. The stock is of good quality, average close to 2 pounds, with fish up to 8 pounds in the larger lakes. Season from beginning of July to the middle of August.
Lake Grungevatn (1,848 ft.) and lake Songavatn (3,200 ft.) are also reached by road from Edland. Long and shallow lake Grungevatn holds trout (average size 8 ounces) and fishing is best in June — July. Lake Songavatn is a big reservoir formed from 8 lakes, and after damming the productivity of the lake has increased. Good chances of big fish (up to 4 1/2 pounds).
Centres: Haukeliseter, Vågslid and Edland , see Haukelifjell in «Hotels in Norway».
Fishing permits: Day tickets to the Kjøla system, approx. kr. 10 per day, from Botn Fjellstue and Prestegård Turisthytte. To Slovatn and Kjelavatn, approx. kr. 15 per week, from Haukeliseter Fjellstue which also sells tickets to the Røldal State Common Ground. Rod fishing in lake Grungevatn has been permitted without fees, but the farmers permission should always asked. Fishing in lake Songavatn must be arranged with the owners, apply through Edland (Telephone) Exchange.

AUST-AGDER AND VEST-AGDER

Conditions have deteriorated so radically that we have decided not to give detailed descriptions of angling waters in these counties. Even before pollution became a grave threat, lakes in this area tended to be sour and the fish small. Today both counties have been hit by the acid pollution transported to Norway from the Continent and Great Britain by prevailing winds, and in some waters fish have completely disappeared. Especially the higher districts have been affected. To this must be added the negative effects of extensive damming for hydro-electrical works. Pollution caused by local industries, urbanization and farming has also played its part.

Lower lakes have been less affected, and in several places it is possible to find passable trout fishing and even some rivers where sea trout run. However, make a note of the fact that some of the best waters along the South Coast are privately owned, and that in most cases the owners reserve fishing for themselves.

ROGALAND

Some coastal districts provide decent sport, but on the whole the islands and lowlands of Rogaland are of little interest to anglers. As you advance inland and especially if you enter the mountain moors and more desolate areas, fishing has been good, but sour pollution has affected the waters, and we must recommend everybody who intend to fish in this area to seek further information before setting off.

BJERKREIM

The main water-cource, Bjerkreimselva river, has been dealt with in the salmon part of this book. But there are several lakes connected with it which we shall deal with presently.

BJERKREIM area (C 14). Travel by train from Oslo to Eigersund in 9 1/2 hours or from Stavanger in 1 hour and from there by bus to Bjerkreim in 1/2 hour. Road distance from Oslo to Bjerkreim is 337 miles, Stavanger 37 miles and Kristiansand 130 miles. Maps: 1212 II (Bjerkreim) and 1212 III (Ørsdalsvatnet).

Lakes like Svelavatn, Hofreiste (558 ft.), Birkelandsvatn (590 ft.), Austrumvatn (1,010 ft.), Vinjavatn and Ørsdalsvatn (210 ft.) belong to the Bjerkreimselv system. Salmon enter Svelavatn and Hofreiste and have even been found in the Vinjavatn lakes. But primarily they are fine trout waters. The same applies to the other lakes mentioned above where trout will average 10 ounces and good

fishing can be expected from May to Aug. All these waters are accessibility road. More distant lakes are Holmavatn (2,624 ft.) and Storavatn (2,300 ft.) north of the Ørsdalen Valley. Very good trout fishing awaits the energetic angler in these parts of Bjerkreim. *Centre:* Helleland (not listed in «Hotels in Norway»). Visitors may also stay in Egersund and Sandnes.

Fishing permits: In the early season trout tickets are sold to lake Svelavatn. Later on those who wish to fish this lake, or the Bjerkreimselv river, must buy salmon tickets. Fishing cards are not sold for the other waters mentioned above and one must come to terms with the local farmers.

FORSAND

In this roadless community there are some lakes in the mountains south of the stupendous Lysefjord. They are situated in very rugged country 2,600 to 3,000 ft. above sea level and are very difficult to reach. Your attention is drawn to the Nilsebu area north of the fjord. Nilsebu lies within the borders of the Hjelmeland community, but as it is reached via Lysebotn we shall deal with it here.

NILSEBU area (C 13). Travel by boat from Stavanger to Lysebotn in 3 1/2 hours and go by bus or car to lake Nilsebuvatn in 1 hour. Either boat across the lake or walk along it in 1 1/2 hours to Nilsebu. Maps: 1313 II (Lyngsvatn) and 1313 II (Lysekammen). Nilsebu lies 2,280 ft. above sea level in rugged country sparsely covered with heather and birch trees. There is good fishing in the Storeåna watercourse. Lake Nilsebuvatn and lake Breivatn are drained by the Storåna. They are both well stocked with trout weighing 6—8 ounces. Larger fish can usually be found in the small lakes around Nilsebu. Season from midsummer to the end of August.

Centre: Nilsebu chalet (Stavanger Touring Club), not listed.
Fishing permits: Fishing is free in the Nilsebuvatn and in the surrounding lakes.

KARMØY

The flat island of Karmøy with fishing villages facing the North Sea, beaches of pure wide sand and picturesque Skudeneshavn harbour has some good trout waters.

SKUDENESHAVN area (B 13). Travel by ferry from Randaberg to Skudeneshavn in 70 mins. or by bus from Haugesund in 1 1/2 hours. Road distance from Haugesund is 25 miles. Maps: Utsira and Bokn.
Trout fishing can be had in a number of small

lakes like Dalsvatn, Hillestadvatn, Kigavatn, Litlavatn, Røyningsvatn and Stiglevatn all accessible in 10 to 30 mins. from the nearest road and none of them situated more than 330 ft. above sea level. The trouble with these lakes is that trout are too numerous with the exception of the Litlavatn — Ilsmyr water reservoirs where trout up to 2 pounds may be taken. Fishing in all these waters is best in May—June.

Centres: Haugesund and Kopervik. Skudeneshavn is not listed in «Hotels in Norway».

Fishing permits: Tickets to Litlavatn—Ilsmyr are available from Sig. Svendsen Sportsforretning, Skudeneshavn. Permission to fish the other lakes can probably be had for the asking.

LUND

This rural community on both sides of E 18 offers fishing in several lakes 150 to 500 ft. above sea level.

MOI area (C 14). Travel by train from Stavanger in 1 1/2 hours. Road distance from Stavanger is 67 miles, Kristiansand 88 miles. Map: Lund.

Trout are numerous and of good quality in lake Bilstadvatn, Ualandsvatn, Heskestadvatn, Eidsvatn, Hovsvatn and Lundevatn all strung out along E 18. Lake Lundevatn, the biggest of the lakes, holds red char as well. Well known fishing spots on lake Lundevatn are Moi, Tronvik and Skålandsvik, also amusing fly fishing from boats underneath the steep mountain walls. Other lakes include Botnavatn (1,050 ft.) reached on foin in a couple of hours from the county road at Bilstad or lake Rusdalsvatn on the county road 10 miles north of Moi. The Storåna river between lake Rusdalsvatn and Hovsvatn is another attractive water.

Centre: Moi.

Fishing permits: Fishing is free on lake Lundevatn. Boats are available to guests staying at Lundevatn Pensjonat, which can also arrange fishing on the other waters mentioned above.

SAUDA

Sauda at the head of the Saudafjord is an industrial township surrounded by wild mountains. The main watercourse has been harnessed, but there is fishing both here and on other waters.

NORDELV—STORELV area (B 13). Travel by express boat from Stavanger in 1 3/4 hours or by ferry in 4—5 hours. The bus from Haugesund takes 4 hours to Sauda. Road distance from Haugesund is 73 miles. Map: Fjæra.

The Nordelv and Storelv rivers have been described in the salmon part of this book. They are also trout waters. The upper Nordelv, above the Høllandsfoss waterfall, runs in small rapids and holds small trout. Lake Fossdalsvatn (2,040 ft.) belongs to this water-course and is reached in 30 mins. from the end of the road at Buer. 10-ounce trout are said to be numerous in this water. There is little water in the upper reaches of the Storelv, but some of the lakes belonging to the system offer good sport, see Breiborg below. Fishing in the Nordelv—Storelv area is reported to be best in Aug.—Sept.

Centre: Sauda.

Fishing permits: There are tickets, at reasonable prices, available from hotels and Sauda Sport, Sauda Bokhandel and J. Helle.

BREIBORG area (B 13). Travel: See Nordelv—Storelv area above. Breiborg lies on Highway 520 some 15 miles north of Sauda. In the Breiborg area trout fishing is said to be good in lake Holmavatn (2,440 ft.) 1/2 hour's walk from Highway 520 and lake Ukkendalstjønn (2,676 ft.) 1/2 hour's walk from Breiborg chalet. Trout in these water are from 10 ounces to 1 pound and of good quality. Trout are more numerous in lake Breiborgvatn and Midtvatn, but the quality is inferior. Lake Førstadvatn, approx. 15 mins. walk from Highway 520 at Litlastøl, holds a moderate amount of trout. Fishing is best in July and Aug. in the Breiborg area. Map: Fjæra.

Centres: Breiborg chalet (Stavanger Touring Club), not listed.

Fishing permits: The area permit is available from Breiborg chalet, Sauda Sport, Sauda Bokhandel and J. Helle. Day, week and season tickets, all inexpensive.

SULDAL

There is more trout fishing in Suldal than in any other Rogaland parish. Most of the fishing, however, includes rather long mountain hikes.

ROALDKVAM area (C 13). Travel by boat from Stavanger to Sand in 1 1/4 hours and then by bus to Nesflaten in 1 hour. Distance by road from Stavanger 95 miles including 1 ferry. Maps: 1314 II (Suldalsvatnet) and 1414 III (Breive).

This area provides fishing in the Kvanndalså and Bleskestadelv rivers. Kvanndalså holds a moderate amount of good quality stock, average weight 8 ounces. At Bleskestadmoen, approx. 2 hour's walk from the nearest road, the Bleskestadelv receives the Sandsvasså which drains lake Sandavatn (3,047 ft.). This again is fed by the Holmevassåna which rises in lake Holmevatn (3,454 ft.). The walk from Bleskestadmoen to Holmevassbu takes approx. 6 hours. Lake Sandavatn has a fine stock of trout, average weight 14 ounces. Fishing in these waters is best in July—September.

Centres: Bleskestadmoen and Holmevassbu are unstaffed huts belonging to Stavanger Touring Club and not listed in «Hotels in Norway».

Fishing permits: Permission to fish and tickets to the Roaldkvam system must be acquired in advance from Mrs. Hanna Roaldkvam, Dronningens gt. 5, Stavanger.

KVILLDAL area (B/C 13). Travel: See Roaldkvam above. Instead of ferrying across lake Suldal drive straight to Kvilldal from Kollbeinstveit. Maps: 1314 II (Suldalsvatnet) and 1313 I (Blåfjell).

This area provides fishing in lake Grunnavatn (2,175 ft.), approx. 45 mins. walk from the end of the road at Kjetilstad, lake Lauvastølvatn (1,952 ft.), approx. 4 hours' walk from Kvilldal and lake Stranddalsvatn (3,280 ft.), approx. 4 hours' walk from the road at Kjetilstad. Both Grunnavatn and Lauvastølvatn are well stocked with 10-ounce trout. Trout are perhaps not so numerous in lake Stranddalsvatn, but the average weight is 1 pound with fair chances of bigger fish. In the first two lakes fishing is probably best in July, in lake Stranddalsvatn in Aug. There is fishing — from a boat preferably — in 33 km long lake Suldalsvatn (225 ft.) which is well stocked, trout and red char. Fishing is especially good where big rivers enter the lake. Trout are said to be particularly big at the upper end of the lake. Season: May—September.

Centres: Kvilldal and Stranddalshytta where Stavanger Touring Club has lodgings for mountain hikers, are not listed.

Fishing permits: Guests at Stranddalshytta will be permitted to fish in the lakes around the chalet. Otherwise permission to fish must be obtained from the local farmers. Fishing is free on lake Suldal, close inshore permission must be asked.

ULLADAL area (B/C 13). Travel by boat from Stavanger to Vadla in 5 hours and proceed by bus up the valley to Ullatan, or go take a ferry from Stavanger to Tau and go by car to Vadla, approx. 45 miles. Maps: Sand and 1313 I (Blåfjell).

The lower reaches of the Ulla river have a run of salmon and sea trout. Higher up (after 6 km) the Ulla becomes a trout water. The river is fed by a number of tributaries which again drain a great number of lakes in the Rogaland Highlands. Lake Sandsavatn is situated 1,968 ft. above sea level and boats are available to guests staying at the chalet. This lake is moderately stocked with trout, weighing approx. 1 pound with the chance of bigger fish. Trout are more numerous in the Svinstøl and Månastølsvatn lakes north of Sandsa. Sandsahytta chalet is reached in 3 hours from the end of the road at Ullatun. Lake Stovedalsvatn (2,719 ft.) is approx. 3 hour's walk from Ullatun. The lake is moderately stocked with good quality trout (10 ounces). The season for the Ulla waters is June—September.

Centre: Sandsahytta chalet, unstaffed, belong to Stavanger Touring Club, not listed.

Fishing permits: Fishing cards to the lower reaches of the Ulla are available from Stavanger and Rogaland Jakt- og Fiskerforening (Hunting and Angling Ass.), Stavanger. The other waters are privately owned and the chalet will be helpful in obtaining the necessary permission to fish.

HORDALAND

This county provides extremely varied fishing ranging from the islands of the skerry-guard to the mountain moors of Hardangervidda. Good fishing on the islands may be had in late April. Fishing on the mountain moors culminates in August.

ASKØY, AUSTEVOLL, BØMLO, FITJAR, FJELL, LINDÅS, MELAND, OSTERØY, RADØY, STORD, TYSNES
All these parishes are situated on the islands west of Bergen and belong to what we term below the Skerry-guard area.

SKERRY-GUARD area (B 12—13). Travel from Bergen by bus and ferry, or by private car, in a couple of hours. The Stord and Bømlo islands south of Bergen requires a somewhat longer journey. Maps: 1115 I (Bergen), Fana, Fensfjorden, Herdla, Marstein, Slåtterøy and Stord.

The lakes and short rivers of this area are far too numerous too be examined in detail. Few of them are situated higher than 300 ft. above sea level and most of them are little known even to the locals. Most of them hold trout only, but quite a few waters have runs of salmon and sea trout. In some lakes red char and/or pike occur. Even rainbow trout are found. On the island of Askøy there are waters with trout up to 2 pounds (Skotnesvatna lakes). Most of the Huftarøy (Austevoll) waters have sea trout runs. Lake Storavatnet on Stord (Fitjar) holds trout and sea trout, the latter averaging half-a-pound. The Sotra (Fjell) lakes have stocks of fine trout and flyfishing should give good results. The Eikemoelv river, in the parish of Lindås, has a fine run of sea-trout and the 20 lakes of the watercourse hold plenty of good-quality trout. On Holsnøy island (Meland) there are fine stocks of trout in a number of lakes. Lake Storavatn is not so good as it used to be. Osterøy is the name of a big island completely surrounded by fjords east of Bergen. On this island lakes are found up to 1,500 ft. above sea level. The lakes of the island seem to be moderately stocked with some big trout. The Radøy lakes are reported to offer fine fly-fishing. Bogetjønn and Ullvatn have big fish up to 2 pounds. Lake Storavatn, in the parish of Stord, is said to be well stocked with 1-pound trout. The waters of Tysnesøy island tend to be overpopulated. Lakes like Fiskevatn and Heglandsvatn have runs of sea trout. Generally speaking fishing in the Skerry-guard waters is best in May—June and August—September.

Centres: The waters of the northern and western islands can be fished from Bergen, though there are small pensions at Lindås, Manger (Radøy) and Ask. The southern islands are not so easy to fish from Bergen, and anglers should seek local accommodation at Storebø (Huftarøy), Bekkjarvik (Selbjørn), Fitjar (Stord), Rubbestadneset and Bremnes (Bømlo) or Leirvik (Stord). Only Stord is listed in «Hotels in Norway».

Fishing permits: Inexpensive tickets are sold to the Stord island lakes by local farmers and Grand Hotel, Leirvik. Tickets are also sold to lake Heglandsvatn on Tysnesøy. But up to now fishing has been free in most of the Skerry-guard waters. To be on the safe side, make inquiries locally.

MASFJORDEN

In this parish there is some trout fishing in the Frøyset water-course west of the Masfjord. These waters are easy to fish from Highway 57 and adjoining county roads. The best fishing, however, is found in the Matre mountains north-east of the fjord.

MATREDAL area (B 12). Travel by bus and ferry to Matre in 4 hours from Bergen and take a taxi to Stordalen. The distance by road from Bergen is approx. 50 miles, including 1 ferry. Map: Masfjorden.
There are a number of lakes in this area at altitudes from 1,350 to 1,500 ft. with varying stocks of trout. Stordalsvatn (dammed, plenty of small trout), Bukkedalsvatn (moderately stocked with trout up to 2-pounds), Krokdalsvatn (usual size 1 to 2 pounds, fine quality). In Krokdalsvatn fish up to 5 pounds may be caught. Walking time to Krokdalsvatn is approx. 1 hour, to Bukkedalsvatn 30 mins., while Stordalsvatn is by the lodge where boats are available. Fishing in these

and other lakes is said to be best in July—August.
Centre: Stordalen Fjellstue (mountain lodge), not listed.
Fishing permits: Fishing is free to guests staying at the lodge.

ODDA

The municipality of Odda is situated on both sides of the Sørfjord — the innermost branch of the Hardangerfjord — and includes a fair slice of the Hardangervidda mountain plateau. The waters on the Hardangervidda are hard to reach from Odda, but some of them can be fished from Litlos (see Ullensvang below).

SELJESTAD area (B 13). Travel by bus and ferry from Bergen to Seljestad in 7 hours, by bus from Haugesund in 3 1/2 hours or by train from Oslo to Bø in 3 hours and then 6 hours by bus. Road distance from Bergen 115 miles and 1 ferry, from Haugesund 75 miles, from Oslo 236 miles. Map: Fjæra.
The Løyningselv river drains the lakes Botnavatn (2,754 ft.), Nyastølsvatn (2,030 ft.) and Løyningsvatn (1,955 ft.). Botnavatn and Nyastølsvatn are reached on foot from Løyning. Trout are of moderate size and not too plentiful in these waters. Fishing is best in June and July. Lake Reinsnosvatn (1,935 ft.) is reached by road from Highway 47. Trout are reported to be numerous (usual size 10 inches) and fishing is permitted from May 15 to Sept. 15.
Centre: Seljestad.
Fishing permits: Tickets to these waters are available from Solfonn Hotel and Seljestad Motel.

EIDFJORD

This municipality provides extensive and varied fishing on the Hardangervidda mountain plateau.

BJOREIDALEN area (C 12). Travel by train from Oslo to Haugastøl in 5 hours, or from Bergen in 4 hours, and then by bus in 1 hour to Tråastølen. From Tråastølen on foot in 1 hour to Bjoreidalen or by car along a primitive road. The distance by car from Oslo to Tråastølen is 181 miles, from Bergen 122 miles. Map: 1415 I (Bjoreio) and 1515 IV (Hein).
The Boreidalen Tourist Lodge is situated 3,420 ft. above sea level. The nearest place to fish is Lake Tinnhølen and its outlet, a good spot for anglers, with satsifactory stocks of trout reaching fair sizes (2 to 3 pounds) of good quality. The water course is however, heavily fished. Fishing in the lake is partly done from boats, which can be hired from the

tourist lodges. Spinning rods are prohibited in the rivers. Season: Aug.—Sept.
Centres: Dyranut, Bjoreidalen and Hellehalsen mountain lodges, none of which are listed.
Fishing permits: Fishing takes place within the Eidfjord State Common ground. Tickets, approx. kr. 15 per week, kr. 25 per month or kr. 35 per season, are available at all lodges.

HALNE area (C 12). Halne lodge lies on Highway 7 just 7 miles east of Tråastølen, see Bjoreidalen above. Maps: 1415 I (Bjoreio) and 1515 (IV (Hein).
Fishing in lake Halnefjord (3,690 ft.) or in Eidfjord State Common Ground west of the county border. Halnefjord has a good even stock of trout of good size and quality. Mostly boat fishing, boats can be hired from the lodge. In the State Commun Ground there is a varying stock of trout, on the whole of good quality. Close to Highway 7 there has been heavy fishing and the stock is often low. Season from about July 10 to Aug. 20.
Centre: Halne Mountain Lodge, not listed.
Fishing permits: Fishing on the lodge's permit in lake Halnefjord is free to guests. Tickets to the State Common Ground, approx. kr. 15 per week, kr. 25 per month or kr. 35 per season, available at the lodge.

HEDLO—VIVELI area (B 12). Travel by train and bus to Vøringfoss on Highway 7, see below. Hedlo is reached in 5 hours on foot along a cairned path from Vøringfoss. Viveli is reached on foot on approx. 1 hour from the end of the road in the Hjølmodal, which lies approx. 205 miles from Oslo and 115 miles from Bergen. The steep road towards Viveli should not be tried by nervous motorists inclined to dizziness. Map: 1415 IV (Eidfjord).
Hedlo is situated 2,850 ft. above sea level. Fishing is offered in a 3-mile stretch of the Veig river. Typical mountain fishing, average stock of trout, usual size from 6 to 13 ounces. Fishing is mostly done from the banks. All the lakes in the neighbourhood are privately owned, and fishing is only permitted by agreement with the owners. Season from first half of July to end of August. Viveli as situated 2,692 ft. above sea level in a beautiful mountain valley. Fishing is offered in 4 miles of the Veig river and 3 to 4 miles of the Vivo river, also several lakes and lakelets belong to this fishery. Fairly good stock of trout in the rivers and small lakes. Season from July 15 to end of August.
Centres: Hedlo and Viveli mountain lodges, not listed.
Fishing permits: Fishing is free to guests (if the catch is handed to the lodge kitchen at Hedlo).

SANDHAUG area (B 12). Travel by train and bus to Dyranut (next to Tråastølen), see Bjoreidalen above, and walk in 6 hours to Sandhaug. Map: 1415 II (Nordmannslågen). Sandhaug lies in an open, treeless valley. Fishing in the large lakes, Nordmannslågen (4,080 ft.) and Lakjen (4,077 ft.) and in the river between them. Also in several tarns reached on foot in 1 to 3 hours from the lodge. Good stocks of trout (1 pound up to 8 pounds) of fine sporting quality. The central parts of the Kvenna water course have been heavily fished. Boats are mostly used in the big lakes and can be hired from the lodge. The rivers are fished from the banks. Spinning rods is not allowed in the rivers. Season from beginning of August to early September.
Centres: Sandhaug (Norwegian Touring Club) and Besså mountain lodges, not listed.
Fishing permits: The Eidfjord State Common Ground tickets approx. kr. 15 per week, kr. 25 per month and kr. 35 per season, are for sale at the lodges.

VØRINGFOSS area (B 12). Travel by train from Oslo to Haugastøl in 5 hours and bus to Vøringsfoss in 10 hours, or Bergen by bus and ferry in 7 1/2 hours. Distance by road from Oslo is 191 miles, from Bergen 113 miles. Maps: 1415 IV (Eidfjord) and 1415 I (Bjoreio).
Trout fishing in the Bjoreia river above the Vøringfoss waterfall, approx. 2,600 to 3,000 ft. above sea level. Bjoreia has a fine stock of trout. The fish are bigger in the upper reaches of the water course, but more numerous further down.
Centre: Vøringfoss (see Eidfjord in «Hotels in Norway»).
Fishing permits: Day tickets, approx. kr. 20, available at Fossli and Maurseth hotels.

ULLENSVANG

This municipality with the villages of Lofthus and Kinsarvik is one of the great tourist areas on the Hardanger fjord. Both sides of the Sør fjord belongs to Ullensvang, as well as considerable parts of the Hardangervidda mountain plateau.

HEIMFJELL (B 12). Travel to Ringøy/Bu by train and bus from Oslo in approx. 7 hours, by bus from Bergen in approx. 4 hours. Distance by road from Oslo 214 miles, Bergen 92 miles, Haugesund 117 miles and Stavanger 166 miles. From Ringøy a cairned path leads to Dalamot Turisthytte in approx. 5 hours. Map: 1315 I (Ullensvang).
Fishing in rivers, tarns and lakes approx. 2,600—3,300 ft. above sea level. Stocks of medium-sized trout of good quality.
Centre: Dalamot of Mountain Lodge (unstaf-

fed) belongs to Bergen Touring Club, not listed.
Fishing permits: Tickets, approx. kr. 10 per day, kr. 40 per week and kr. 100 per season, from the Kinsarvik tourist office.

KINSO (B 12). Travel times and distances approx. as Heimfjell above. Kinsarvik lies 11 miles west of Ringøy. From Kinsarvik along a steep, cairned path to Stavali Turisthytte in 4—5 hours. Map: 1315 I (Kinsarvik).
Stavali is centrally placed in this area. From the lodge fishing may be enjoyed in lake Stavalivatn, the Stavali river, lake Lonavatn and several other waters situated 3,000 to 3,300 ft. above sea level. All waters hold trout of excellent quality.
Centre: Stavali Mountain Lodge (unstaffed) belongs to Bergen Touring Club, not listed.
Fishing permits: See Dalamot above.

LITLOS (B 12). From Stavali a cairned path leads via Torehytta (unstaffed) to Litlos in 2 days.
Litlos is situated in Ullensvang State Common Ground where there are many lakes rivers fairly well stocked with trout. The common ground may also be fished from Torehytta Mountain Lodge. Litlos lies on the Kvenna water course at the north end of lake Litlosvatn (2,740 ft.) in tressless mountain country. The nearest lakes are Kollsvatn and Kvennsjøen. Spoons are not permitted. Typical high mountain fishing. Good stocks of fine trout, usually about 1 pound. Some lakes in the vicinity are closed to anglers. Season July 10 to approx. Aug. 20.
Centre: Litlos Mountain Lodge belongs to the Norwegian Touring Club, not listed.
Fishing permits: Tickets to Ullensvang State Common Ground, approx. kr. 25 for 2 days, kr. 50 per week and kr. 100 per season available at the lodge.

VOSS
The village of Voss is a famous tourist centre on the Bergen Railway. The municipality of Voss includes wast mountainous tracts streching almost to the Sognefjord in the north and to the Hardangerfjord in the south.

VOSS area (B 12). Travel by train from Bergen in 1 1/2 hours, from Oslo in 7 hours. Road distance from Bergen 104 miles, from Oslo 250 miles and 1 ferry. Maps: Voss and Vossestrand.
Fishing partly in the main water course, partly in the mountains. The Strondaelv river drains the lakes Lønavatn (250 ft.), Melsvatn and Lundarvatn to fall into lake Vangsvatn (151 ft.). E 68 runs along the main water course. In the village of Voss, it is joined by

the Raundalselv tributary. There is a county road along this river. Both in the lakes and the Strondaelv river there is a moderate stock of trout of varying quality. Trout in the lower reaches of the Raundal river are small and of inferior quality. Higher up the river conditions are better. In the mountains north of Voss there are a great number of lakes. Most of them have good to fair stocks of trout of moderate size and uneven quality. There are some unstaffed huts in this area, contact Voss Touring Club. Season: In the valley May—-Sept., in the mountains middle of June to end of August.
Centre: Voss.
Fishing permit: The Voss area permit, approx. kr. 20 per week, kr. 50 per season, is sold by sports shops in the village.

OPPHEIM area (B 12). Travel: See Voss. Oppheim lies 14 miles (45 mins.) by bus, north of Voss. Map: Vossestrand.
Trout fishing in the Strondaelv river, lake Oppheimsvatn (1,082 ft.), lake Myrkdalsvatn (754 ft.) and the Myrkdalselv river. Lake Oppheimsvatn is well stocked with trout weighing from 6 to 10 ounces, chances of bigger fish. Lake Myrkdalsvatn holds a moderate amount of 10-ounce trout. The Strondaelv is moderately stocked with trout of uneven quality and the Myrkdalselv has plenty of small trout with bigger fish a definite possibility. E 68 follows the Strondaelv and Highway 13 the Myrkdalselv. All waters can be fished from May to Sept., but the best river fishing is during spate periods in late summer.
Centre: Oppheim.
Fishing permits: The Voss permit covers part of this area. Lake Myrkdalsvatn with a number of small lakes, tarns and rivers is covered by a special ticket available locally.

SOGN AND FJORDANE
This county of majestic fjords is well known for its salmon waters. But there are also some big lakes, which are very well stocked with trout, and numerous small lakes where good sport can be had. In the salmon rivers fish may be helped to by-pass a waterfall or two, but there always comes a fall that stops the run. Above that fall trout take over in the Sogn and Fjordane rivers, and there are plenty of them.

FJALER
South of the Dalsfjord interesting fishing is provided by the Flekke—Guddal water course.

FLEKKE area (A/B 12). Travel by express boat from Bergen to Rysjedalsvika in 2 1/2 hours and then by bus to Dale in 2 hours.

The distance by car from Bergen via Lavik is approx. 100 miles and 2 ferries. Map: Lavik. The Flekke—Guddal water course, or the Rennestraum system, drains lake Hovlandsdalsvatn (167 ft.), lake Nautsundvatn, lake Hovlandsvatn (52 ft.), lake Breivatn (30 ft.) and lake Rennestraumsvatn (23 ft.) before entering the Flekkefjord. Salmon and sea trout run as far as the Harefoss waterfall at the outlet of lake Nautvatn. Salmon are reported to be big, sea trout rather small and trout will areage 10 ounces. There are also some red char. Lake Hovlandsdalsvatnet is said to contain too many trout and red char, and the size is accordingly smaller than in the lower lakes. Season: May—Oct., fishing is probably best in Aug.—Sept. Highway 57 and county roads make the system easy to fish.

Centre: Dale.

Fishing permits: The system is divided into zones, tickets are sold by the Flekke Post Office.

FØRDE

The village boasts the magnificent Førde or Jølstra salmon river, but there is also trout fishing to be enjoyed in this and other waters.

FØRDE area (B 11). Travel by boat from Bergen to Rysjedalsvika in 2 1/2 hours and then 2 hours by bus to Førde. The distance by car from Bergen is 106 miles and 3 ferries, from Oslo 300 miles and 2 ferries. Map: Førde.

Trout fishing in the Førdeelv river above the salmon run. This includes lake Movatn (128 ft.) and the lakes Åsvatn (429 ft.) and Holsavatn (429 ft.) in the Holsa tributary above the Huldrefoss waterfall. There is a good stock of trout in the main river and plenty of trout in Åsvatn and Holsavatn, but of uneven quality, average weight approx. 8 ounces. Highway 5 makes access to the fisheries easy. Sesaon: June—September.

Centre: Førde.

Fishing permits: Fishing is free in the lakes. A boat on lake Movatn can be hired from Olav Aasen, Moøyra. Tickets to the Førdeelv above the salmon run, inexpensive, are available at Sunnfjord Hotel, Førde.

GAULAR

This parish's fame rest on the Gaula salmon river. After the salmon has had its 12 km run to the Fossefoss falls, there is plenty of trout fishing in the water course.

BYGSTAD area (B 12). Travel: See Førde above. The village of Bygstad lies 14 miles south of Førde. Maps: Førde and Vevring. Small trout can be caught in lake Lange-

landsvatn (1,085 ft.) and lake Skilbreivatn (827 ft.) close to Highway 14 south of Førde, but better sport is enjoyed and bigger fish killed off the beaten track in lakes 600—2,900 ft. above sea level. These lakes are owned by Bygstad farmers and fishing is offered in 5 different zones. All lakes are reached on foot, but if you prefer, the easy way to your sport, take a taxi plane from Førde.

Centres: Førde and Bygstad (not listed).

Fishing permits: Inexpensive tickets to Langelandsvatn and Skilbreivatn, approx. kr. 5 per day and kr. 20 per season, can be bought in Førde Sport or Sunnfjord Hotel, Førde. Tickets to the 5 zones of mountain lakes are also available here. They are also sold by Skilbrei Post Office and the shopkeepers O. A. Lunde, Bygstad and M. Øvrebø, Hjelmeland.

VIKSDALEN area (B 11). Travel: See Førde above. The centre of Viksdalen lies 27 miles east of Førde. Maps: Årdal (Series 1501), Førde and Kyrkjebø.

Trout fishing in the Gaula river and the Eldalselv tributary. The Gaula drains two big lakes, Haukedalsvatn (974 ft.) and Viksdalsvatnet (479 ft.). In between lies lake Lauvatn and beautiful Vallestad waterfall. The Eldalselv rises in lake Nyastølsvatn (approx. 2,300 ft.) and drains a number of lakes, Holmevatn, Byttevatn, Myrevatn, Føllingsvatn, before entering lake Viksdalsvatn. There is a good stock of trout both in the rivers and the lakes. In some of the lakes trout are too numerous. Some claim that lake Haukedalsvatn is the best of all Sogn and Fjordane lakes. It used be overpopulated, but a mysterious disease reduced the stock considerably a couple of years ago, with the result that the size and the quality of trout improved greatly. The Viksdalen area is easy to fish from Highways 5 and 610. Season: June—September.

Centre: Viksdalen.

Fishing permits: Tickets to the Gaula water course between Årteig and the Eikelandsfoss (including half of lake Viksdalsvatn and the Hestadfjord lake) can be bought, at reasonable rates, in these shops: Olaf Lien and Kirkelid, Hestadgrend and J. O. Tyssekvam, Sand. Tickets covering the rest of the area, also inexpensive, are available from the Hellebust, Viken and Hoff pensions, Gjermundstad camping and local shopkeepers.

GLOPPEN

Gloppen offers fishing in two widely separated areas, Breim and Hyen.

BREIM area (B 11). Travel by boat from Bergen to Rysjedalsvika in 2 1/2 hours follo-

wed by 4 1/2 hours on the bus to Byrkjelo. Road distance from Bergen approx. 260 miles and 2 ferries, from Oslo (via Lærdal) 315 miles and 2 ferries. Map: 1318 III (Breim). Lake Breimsvatn (200 ft.) is 20 km long, set in scenery of exceptional beauty. Fishing the lake at random will seldom give good results, but the proprietors of local pensions will advise where best to fish. It is possible to catch 20 trout in three to four hours, average size 10 ounces, but larger specimens are sometimes caught, even up to 12—14 pounds. Bank fishing is available right outside the former Gordon Pension, or at the Breimselv river mouth. Excellent bank fishing also at Kandal on the west side of the lake. A side road leads from Byrkjelo up the Myklebust Valley and along a string of river rapids, pools and lakes where good fishing may be expected too, in dream-like surroundings.
Centres: Byrkjelo and Sandane.
Fishing permits: The fishing area is divided into zones. Tickets, approx. kr. 10 per day or kr. 50 per season, are available at local pensions.

HYEN area (B 11). Travel by boat from Bergen to Sandane in 17 hours and from there by bus and ferry to Hyen in 2 hours. By car from Bergen 154 miles and 3 ferries. Maps: 1218 II (Fimlandsgrend) and 1218 III (Naustdal).
Trout fishing in several lakes and rivers including lake Storfjorden (410 ft.), Skjellbreivatn (820 ft.), lake Storevatn (1,312 ft.), Rombergvatn (1,312 ft.) and lake Røyrvikvatn (492 ft.). The lakes are accessible either from Highroad 615 or local roads. Lake Rombergvatn, which is 1 hour's walk away, holds trout and red char, average weight 1/2 pound. In Røyrvikvatn both red and char are numerous, whereas lake Skjelbreivatn and Storevatn have good stocks of trout weighing 1/2 to 1 pound. Season: June—August.
Centre: Hyen.
Fishing permits: Tickets (day, week, season) are sold by O. Rønnekleiv, Hyen to all lakes except lake Storevatn. Tickets to this lake are available at Gjengedal. Boats in most of the lakes may be rented from local farmers.

JØLSTER

The Jølster are is not only beautful, but the big lake and the river draining it offer very good trout fishing.

JØLSTER area (B 11). Travel by boat from Bergen to Rysjedalsvika in 2 1/2 hours. The bus from Lavik takes 3 hours to Vassenden and 3 1/2 hours to Skei. Road distance from Bergen to Skei is 133 miles and 3 ferries, from Oslo 314 and 2 ferries. Maps: Førde and 1318 III(Breim).

The 32 km long lake Jølstervatn (676 ft.) is an unusually productive water. The very large trout (9 to 11 pounds) are not easily caught on rod. The whole length of the lake may be fished from a boat with spoon or fly, and trolling is also permitted. Do not waste time rowing the lake at random, as advice on where to fish at any given time is readily given at Skei Hotel or Vassenden Pension. Good fishing spots are the river mouths at Ålhus and Årdal where 6 to 10 ounce-trout are plentiful. From Årdal there is also a road leading to the small, but fine lake Dalevatn. The river leading down to Førde at the head of lake Breimsvatn is another water where trout are numerous, although ratter small in size. If you follow the Stardal river to Fonn you will not only see the Jostedal glacier, but probably hook some trout as well. Boats on lake Jølstravatn can be hired from Jølstraholmen Camping and Jølvassbu Camping as well as from Tor Aarnes and Knut K. Sandal, both living at Sandal on the south side of the lake. Boats are also available to guests staying at Skei and Vassenden.
Fine fishing can be enjoyed by experienced anglers (with small dry or wet flies and fine casts 0,20—0,25 mm) in the Jølstra river below the lake, in spite of the fact that this water is heavily fished. All the fisheries in Jølster are accessible by car. Season: June—-Aug. Closed season Oct.15 — Dec. 31.
Centre: Jølster.
Fishing permits: The inexpensive Jølster ticket, covering 12 lakes and 10 river, costs approx. kr. 7.50 per day or kr. 25 per season, available from hotels, pensions, camping sites and shops in the area. The Jølstra river ticket, approx. kr. 10 per day and kr. 50 per season, can be bought at Vassenden Pension, the camping sites, Sunnfjord Hotel and Førde Sport.

LÆRDAL

Lærdal is known to anglers in many countries because of its famous salmon river. For energetic walkers Lærdal provides fine trout fishing too.

LÆRDAL—MARISTOVA (B/C 11). Travel by boat from Bergen to Revsnes in 5 1/2 hour and then by bus to Maristova in 2 hours. By train from Oslo to Fagernes in 4 hours and bus to Maristova in 3 hours. Road distance from Bergen is 174 miles and 1 ferry, from Oslo 169 miles. Map: Filefjell.
Fishing in several lakes situated 3,000 to 4,500 ft. above sea level. E 68 goes along lake Nedre (Lower) Smeddalsvatn (3,116 ft.), the other waters are reached on foot (max. 2 hour's walk). The lakes contain a fair stock of mountain trout, average size 10 ounces, with

fish up to 2 pounds. Fishing is best in July and August.
Centre: Maristova.
Fishing permits: Fishing is free for resident guests at Maristuen Hotel.

SOGNDAL AND LUSTER

Sogndal village is a lively tourist spot, Luster is a beautiful parish on the Lusterfjord (the innermost branch of the Sognefjord). Together they provide some interesting trout fishing.

SOGNDAL area (B 11). Travel by boat from Bergen in 4 1/2 hours to Hermansverk and then 45 mins. by bus to Sogndal. From Oslo take the train to Gol in 3 hours and go by bus and ferry to Sogndal in 4 hours. Distance by road from Bergen 176 miles and 1 ferry, from Oslo 214 miles and 1 ferry. Maps: Sogndal and 1418 II (Mørkrisdalen) and 1418 III (Jostedalen).
Trout fishing in Annestølsvatn (approx. 1,300 ft.), Dalavatn (1,296 ft.), Hunnsvatn (2,500 ft.), the Laugaelv river, Naversetvatn (2,952 ft.), the Sogndalselv river, Voladnvatna (2,857 ft.) and other lakes and rivers. All the waters mentioned have good stocks of trout. In some of the lakes trout are too numerous and accordingly small. Average size of trout in the Sogndalselv river is 10 ounces with fish up to 2 pounds. Some of these waters are accessible by car, most of them demand 1—2 hours' walks in rugged country. The lower waters will probably yield the best results in May—June and Aug., the more elevated lakes in July—Aug. Closed season: Sept. 25 — May 15.
Centre: Sogndal.

HAFSLO — GAUPNE area (B 11). Travel: See Sogndal above. Hafslo and Gaupne lies on Highway 55 — 10 and 20 miles north of Sogndal respectively. Maps: 1417 IV (Solvorn) and 1418 III (Jostedalen).
Fishing in lake Hafslovatn (646 ft.), lake Veitastrondsvatn (656 ft.), the Jostedøla river and other waters. Highway 604 runs along the Jostedøla and a county road skirts the lakes. Trout are said to be numerous in lake Hafslovatn, average weight 1 pound; 10-pounders a possibility. Lake Veitastrondsvatn has a moderate stock of 1-pound trout, similar to the Jostedøla river. Fishing is best in July and Aug. Close season for Hafslovatn and Jostedøla Oct. 1 to May 15.
Centres: Marifjøra, Hafslo and Jostedal. Gaupne and several small pensions in the Jostedal Valley are not listed in «Hotels in Norway».

STRYN

Stryn, at the head of Nordfjord, features beuty spots like Olden and Loen with lakes and glaciers. Some of those lakes hold fair stocks of trout.

LOEN — OLDEN area (B 11). Travel by boat from Bergen in 19 hours or by boat to Rysjedalsvika in 2 1/2 hours and bus to Olden/Loen in 5 hours. From Oslo by train to Otta in 5 1/2 hours and next day 7 hours by bus to Loen/Olden. Road distance from Bergen 171 miles and 3 ferries, from Oslo 316 miles. Maps: 1318 I (Stryn), 1318 II (Briksdalsbreen) and 1418 IV (Lodalskåpa). Trout are numerous in lake Oldevatn (121 ft.) and of good quality. Red char are numerous and small in size. Lake Loenvatn (142 ft.) holds many trout, average size 10 ounces. There is also fishing in lake Hornindalsvatn (170 ft.) — the deepest lake in Europe — and lake Strynsvatn (82 ft.). Lake Hornindalsvatn has a fair stock of 1/2-pound trout. Red char weighing approx. 8 ounces are very numerous. Raftevold Hotel has rowing boats for its guests. Lake Strynsvatn is moderately stocked with rather small trout and red char. Season: June — Aug. and preferably in warm weather.
Centres: Hjelledal (see Stryn in «Where to Stay») Hornindal, Loen, Olden, Stryn and Videseter.
Fishing permits: Up to now (1981) fishing has been free in Hornindalsvatn and Strynsvatn. Tickets to lake Oldevatn are sold by the farmers along the lake and the Information kiosk in Olden. Tickets to lake Loenvatn are also sold by local farmers and by the two camping sites on the lakes.

VIK

In Vik at the south side of the Sogne fjord fishing has been seriously affected by damming and hydro-electrical developments, but there are still a few good trout lakes in the mountains .

VIK (B 12). Travel by express boat from Bergen in 4 1/2 hour, or via Voss by train and bus in 3 hours. From Oslo by train to Gol and bus and ferries to Vik in approx. 9 hours. Distance by road from Bergen is 145 miles, from Oslo 246 miles and 2 ferries. Map: Vik. The mountain lakes hold trout only. They are fairly well stocked with fish weighing from 6 ounces to 2 pounds. Årebotnvatn, Kvilesteinsvatn, Muruvatn, Skjelingsvatn and Holskardvatn lakes, all found between 3,000 and 3,300 ft. above sea level, were all fine trout waters, but fishing is not what it used to be. Highway 13 across the Vikafjell mountains passes trough this area.

The other lakes in the Vikafjell, Vangsnes-fjell and Arnafjell mountains are situated between 2,300 and 3,900 ft. above sea level, and all undammed waters are regularly supplied with fry. These lakes contain very much trout, some are in fact «overpopulated». July — Aug. is the best season, and flies, spoons and worms are used. These waters are privately owned, but most owners are members of the Vik Ground Owners' Association, which issues fishing permits. The upper reaches of the Vikja river hold some trout, but damming has reduced fishing considerably.
Centre: Vik.
Fishing permits: Tickets for sale from Johs. Hove A/S, Vik Tourist Information and Olav Mørke's shop in the Myrkdalen valley.

MØRE AND ROMSDAL
Top of the Fjord Country — adorned with fjords and alpine mountains, draped with waterfalls and enriched with salmon and sea trout waters. This fabulous county is also speckled with lakes containing trout and red char. Some of the classical fishing in the mountains have gone with water power developments, but on the islands and in the coastal districts anglers have discovered new waters in which to cast their flies with fair prospects of rich yields.

KRISTIANSUND AND FREI, HALSA, TINGVOLL AND TUSTNA
The capital of Nordmøre itself offers only limited fishing, but the waters that can be reached from Kristiansund are almost unlimited.

KRISTIANSUND area (B 10). Travel by plane from Bergen or Oslo to Kristiansund in 1 hours, or by boat from Bergen in 22 hours, by train from Oslo to Oppdal in 6 hours followed by 4 1/2 hours on the bus to Kristiansund. Road distance from Oslo 371 miles, Bergen 406 miles and 6 ferries. Map: 1321 II (Kristiansund).
The nearest fishing is in lake Rensvikvatn (98 ft.) on Higway 16 only 4 miles south of the town. Good quality trout up to 9 pounds, best fishing in May — June. If you take the ferry across the fjord to Tustna (45 mins.) there is more fishing to be found, both on the Tustna island and the neighbouring island of Stabben. Lakes here offering bright prospects are Jørgenvågvatn (164 ft.), Linvågvatn (65 ft.) Nonshaugvatn (984 ft.) and Sagavatn (98 ft.). All these lakes hold good stocks of fine trout. There are other lakes on the islands where trout are more numerous, but smaller. With the exception of Nonshaugvatn

these lakes are reached by car. Season: June — Aug.
Centre: Kristiansund.
Fishing permits: Rensvikvatn has been leased to Kristiansund and Nordmøre Hunting and Angling Association and can be approached through the Tourist Office. Tickets are sold locally to Jørgenvågvatn and Linvågvatn. Permission to fish Nonshaugvatn and Sagavatn must be obtained from the farmers.

HALSA — TINGVOLL area (B 10). Travel: See Kristiansund. Halsa village is 16 miles (and 2 ferries) east of Kristiansund. Tingvoll village 27 miles (and 1 ferry) south of Kristiansund. Map: Kristiansund(M 515). The most promising Halsa waters seem to be Botnavatn (984 ft.), Englivatn (656 ft.), Liabøvatn (820 ft.) and Ljosvatn (1,148 ft.). They are all well stocked with fine quality trout. In Englivatn and Ljosvatn there are plenty of red char too. There is a road to Englivatn. Liabøvatn lies only 15 mins. walk from the nearest road. Botnavatn and Ljosvatn are within easy walking distance. Season: June — August.
Tingvoll lakes include among others Fjellsæ-tervatn (984 ft.), Grimstadvatn (131 ft.), Grunnsjøen (164 ft.), Herredsdalsvatn (984 ft.), Lillevatn (328 ft.), Nøsavatn (131 ft.), Salvatn (1,312 ft.) and Storvatn (164 ft.) all of which are reported to be well stocked with trout — some of them hold red char as well — of good quality and size. Some of the lakes (Grimstadvatn, Grunnsjøen, Herredsdalsvatn , Lillevatnet and Nøsavatn) are situated near roads, the remainder are reached on foot in approx. 1 hour. Season: June — August.
Centres: Tingvoll (not listed), Kristiansund and Halsa, see Halsanaustan.
Fishing permits: Fishing cards to all Halsa and Tingvoll lakes mentioned above are sold locally.

MOLDE AND EIDE, FRÆNA AND GJEMNES
Molde — town of roses and panoramic views — has some good trout fishing too. Some within the town limits, more in the surrounding parishes but within easy reach of the town.

MOLDE area (B 10). Travel by boat from Bergen in 18 hours, or by train from Oslo to Åndalsnes in 8 hours and then 2 hours by bus to Molde. By plane from Bergen or Oslo in approx. 1 hour. Road distance from Bergen is 365 miles and 5 ferries, from Oslo 318 miles. Maps: 1320 IV (Eide) and 1220 I (Hustad). Small lakes and tarns in the Moldeheia hills, 1,000 to 1,500 ft. above sea level and reached in 1/2 hour to 2 hours walk from the nearest road, contain plenty of small-size trout. On Highway 67 — 22 miles north of Molde — - lake Nosvatn (33 ft.) has a fair stock of trout and migratory char. Also sea-trout and salmon. The short river to the sea has good runs of sea trout and salmon in spate periods. Best fishing in spring and autumn. Lake Hostadvatn (131 ft.) in Fræna contains both red char (numerous), trout, sea trout and small salmon (after spate periods in the Farstadelv river). Highway 663 skirts the lake some 25 miles north of Molde. Make a note also of the Aureosen — Tverrlivatn water course only 12 miles from Molde. There are plenty of trout up to 12 ounces in these waters and some sea trout and small salmon. Trout fishing is best in May, sea trout run in Aug. — Sept. The Hustad water course, including the lakes Skjellbreia, Langvatn (187 ft.) and Frelsvatn, run along Highway 663 approx. 22 miles north of Molde. Fish is too numerous in Skjellbreia, numerous and of better quality and Langvatn, where size varies from 10 ounces to almost 2 pounds. Red char also occur in these waters and runs of sea trout and salmon. Trout fishing is most enjoyable in the spring (May).

The Gjemnes waters include lake Fosterlågen, the Batnfjordselv river, and Fursetfjell lakes. Lake Fosterlågen (492 ft.) lies south of Highway 665 and approx. 22 miles from Molde. It contains trout and red char of uneven quality and moderate size. The river between the lake and Osvatn (53 ft.) offers first-class fishing, especially in July. Trout in these waters will average 10 ounces with sea trout up to 25 pounds a possibility in the autumn. The Batnfjordselv river is reached on Highway 66 some 20 miles east of Molde. This is a typical spate river with surprisingly big runs of small salmon and sea trout in Aug. But to return to trout waters, there are at least 15 lakes containing trout on the Fursetfjell mountain at altitudes from 820 — 2,000 ft. where trout are very numerous, but of uneven quality and rather small in size.
Centre: Molde. Small pension also at Eide.
Fishing permits: Fishing is free in the Moldeheia tarns. Fishing is also said to be free in the Aureosen — Tverrlivatn waters, but permission must be asked locally. The same goes for fishing in the Fursetfjell mountains. Tickets for lake Hostadvatn are inexpensive and available locally. Also to the Hustadelv watercourse inexpensive tickets are available locally. Tickets to the Batnfjord river, and the Fosterlågen — Osvatn waters, are likewise available locally at reasonable prices. Visitors should contact the Molde Travel Ass. concerning fishing permits. They will also supply you with a map showing the angling possibilities in this area.

NESSET

Lake Meisalsvatn (1,968 ft.) between Boggestrand and Eidsøra is a fine lake with a good stock of trout. There are also some small lakes near Highway 62 on the Skjørseterfjell mountain, 1,300 to 1,600 ft. above sea level and approx. 1/2 hour on foot from the road. Map: 1320 I (Tingvoll).
Trout here are numerous but small in size. Fishing in these waters is considered to be free. Most of the fishing in Nesset, however, is concentrated in the Eikesdal area.

EIKESDAL area (B 10). Travel: See Molde. From Molde take a bus to Øverås in 2 1/2 hours and ferry across lake Eikesdalsvatn in 1 1/2 hours to Reitan. From the ferry you will se the highest waterfall in Europe, the Mardalsfoss, vertical frop 974 ft., total fall 2,148 ft., although considerably reduced thanks to damming. Maps: 1420 III (Sunndalsøra) and 1419 IV (Aursjøen).
Lake Eikesdalsvatn contains salmon, sea trout, trout and small red char (numerous). Lake Lillevatn (330 ft.) 3 miles up the valley from Reitan is well stocked with sea trout, trout and red char with trout more numerous than the othere species (average weight 10 ounces). Fishing is also reported to be good in the rivers Breimeiga and Kjøtåa. Fishing is best in July and Aug.
Centre: Reitan (see Eikesdal in «Hotels in Norway»).
Fishing permits: Available at Reitan pension.

RAUMA

This district is famous for its great salmon river — the Rauma — its scenery and the highest perpendicular mountain walls in Europe. But there are smaller rivers holding trout and sea trout, among them the Innfjordelv, the Istra, Isa, Glitra and Visa rivers. There is also trout fishing in numerous lakes.

ÅNDALSNES (B 10). Travel by train from Oslo in 7 hours, or by plane from Bergen and Oslo in less than 1 hour to Molde, followed by 1 1/2 by bus to Åndalsnes. Distance by road from Oslo is 283 miles, from Bergen via Vadheim and Geiranger approx. 300 miles and 3 ferries. Maps: 1320 III (Åndalsnes), 1319 I (Romsdalen) and 1319 IV (Valldal). Several lakes can be fished from Åndalsnes. Most of them are accessible by car, to others there is a short walk as well. Lake Gjersetvatn is situated on Highway 64. Lake Herjevatn (1280 ft.) to Åfarnes is reached on the toll road to Nysetra and Selsetervatn and Breivikvatnet lakes. (1640 ft.) by the Skorgedalen toll road. In addition there are many lakes in the Romsdal mountains.
Centre: Åndalsnes.

Fishing permits: Available from the Åndalsnes Tourist Office, camping sites and farms in the area.

SMØLA

The flat island of Smøla has seldom, if ever, been visited by anglers from abroad. To-day it must be considered one of the best areas in South Norway.

SMØLA area (B 10). Travel: See Kristiansund. From there go by ferry to Straumen (Smøla) in 1 1/2 hours. Bring your car along, if you can, because most of the fisheries are situated close to Highway 669 or local roads: Map: 1321 I (Smøla).
More than 30 lakes await you on Smøla. They are almost identical as far as conditions are concerned, situated 10 to 100 feet above, sea level, well stocked with trout weighing approx. 1/2 pound. Sea trout of good quality and size occur in all waters. Fishing is good from May to Sept., but the best fishing is enjoyed in March and April. There are also four fine sporting rivers. The Fuglevågselv holds plenty of trout and has a fine run of sea trout in Aug. Hinnåa is primarily a trout river. The Hopelv river offers fine spring fishing with sea trout runs later on. The Roksvågelv contains good quality trout with sea trout runs in the autumn.
Centres: Small pensions at Dyrnesvågen and Lervik (see Smøla in «Hotels in Norway»).
Fishing permits: Tickets to almost all waters on Smøla are sold locally.

SUNNDAL

There are to many dams in this district, but the reservoirs are meticulously cultivated and offer decent sport, and there are areas completely untouched by the dam-builders.

LITLEDALEN area (B 10). Travel by train from Oslo in 6 hours to Oppdal and spend 1 1/2 hours on the bus to Sunndalsøra. Or go by boat from Bergen to Kristiansund in 22 hours — or by plane in 1 hour — and take the bus to Sunndalsøra in 3 hours. Road distance from Oslo is 453 miles, from Trondheim 106 miles, from Bergen 453 miles and 5 ferries. Map: 1420 III (Sunndalsøra) and 1419 IV (Aursjøen).
This is the reservoir area where lake Holbuvatn (2,605 ft.) holds a fair stock of good-quality trout and grayling and Store (Great Krøsvatn (2,850 ft.) is regarded as a fine sporting lake. So are the Purktjønna tarns (2,920 ft.) one hour's walk from the Sunndalsøra—Aursjø road. Here there are boats for hire. The Reinsvatn reservoir (2,880 ft.) is well stocked with fine trout and boats are available. Lake Sandvatn is another reservoir

2,780 ft. above sea level and it is stocked with trout and grayling of good quality. This also applies to lake Torbuvatn (2,800 ft.). The best season for trout fishing in all these waters is most probably Aug. Grayling are easier to catch in June and July. Closed season: Sept. 15 to May 15. With the exception of the Purketjønn tarns all these lakes can be fished from the Sunndalsøra — Aursjø road.
Centre: Sunndalsøra.
Fishing permit: Available at hotels, pensions and camping sites.

INNERDAL area (B 10). Travel: See Sunndalsøra. Innerdal lies some 15 miles north-east of Sunndalsøra. The last 3 miles to the area is only a crosscountry road (45 mins. walk). Map: 1420 II (Romfo).
The Innerdal Valley is considered one of the most beautiful in Norway. Popular rock climbing area. Fishing in the lakes Store and Lille Innerdalsvatn. (approx. 1,300 ft.) and in the Innerdalselv river (close by the lodge), or in lake Langvatn (2 1/2 hours' walk), Nedre Renndalsvatn (1 1/2 hour's walk) and in other mountain lakes further away. There is a large stock of trout in Innerdalsvatn, from moderate to small in sixe. In Langvatn and Nedre Renndalsvatn there is a stock of fine size and excellent quality. In Store (Great) Innerdalsvatn fishing is mostly done from boats, in Lille (Little) Innerdalsvatn from both boats and the banks. Boats available to guests. Season from June to beginning of September.
Centre: Innerdal (Innerdalshytta and Renndalsetra lodges — not listed in «Hotels in Norway»).
Fishing permit: Fishing is free to resident guests.

SURNADAL

In the wide valley of Surnadal flows the Surna salmon river. In the Nordmarka hills north of the valley and the Todal area to the south, trout fishing is offered to visitors.

NORDMARKA area (B 10). Travel by bus from Trondheim to Surnadal (Skei) in 3 hours or from Kristiansund in 3 1/2 hours. Distance by road from Oslo 479 miles and 1 ferry, from Trondheim 79 miles and from Kristiansund 40 miles and 2 ferries. Maps: 1421 III (Halsa) and 1421 II (Vinjeøra).
In Nordmarka there is fishing in several waters, most of them accessible by road. Lake Geitøyvatn (1,085 ft.) and lake Krokvatn (1,088 ft.) hold plenty of trout and char of fair quality. In lake Langvatn (830 ft.) trout up 4 pounds are caught. Fishing in Mangevatna lakes (1,640 ft.) means easy walking.

Fishing in all Nordmarka lakes is best in July — August.
Centre: Surnadal.
Fishing permits: Tickets are sold to Geitøyvatn, Krokvatn and Langevatn. To fish the Mangevatna lakes permission must be acquired from the owners.

TODALEN area (B 10). Travel: See Nordmarka above. Kårvatn in Todalen lies 24 miles south of Skei. Maps: 1420 I (Snota) and 1420 II (Romfo).
Kårvatn lodge (2,400 ft.) lies in a steep valley surrounded by mountains. Fishing in the Todalselv river and several mountain lakes. The Todalselv has a good stock of trout, (approx. 1/2 to 6 pounds). The mountain lakes (access on foot) are Naustådalsvatn (2,788 ft.), Neådalsvatna (1,970 — 2,296 ft.), Tverrdalsvatna (2,625 — 2,950 ft.) and others. Naustådalsvatn is reported to be overpopulated, but the other lakes have fair stocks of good quality trout. The Todalselv is best during spate periods all through the summer. The mountain lakes should be fished in Aug. — Sept.
Centre: Kårvatn Chalet (Trondheim Touring Club), not listed.
Fishing permits: Tickets both to the river and the lakes are sold by Kårvatn Chalet.

VANYLVEN
The peninsulas of the Vanylven parish have some fine trout waters. The Brandal water course has been harnessed by the local power station, but the lake Olalivatn (approx. 1,300 ft. above sea level) is still a good water with stocks of fine trout.

SYVDE area (A 11). Travel by bus and ferries from Ålesund in approx. 3 hours. The distance by car from Ålesund is approx. 40 miles, 2 ferries. Maps: 1119 III (Vanylven) and 1119 II (Volda).
The mountain lakes between Syvdsbotn, Åheim and Dalsfjord form one of the best fishing areas of the Sunnmøre province. Lake Setervatn (750 ft.), only a short walk from the road at Øverberg, Storlivatn and Myrkevatn (approx. 1,800 ft., one hour's walk from Åsen in Rovde, are stocked with trout weighing 2—6 pounds. In Sarpevatn and Dansevatn trout (12 to 16 ounces) are numerous.
Season: July — August.
Centre: Syvde (not listed in «Hotels in Norway»).
Fishing permits: Fishing have been free up to now in Setervatn, Storlivatn and Myrkevatn. Tickets to Sarpevatn and Dansevatn are available at Dansesetra.

VOLDA AND ØRSTA
The neigbouring villages of Ørsta and Volda are richly endowed with scenery and trout waters.

VOLDA area (A/B 11). Travel by bus and ferry from Ålesund to Volda in 2 hours. The distance by car is 42 miles and 1 ferry . Maps: 1119 II (Volda) and 1219 III (Hjørundfjord).
On the other side of the Voldafjord (ferry to Folkestad) there is fine fishing in the Kils water course consisting of two lakes and 3 rivers. The length of the water course is 2,8 km between lake Bjørkedalsvatn (82 ft.) and the fjord. Trout in this water will average from 1 to 2 pounds, but salmon up to 20 pounds have been killed. The Austefjord water course east of Volda offers plenty of fishing between lake Kaldvatn (230 ft.) and the fjord. In between are the lakes Langvatn, Eidsvatn, Bolingen and Litlevatn. Trout and red char in lake Kaldvatn, the other lakes hold some salmon and sea trout as well. Fine stocks of trout (approx. 1/2 pound) and red char (14 ounces). The third water course is formed by the Åmela river. This river drains lake Storlivatn (1,765 ft.). and a number of fine lakes with plenty of trout and then falls into the Dalsfjord at Åmelfot 12 miles and one ferry south of Volda. A few salmon and trout run a few hundred yards up the river. Trout in the lakes will average 1 pound.
Season: July — Aug for all waters in the Volda area. The Kils- and Austefjord water courses are accessible by car. The Åmella calls for a good deal of walking.
Centres: Volda and Kaldvatn (see Volda).
Fishing permits: Tickets to Kilsvassdraget (water course) from Volda Sport or Marius Kile, Kile. Permission to fish the Austfjord and Åmela systems must be acquired from the farmers.

ØRSTA area (A/B 11). Travel by bus and ferry from Ålesund in 2 hours. Road distance from Ålesund 37 miles. Maps: 1119 II (Volda) and 1219 III (Hjørundfjord).
Lake Vatnevatn (315 ft.) on Highway 655 12 miles south of Ørsta village holds plenty of trout and red char, average weight 10 ounces. Fishing here is best in June. Lake Hovdevatn (380 ft.) 4 miles south of Ørsta is moderately stocked with trout (1 pound) and red char (1/2 pound). No fishing on Mondays and Tuesdays. Fishing here to is probably best in June. If one continues along Highway 655 and ferries across the magnificent Hjørundfjord one arrives at Norangsdal 21 miles east of Ørsta. The Norangsdalselv river flows through the valley draining a number of lakes. The uppermost lakes, Geirskrevatn and Jupevatn (approx. 1,000 ft.), are overpo-

pulated and trout are small. Stavbergsvatn and the Nobbevatna lakes further down offer fine sport, good-quality trout and red char. Lyngstålsvatn, the next lake is overstocked with red char, but trout fishing should be fair. Below this lake the river is a salmon and sea trout water. Season: July and Aug. If you are inclined to walk, the Tussavatn (1,980 ft.) and Trolldalsvatn (2,950 ft.) 2 hours' walk from Bjørke at the head of the Hjørundfjord, will yield fair sport. Fishing is best in Aug. Bjørke lies 31 miles east of Ørsta.
Centre: Ørsta.
Fishing permits: Inexpensive tickets to lake Vatnevatn, are sold by Vatne Landhandel (general store). Tickets to Hovdevatn from local farmers. Tickets to the Norangsdal water course from Union Hotel, Øye and Øye Landhandel. Fishing is free in Tussavatn and Trolldalsvatn.

ÅLESUND AND GISKE, HAREID AND HARAM

Ålesund is like a fish-hook thrown out into Atlantic. And there are fine fish to be caught not only in the sea, but also in lakes on the islands and on the mainland.

ÅLESUND area (A 11). Travel by plane from Oslo or Bergen in approx. 1 hour to Ålesund, or by boat from Bergen in 13 hours, or train and bus from Oslo in 11 hours. Road distance from Olso 514 miles, from Bergen 232 miles and 6 ferries. Maps: 1119 I (Ålesund), 1120 II (Vigra) and 1220 III (Brattvåg).
Lake Alnesvatn on the island of Godøy is a fine lake, situated approx. 650 ft. above sea level. It holds plenty of sporting trout (average weight 1 pound) and can be fished from April to Sept. Closed season: Sept. 15 to April 15. Ferry from Ålesund 25 mins. On the island of Hareid lake Liavågvatn (130 ft.) is the best water. It holds a fair amount of 1/2 pound trout with chances of bigger fish. Sea trout run in the autumn. Lake Brusdalsvatn (165 ft.), 10 miles east of Ålesund, holds plenty of small char and some really big trout. Several 17- and 20- pounders have been caught in the last years. There are also a few good lakes in the mountains south of Brusdalsvatn. The most promising lakes in Haram seem to be Slyngstadvatn (227 ft.), Søvikvatn (656 ft., path from Hildre, approx. 3 miles) and Vatnevatn (66 ft.). All these lakes hold fair stocks of 1/2 pound trout. Lake Vatnevatn should be fished from a boat. With the exception of Søvikvatn these lakes are reached by car, distance from Ålesund approx. 25 miles. All the lakes in the Ålesund area have a long season.

Centre: Ålesund.
Fishing permits: Tickets to lake Alnesvatn are sold locally. Free rod-fishing is permitted in Liavågvatn. Up to now fishing has been free in lake Brusdalsvatn. Rod-fishing has been free in Slyngstadvatn. Permission to fish lake Søvikvatn must be obtained from the farmers. Tickets are sold locally to lake Vatnevatn.

SØR-TRØNDELAG

There is fishing in the mountains, on the moors, in the valleys and the fjords and on the islands of this county around the city of Trondheim. Make a note of the fact that grayling are sporting fish on the Trøndelag moors and also that red char take more willingly than in counties further south.

HITRA

The island of Hitra is known for its red deer and for its 934 fishing waters. Only a few of these are situated more than 300 ft. above sea level. There are roads round the island, but only a few lead into the interior. Thus fishing the Hitra waters requires a good deal of walking in flat, mossy country.

HITRA area (B 9—10). Travel by bus and ferry to Hitra (Sandstad) in approx. 4 hours from Trondheim. The distance by car from Trondheim is 88 miles and on ferry. There is also a ferry (3 hours) from Kristiansund to Hitra (Forsnes). Maps: 1422 II (Hitra), 1422 III (Sør-Frøya) and 1421 IV (Skardsøy).
We can only mention a few of the Hitra waters. Lake Barlifjellvatn (walk from Balsnes on Highroad 713) is well stocked with trout weighing up to 2 pounds. Lake Kjørstadvatn (west of Forsnes) has a fine run of sea trout in July — Aug. Lake Laksåvatn (near Highway 713) where big sea trout may be caught. The Lomemmertjønna tarns where the Laksåvik water course rises is reported to hold big trout. Similar conditions exist in lake Mørkedalsvatn — the uppermost water in the Skumfoss water course — where fine trout may be caught. The Hitra waters can be fished from May to September.
Centre: Small pension at Ansnes, listed under Hitra in «Hotels in Norway».
Fishing permits: Hitra is divided into 4 fishing areas. Tickets to these areas are sold on the ferries. Fishing cards for sea trout and small salmon fisheries are available from local shops.

MELHUS

This agricultural parish south of Trondheim has a few lakes of interest to visitors. These waters may be fished from Trondheim

86

MELHUS area (C 9—10). Travel by train or bus from Trondheim in 1/2 hour. Melhus village lies only 12 miles south of Trondheim. Maps: 1621 III (Støren), 1621 IV (Trondheim) and 1521 II (Hølonda).
Gaula river has been dealt with in the salmon section. Lake Håan (1,394 ft.) is reached on a toll road from Lundamo. Good trout fishing, fish up to 6 pounds, average size 10 ounces. Lake Samsjøen (1,627 ft.) belongs to the same system and is said to be well stocked with trout (12 ounces to 2 pounds). Season (both lakes): June — July. Lake Ånøyen (343 ft.) lies on Highway 708 south of Melhus. Good stock of trout (up to 18 pounds) and some red char (average weight 12 ounces). Season: May — September.
Centres: Trondheim and Melhus (not listed).
Fishing permits: Tickets to Håan and Samsjøen are sold by Lundamo Kafe. Tickets to Ånøyen from Hove camp, or permission from local owners.

OPPDAL
The mountain village of Oppdal offers fishing in several widely scattered areas.

OPPDAL area (C 10). Travel by train from Oslo in 6 hours or from Trondheim in 2 hours. Road distance from Trondheim 76 miles, from Oslo 331 miles. Map: 1520 III (Oppdal).
There are several waters in the area including lake Gjevilvatn (2,165 ft.). This big lake, however, is too deep to yield good sport, it contains quite a few red char (very little trout) weighing up to 18 pounds. Best sport is probably to be found in the Åmotselv river, a tributary to the Driva, south of Engan. Approx. 3 hours' walk from Åmotsdal farm to the best fishery, which is located between the Urvassbekk tributary and lake Åmotsdalsvatn (4,200 ft.). This stretch of water is moderately stocked with trout (6 to 8 ounces). Season: End of July — Aug. *Centre:* Oppdal. The river is more conveniently fished from Åmotsdalshytta (unstaffed chalet belong to Kristiansund Touring Club), situated approx. 5 hours' walk from Åmotsdals farm.
Fishing permit: The above-mentioned waters belong to Oppdal Common Ground, fishing permits from sports shops in Oppdal.

DRIVSTUA — KONGSVOLL area (C 10). Travel: See Oppdal. Drivstua is situated 14 miles and Kongsvoll 25 miles south of Oppdal on E 6. Maps: 1520 III (Oppdal) and 1519 IV (Snøhetta).
Fishing in lakes and river belonging to Drivstua and Kongsvoll State Common Grounds. Here is the Vårstigåa, which rises in Vårstigtjønna 3,956 ft. above sea level and

falls into the Driva between Kongsvoll and Drivstua some 2,300 ft. above sea level. Fishing is said to be good on a 1 km stretch just below Vårstigtjønna, moderate stock of 8-ounce trout. Fishing also in the upper reaches of the Kaldvella tributary and in lake Kaldvellsjøen (4,100 ft.) 2 1/2 hours' walk from Kongsvoll. The lake holds plenty of trout (average weight 10 ounces) of inferior quality. The trout in the river are smaller, but of somewhat better quality. The best fish in this area is perhaps found in lake Stroplsjøen (4,200 ft.). Here there are plenty of trout, weighing approx. 8 ounces. 3 1/2 hours' walk from Kongsvoll. Fishing in the area is at its best in July and August.
Centre: Kongsvoll (see Oppdal in «Hotels in Norway»).
Fishing permits: A limited number of fishing cards to Kongsvoll State Common Ground (Kaldvella and Stroplsjøen) are available at Kongsvoll and Hjerkinn railway stations. Tickets to Drivstua State Common Grounds (Vårstigåa) are sold by sports shops in Oppdal, approx. kr. 30 per week.

STORLI area (B 10). Travel: See Oppdal. Storli lies 26 miles east of Oppdal. Map: 1520 III (Oppdal).
The Storli Valley offers fishing in several waters. Some of these are situated on or near the Lønset — Storli road, others in the Trollheimen Mountains. Lake Dalsvatn (1,968 ft.), lake Ångårdsvatn (2,065 ft.) and the Lona river belongs to the first catergory, the Tovatna lakes to the second (1 hour's walk from Storli). The waters contain good to moderate stocks of trout, weighing from 10 ounces up to 9 pounds. Ångårdsvatn is slightly overpopulated. Season for this area: June — July. Closed season: Sept. 15 — Oct. 15.
Centres: Storli and Vassli farms are not listed in «Hotels in Norway».
Fishing permits: Available at Storli and Vassli.

OSEN
This municipality is off the beaten track, though most of the waters are easily accessible from Highway 715.

OSEN area (B 9). Travel by train from Trondheim to Steinkjer in 2 hours and by bus to Osen in approx. 3 hours, Road distance from Trondheim is 130 miles. Maps: 1623 IV (Osen) and 1623 I (Jøssund).
Most of the fishing belong to the Steindalselv system, which contains salmon up to Nordmelandsfoss waterfalls (3 km). Lake Elgsjøen (734 ft.) lies 2 km from a local forest road and holds numerous 8-ounce trout and red char.

Fiskløsvatn (literally «lake without fish») is situated 1,135 ft. above sea level and 1 km from the road. Good lake, fine quality trout, average weight 8 ounces — according to reports — and rod fishing only. Lake Kangsvatn (712 ft.) is also reached on foot, approx. 1 hour from Highroadb 715, fine trout and good sport. Season: June — Sept.
Centres: There is a guest house in Steinsdalen (Osen), but one may well lodge in Steinkjer or Namsos and fish the Osen waters.
Fishing permits: Most waters belong to the Osen State Common ground, and inexpensive tickets are sold at Namdalseid and Steinsdalen.

RØROS AND ÅLEN

There are several waters in this area, partly small lakes on the mountain plateau, partly great watercourses like the Glomma river and the waters in the northern Femund district. In Ålen tickets to the State Common Ground are not available to foreigners.

RØROS area (C 10). Travel by train from Trondheim in 2 3/4 hours or from Oslo in 6 hours. Road distance from Oslo 248 miles, from Trondheim 98 miles. Map: 1720 III (Røros).
Glåmos, or the outlet of the Glomma river from lake Aursunden, is a very good stretch of river with numerous trout and grayling. Fish up to 3 pounds are a definite possibility. Season: July and August.
Centre: Røros.
Fishing permit: Tickets (casting from the bank) are available at Glåmos Samvirkelag (Co-op).

BREKKEN area (C 10). Brekken lies 22 miles east of Røros centre and is reached by bus in 45 mins. Highway 31 and local roads leads towards the fishing waters. Maps: 1720 II (Brekken).
Lake Bolagen (2,637 ft.) is well stocked with good quality trout. The fishing is much sought after and must be booked well in advance from John Ryen, Brekken. It is let with boat for 24 hours at the time. The Bolagstjern tarn (2,664 ft.) belongs to Brekken Common Ground. It contains a fair amount of quality trout. Davolsjøen (2,910 ft.) is also part of the common ground (which comprise hundreds of lakes). Both trout and red char are numerous in this water. Short walks from the nearest road lead to the abovementioned waters. The Grubevolltjern tarn (2,509 ft.) lies only 400 yards from the Myrmoen — Stugudal toll road. Well stocked with trout and char. Season: July and August.

Centres: Brekken and Vauldalen (listed under Røros), or Røros.
Fishing permits: Fishing in lake Bolagen must be arranged with the owner. Tickets to Brekken Common Ground are available locally.

FEMUND area (C 10). Lake Femund (Sørvika) lies 22 miles south-east of Røros centre and is reached by bus in 1 hour. Boat from Sørvika to the mouth of the Røa river. Map: 1719 I (Røa).
The Mugga system rises in the Vingelen mountains, drains a couple of lakes on the Swedish side of the border and forms in Norway several pools and small lakes where good sport can be expected. Between lake Femund (2,175 ft.) and the first waterfall the Mugga contains perch, pike, gwyniad and grayling. Above the first waterfall the river is well stocked with trout. On both sides of the Mugga there are lakes that feed the river. In these lakes trout, perch and pike are numerous. Season: July and August.
Centre: There are no roads and no accommodation along the Mugga. Most anglers bring their tents and camp.
Fishing permits: The area belongs to Røros State Common Ground. Tickets at reasonable prices are available from the Røros Tourist Office.

ÅLEN area (C 10). Ålen lies on Highway 30 — 20 miles north for Røros. Map: 1720 IV (Ålen).
Ålen area offers fishing in the Båttjerndal Valley. Several small lakes and tarns, all well stocked with mediumsized trout. A local road leads to these waters which are situated approx. 2,600 ft. above sea level.
Centre: Ålen (not listed) and Røros.

SNILLFJORD

This parish of small fjords, little valleys and low mountains west of Trondheim is not without attractions to anglers.

SLØRDAL area (B 10). Travel by bus from Trondheim to Slørdal in 2 1/2 hours. Road distance from Trondheim is 62 miles. Maps: 1521 IV (Snillfjord) and 1522 III Ørland).
The Slørdal system follows Highway 714. Melvatn (410 ft.) and lake Slørdalsvatn (393 ft.) hold plenty of trout, average weight 8 ounces, good quality. Also some small red char. Tjernet (204 ft.) lies north of Slørdalsvatn and has even more trout. Before entering the Åstfjord the river forms a little lake in which sea trout and salmon occur.
Season: May — September.
Centre: No accommodation locally. Nearest hotel in Orkanger (listed) 30 miles away.
Fishing permits: Available from G or J. Slørdal.

SELBU AND TYDAL

Vast hydro-electric developments have changed both the topography and fisheries. All the same the area has several good fishing waters. Among the best are the lakes Stugusjøen and Nesjøen and the Nea river. These contain trout and red char. Ice fishing starts in the middle of April and continues until the ice breaks up. Many of these lakes are dammed, and the ice can be dangerous.

The Nea Valley has been dammed and the former Essandsjø transformed into a huge reservoir Nesjøen (3,300 ft.). The outlook for this reservoir is uncertain, but it will probably hold a lot of red char and little trout. Lake Gammelvollsjøen (1,500 ft.) is also dammed, small trout and red char are numerous. Situated on the Ås — Essandsjø toll road. Mosjøen (1,840 ft.) on the main road belongs to the Tya water course and is reported to contain a fair stock of trout and red char, average size 8 ounces. The Tya rises in lake Stugusjøen (1,970 ft.) where trout up to 6 pounds have been caught, but where red char is the dominant species. Fishing regulations forbid the use of your own boat in lake Nesjøen and some smaller lakes. However, boats to lake Nesjøen may be rented from Nesjøen Båtutleie (boat rental) in Litjelvdal, approx. 11 miles from Stugudal. Boats are rented with oars, but you are permitted to use your own outboard motor. Boats to Stugusjøen can be rented from the guest houses.

Centre: Tydal.
Fishing permits: Tickets are sold by pensions and guest houses as well as by the boat rental stations.

ÅFJORD

A parish that offer fishing galore in fjords, lakes and rivers.

ÅFJORD area (B 9). Travel by ferry and bus from Trondheim to Åfjord in 2 1/2 hours. Distance by road from Trondheim is 55 miles and 1 ferry. Maps: 1622 IV (Åfjord), 1522 I (Bjugn) and 1623 III (Roan).

The Norddalselv and Stordalselv river have been described in the salmon section. The upper reaches of both these waters, and lakes belonging to their systems like Krokvatn (918 ft.) and Stordalsvatn (69 ft.), hold other fish. In Krokvatn there is a fair amount of red char, Stordalsvatn is moderately stocked with trout. Also fishing in «independent» lakes such as Grovlivatn (587 ft.), well stocked with trout and red char, Håvikvatn (713 ft.), trout up to 5 pounds, Lonan (600 ft.). plenty of good-quality trout and lake Mørivatn (56 ft.), where trout and red char are numerous and both sea trout and salmon occur. Storvatn

(285 ft.) contains both trout and red char well above average size. Angling in Krokvatn means walking 1 1/2 hours, Grovlivatn 1 hour (on a local forest road), Håvikvatn 2 hours, Lonan at least 1 hour. The other waters mention above are reached by road.

Season: June — August.
Centre: Åfjord (not listed).
Fishing permits: Available from Årnes Sport and Radio.

NORD-TRØNDELAG

In the parish of Snåsa alone there are some 2,000 lakes and tarns and the majority hold fish. It has been said that possibilities for angling in Nord-Trøndelag are unlimited. That is perhaps an overstatement. The lakes in the «lowlands» around the Trondheimsfjord and the coastal districts hold too many trout, and the quality is often inferior from an angler's point of view, but as one advances to higher ground on the Snåsa, Lierne and Røyrvik mountain moors, quality improves and good sport may almost be guaranteed.

LIERNE

This vast and sparsely populated mountain parish, formerly Nordli and Sørli, has a great variety of big and small lakes. Some of these are reached by road, but most of them are situated in the roadless mountains.

NORDLI area (C 8). Travel from Trondheim to Formofoss by train in 3 hours and then 2 hours by bus to Nordli. Maps: 1923 IV (Nordli) and 1923 I (Murusjøen).

In the region a number of large lakes are close to Highways 74 and 765 or local roads, and several smaller ones which are approached on foot. Here are some of the big lakes: Kvesjøen (1,033 ft.) Laksjøen (1,276 ft.), Sandsjøen (1,312 ft.) and Lauvsjøen (1,764 ft.). Kvesjøen holds trout (up to 16 pounds), red char, grayling and pike. Laksjøen and Sandsjøen are well stocked with trout and red char. Trout will scale 10 ounces with fish up to 10 pounds a possibility. The same applies to Lauvsjøen where red char may weigh as much as 4 pounds. These lakes should be fished in the latter half of June and July, and preferably from boats. Otersjøen (1,128 ft.) is situated near Highroad 74. Good stocks of trout (8 ounces up to 10 pounds) and red char (6 ounces upwards to 2 pounds). Lake Bugvatn is situated 2,168 ft. above sea level and 10 miles from the nearest road, but it is stocked with fine trout, average weight 10 ounces with specimens up to 2 pounds. The Lutra river which rises in the Hartkjølen mountains almost 4,600 ft. above sea level and falls into lake Sandsjøen is known to be a good trout river especially the lower reaches. The higher waters in the Nordli area offer the best fishing in July — August.

Centres: Skjellbrei and Holand (not listed in «Hotels in Norway»).

Fishing permits: Inexpensive fishing permits to these waters are sold locally. Kvesjøen tickets are available from Arne Kvemo, Kvelia. Tickets to Lutra from Holand Gjestgiveri (Guest House) and to Tisvatn from Bjarne Ness, Nordli.

SØRLI area (C 8). Travel: See Nordli. Mebygda/Jule lies 25 miles south of Nordli. Maps: 1923 II(Sørli) and 1923 III(Blåfjellhatten).

There are even more waters in Sørli than in Nordli and, as in Nordli, the biggest lakes are found along the main road (Highway 765). The best of these is probably Ulen (1,122 ft.) and the best fishing spot here is Julestrømmen, or the river between lake Lenglingen and Ulen. Trout and red char of fine quality, fish will average 12 ounces, but trout up to 15 pounds have been caught. In the mountains west of the main water course are some fine lakes, situated 1,600 to 2,600 ft. above sea level and reached on foot. Make a note of Arvatn, Blåfjellvatna, Gussvatn and Midtvatn. They all belong to Finnli State Common Ground and they are well stocked with 1-pound trout. Lake Gussvatn and lake Arvatn have plenty of small red char as well. Good river fishing is provided by Innerdalsåa, especially below the Innerfoss fall where the river contains plenty of trout (up to 8 pounds) and red char. Above the waterfall there are trout only, weighing 8 to 12 ounces. The river is reached by road from Jule. The main water course can be fished in June — July, the mountain waters should be fished in late July and August.

Centres: Sørli and Jule (not listed in «Hotels in Norway»).

Fishing permits: State Common Ground tickets are sold several places locally. Tickets to Innerdalsåa, approx. kr. 10 per day, from Edith Juleshaug or Fr. Næss, Sørli. Tickets to Julestrømmen from Samfunnskaféen or Sørli Handel (local shop), Sørli. Tickets to Ulen from Jon M. Skåle, Sørli. All tickets are reasonable or inexpensive.

MERÅKER

The waters of Meråker tend to be overpopulated, yet they are so strategically placed near E 75 and the Swedish border that we have decided to include them among the Nord-Trøndelag fisheries.

MERÅKER area (C 9). Travel by train from Trondheim to Meråker in 2 hours. Road distance from Trondheim is 64 miles. Maps: 1721 I(Meråker) and 1722 II(Feren). Some of the best Meråker waters are Halsjøen (1,955 ft.) in roadless country close to the Swedish border and lake Langen (1,640 fr.), reached in approx. 1 1/2 hours from the Meråker — Feren road. Both lakes are situated north of the main valley and they are moderately stocked with trout of good quality. There is also lake Storkjerringvatn (2,734 ft.) in the mountains 4 miles north of Skurdalsvollen farm. South of the Stjørdal Valley the Lødølja river — 3 hours' walk from Stordalen — is well stocked with trout and red char and should offer good sport. The same applies to the upper reaches of the Vatnelv river, where trout are reported to scale 10 ounces and red char are only too numerous (and small in size). And why not try the Tevla which runs along E 75? In its upper reaches this river drains three tarns which are said to be well stocked with red char and trout.

Centre: Meråker.

Fishing permit: Tickets covering the area, approx. kr. 15 per day, are available at the Information Kiosk, Meråker Railway Station, Brenna Camping, Teveltunet Guest House and Hegseth Sport.

NAMSSKOGAN

This parish on both sides of the Namsen river offers fishing mainly in the mountains on the west side of the valley. There is some trout in the Namsen and also a kind of relict salmon, known as 'Namsblanken', which is small in size.

NAMSSKOGAN area (C 8). Travel by train from Trondheim to Namsskogan in 4 hours. Road distance from Trondheim is 178 miles. Maps: Trones and Frøiningfjell.

The best trout fishing in the Namsen is found at 'Namskroken' east of Smalåsen station, where the river turns towards the south. Lake Smalvatn (781 ft.) at Smalåsen station has plenty of trout, average weight 8 ounces. Lake Mellingen (788 ft.) lies only 2 miles east of E 6 at Smalåsen. Mellingen is reported to be moderately stocked with trout weighing up to 2 pounds. The Gåsvatna lakes are situated some 4 miles from E 6. In Østre Gåsvatn (1,575 ft.) both red char and trout are numerous and of good quality, up to 4 pounds. Further south in the Namdal Valley many lakes are within reasonable walking distance of the Strompedal mountain road. Among these are the Ausvatna lakes (689 ft.) which hold plenty of trout, scaling approx. 1/2 pound. The Namsskogan waters can be fished from the middle of June to the end of August.

Centre: Brekkvasselv (not listed) and Namsskogan with modest pensions.
Fishing permits: Inexpensive tickets to Namsen, Mellingsvatn and Østre Gåsvatn are sold by Abels Gjestgiveri, Smalåsen and Mellingsmoen camping. Tickets to lakes along the Strompedalsroad are available from Van Severen, Trones and Bangdalsbruket, Kjelmoen.

OVERHALLA

This parish on the lower Namsen is always associated with salmon fishing, but there are several waters in the wooded hills where good trout fishing may be had.

OVERHALLA area (C 8). Travel by train from Trondheim to Overhalla in 4 hours. Distance by road from Trondheim is 144 miles. Maps: 1723 I(Overhalla) and 1723 IV (Namsos).
Lille Brokvatn, Eriktjønna, Lilleflisingen, Lillesøien, Rognvatn, Storflisingen and Tømmersjøen are situated from 300 to 1,300 ft. above sea level. Some of these waters are accessible by car on local forest roads, and they are all fairly well stocked with 8—12 ounce trout. Season: July — Aug. Closed season: Sept. 15 — Nov. 15.
Centre: Namsos and Grong and Skogmo.
Fishing permits: Tickets to these lakes are sold locally.

RØYRVIK

Some of the fishing in the parish lies within the borders of the Børgefjell National Park.

RØYRVIK area (C 8). Travel by train from Trondheim to Brekkvasselv or Namsskogan in 4 hours and bus to Gjersvik in 1 hour. Road distance from Trondheim is 185 miles. Maps: Namsvatnet and Børgefjell.
Fishing in the bigger lakes of Vektaren (2,130 ft.) and Huddingsvatn (2,192 ft.), in the river Huddingselv and several smaller lakes within 15 mins, to 1 1/2 hours' walk from the road. Boats for hire at the tourist lodges. In the bigger lakes fishing is mostly done from boats. The fish are trout and char, but some lakes have trout only. Very good stock, usual size from 12—25 ounces up to 6 pounds, excellent quality. Fishing also in State Common Ground lakes in the Børgefjell National Park north of lake Namsvatn. Fishing in the National Park means long walks and an out-door life.
Centres: Limingen Gjestegård, Vekterli Turistheim (both not listed) and the chalets rentals at lake Namsvatn, lake Huddingsvatn and the Huddingselv river.
Fishing permits: Tickets to lake Vekteren, lake Huddingsvatn and the surrounding lakes are sold by local farmers. Tickets to the State

Common Ground, including Børgefjell National Park, and to the waters of Røyrvik Jakt- og Fiskeforening (local hunting and angling ass.) are available from Røyrvik Auto.

SNÅSA

This is the parish with unlimited fishing, which also means that it is difficult to give a balanced account of the various possibilities. The majority of the fisheries are far from roads and strenuous walks are part of successful fishing.

SNÅSA area (C 8—9). Travel by train from Trondheim to Snåsa in 3 hours. Distance by road from Trondheim is 118 miles. Maps: 1823 I (Andorsjøen), 1823 III (Snåsa) and 1823 IV (Grong).
Lake Snåsavatn (79 ft.) contains trout, red char, eel and burbot. Red char are numerous and weigh from 6 to 14 ounces. Good stock of big trout, up to 17 pounds (trolling). Lake Andorsjøen (1,058 ft.) lies 3 miles from the nearest road and is densely stocked with trout, average weight 14—16 ounces, with fish up to 3 1/2 pounds. The Andora river drains the lake and joins the Storåselv river. Below Agle this water course is called Grana river. The upper reaches of the Andora has good fishing, trout up to 1 pound. The Imsa river, called Jøstadelva further down, is fed by several tributaries. Reinsjøelv drains lake Reinsjøen, where trout is numerous, and Store Landskoro rises in some good trout tarns in the Imsdal mountains. Trout is smaller in the Imsa itself, but tarns close to the river hold some fine fish. The whole area offers fishing from June to the beginning of Sept. There is a local road along the Jørstadelv river and a local toll road runs along the Imsa.
Centre: Snåsa.
Fishing permits: Tickets to lake Snåsavatn, also covering lake Grønningen (see below) and Store Øyningen are sold by Rohde and Hammer, Snåsa, and Breide Samvirkelag (Co-op). Tickets to the other waters mentioned above are also available here. All tickets are reasonable.

JÆVSJØ area (C 8). Travel: see Snåsa. Map: 1823 II (Gjevsjøen).
Apart from lake Grønningen (1,529 ft.) all these lakes are reached on foot. The best known lakes in this area are Grønningen, Heggsjø, Ismenningen, Reinsjøen, Jævsjøen, Langvatnet, Nåvatnet and Vivatnet. There are also the Kasttjern, Klingertjern and Stigåtjern tarns. The lakes are situated 1,300 to 2,000 ft. above sea level and contain trout and red char mostly. Trout will scale approx.

from 10 ounces to 1 pound with possibilities of bigger fish (up to 16 pounds in lake Jævsjø). The area has been rather heavily fished and the big lakes should be fished from boats. Some river stretches offer good sport, especially the Gauna and its tributaries, where trout are seldom bigger than 14 ounces, but grayling usually scale 1 pound. The Gauna is privately owned. Fishing must be arranged with the Gaundalen farm.
Centres: No accomodation in the area, but some huts can be rented through Snåsa Fjellstyre (Mountain Board).
Fishing permits: Tickets to most of these waters are sold by Rohde & Hammer, Snåsa. The Vivatn ticket costs approx. kr. 50 per season. Fishing in lake Jævsjø must be arranged with the owners of the Jævsjø farms, who also owns the Kasttjern tarns (partly leased for long periods). Tickets to the Klingertjern and Stigåtjern tarns are sold by Rohde & Hammer and Breide Samvirkelag (Co-op).

LURU area (C 8). Travel: See Snåsa. Map: 1823 I(Andorsjøen) and 1823 IV(Grong).
The Luru water course with such tributaries as the Alma and the Medøla provide good and varied sport. The upper reaches of the Luru lies within the Gressåmoen National Park. A local road leads along the river and stops approx. 2 miles from the national park. Trout in the Luru are small in size (8 ounces). In the upper reaches of the Alma there are bigger fish, especially in the tarns and glides, but it is a long way to go there. The Medøla with its glides and rapids is a sporting river, but the fish are small. The river lies far off the beaten track and is seldom fished.
Centres: No accommodation in the area. Snåsa is the nearest centre.
Fishing permits: Most of the area is State Common Ground, inexpensive tickets available from Rohde & Hammer, Snåsa.

NORDLAND
From a scenic point of view Nordland — the first of the 3 big counties in North Norway — is of astounding beaty and variety. The good trout fishing in Nord-Trøndelag continues in Nordland, but as the county narrows and water power developments become more apparent, possibilities become more limited. In the coastal districts — on the innumerable isles — there are waters hardly ever visited by sportsmen. Such waters, however, are likely to suffer from overpopulation.

BODØ
The growing and active town of Bodø has recently incorporated substantial parts of the surrounding countryside. As a consequence quite a few fishing waters both north and south of the Saltfjord became part of Bodø. The best water south of the Saltfjord is probably lake Valnesvatn.

BODØ area (B 6). Travel by plane to Bodø from Oslo in 1 1/2 hours, from Bergen in 3 hours or by train from Trondheim in 11 1/2 hours. Distance by car from Trondheim is 467 miles, from Oslo 811 miles. Maps: Bodø and Kjerringøy.
Lake Bogvatn (492 ft.) is well stocked with red char and trout and so is lake Heggmovatn (420 ft.), though red char here are small in size. Both lakes are reached by road from Hopen. A forest road leads from Kvalvåg to lake Tinnvatn (980 ft.) where trout are of good quality and fair sport may be expected. There is also lake Tussvatn (328 ft.), reached by road from Bertnes, with plenty of 8-ounce trout. Season for all lakes in the area: July — August.
Centre: Bodø.
Fishing permits: Fishing has been free up to now in Bogvatn, cards are sold locally to Heggmovatn, Tussvatn and Tinnvatn (ask Bodø Tourist Office).

KJERRINGØY area (B 6). Kjerringøy lies 24 miles (one ferry) north of Bodø. Map: Kjerringøy.
The principal Kjerringøy waters are Fjærevatn (10 ft.), Storvatn (10 ft.) and Sørvatn (16 ft.). Lake Storvatn and lake Sørvatn are reached in 1/2 hour and Fjærevatn in 1 hour from Fjære on foot. In all 3 lakes both trout and red char are fairly numerous. Season: July — August.
Centre: Kjerringøy where the old trading post has been turned both into a museum and a charming hostel, not listed.
Fishing permits: Tickets to these lakes are sold at Fjære.

BRØNNØY
The township of Brønnøysund next to the famous Torghatten mountain might be considered for a fishing holiday, especially if one is willing to combine deep sea and inland fishing.

BRØNNØYSUND area (B 8). Travel by plane from Trondheim in 1 1/2 hours or by boat in 13 hours. Distance by road from Trondheim is 240 miles. Map: Velfjord.
Lake Hornsvatn (10 ft.), Movatn (10 ft.) and Tilremsvatn (33 ft.) are all situated close to Highway 17. According to reports trout are numerous and of good quality in these waters. The Rødlivatna lakes (72 ft.) lies 1 1/2 miles from the nearest road and are said to be well stocked with trout and red char.

Season: June — August.
Centre: Brønnøysund.
Fishing permits: Tickets to Hornsvatn, Movatn and Tilremsvatn are available from Sør-Helgeland Tourist Office, Brønnøysund. Permission to fish the Rødlivatn lakes must be acquired from the owners.

FAUSKE, HAMARØY, SALTDAL AND SØRFOLD

This vast area consisting of several municipalities has been turned into one angling district, where one fishing card is valid for all waters on state ground from Tysfjord in the north to the Saltfjell mountain in the south. Here is trout and char fishing in the Lønsdal river, the upper and lower Viskisvatn lakes and lake Kjemåga within the Saltdal area. The Lønsdal river runs along E 6, the lakes are reached in approx. 1 hour from the road. The Sørfold area is said to provide fishing in some 20 lakes situated from 6 to 2,000 ft. above sea level. Fishing in the best Sørfold waters certainly means a lot of walking (up to 6 hours). The Hamarøy area is easier to fish as E 6 runs along the main water course, the Sagvasselv river, with its string of lakes. In all these areas, fishing is best in July and Aug. The most varied and interesting fisheries are provided by Fauske or — to be more exact — by the Sulitjelma area.

SULITJELMA area (C 6). Travel: See Bodø above. Fauske lies on E 6 (and the North Norway Railway) 40 miles east of Bodø. From Fauske it is 25 miles, or one hour by bus, to Sulitjelma. Maps: Sulitjelma, Saltdal and Junkerdalen.
Some of the lakes in the area really belong to Saltdal, but they can only be fished from Sulitjelma. These are Beritvatn, Dødvatn, Fuglevatna, Nenajavarre, Rosni, Sølvvatn and others. These lakes are situated 2,000 to 3,000 ft. above sea level, 6 to 25 miles south of Sulitjelma centre, and they are reached on foot in 20 mins. to 3 hours from the Sulitjelma — Balvatn road. All the lakes mentioned are stocked with fine trout weighing from 14 ounces to 2 pounds. Fishing according to our reports is best from the middle of July to the middle of Aug. The season is closed from Sept. 15 to Jan. 1. Here are some of the other lakes in this area: Calalvejavrre, Kjelvatn, Lomijavrre, Mourkijavrre, Saakivatn, Skuortajavrre, Sorjusjavrre, Saakivatn and Villumvatn. These waters lie 1,650 to 3,000 ft. above sea level. Some of them are accessible by car from Sulitjelma. Most of them lie 1 to 4 hours' walk from the nearest road. In all these lakes 1-pound trout are fairly numerous and bigger fish a definite possibility. Lomijavrre and Mourkijavrre are

red char waters mainly. Season: July 1 — Aug. 15. Closed season: Sept. 15. — Jan. 1.
Centre: Sulitjelma (not listed).
Fishing permits: The general ticket mentioned above is valid in this area. It costs approx. kr. 35 per week or kr. 75 per season and is sold by shops in Sulitjelma.

GRANE

The Vefsna with the Svenningsdalselv tributary are the main waters of this parish. There is also some mountain fishing in the Majastua area.

MAJAVATN area (C 8). Travel by train from Trondheim to Majastua in 5 hours. The distance by road from Trondheim is 197 miles. Maps: Børgefjell and Hattfjelldal.
Fishing in the lakes Majavatn (1,071 ft.), Thomasvatn (1,148 ft.) and Fiplingvatn (1,200 ft.), accessible from road. Fishing mostly from boats. Several lakes in the mountains 1,500 to 2,000 ft. above sea level can be reached on foot. In the lakes the trout are of moderate to medium size. In the Børgefjell mountains (National Park) fishing has been very good, but is now somewhat reduced by icefishing. Several lakes hold red char as well as trout. Season from beginning of July to end of Aug., starting somewhat later in the higher lakes.
Centre: Majavatn.
Fishing permits: The Vefsn Fishing Administration ticket (moderately priced), covers most of the lakes and is available locally. A special ticket is sold to Majavatn.

HATTFJELLDAL

This vast parish offer fishing in Norway's second biggest lake, Røsvatn, and several smaller waters. Energetic walkers and campers may even fish the Børgefjell National Park from Hattfjelldal.

HATTFJELLDAL area (C 7). Travel by train from Trondheim to Trofors in 5 1/2 hours and then by bus to Hattfjelldal in 1 hour. Distance by road from Trondheim is 248 miles. Maps: Hattfjelldal, Røsvatn, Krutfjell and Skarmodalen.
Red char are only too numerous in lake Røsvatn (1,250 ft.), but not so easy to catch even from a boat. Fishing also in the Elsvatna, Krutvatna and Unkervatn lakes situated 1,000 to 2,000 ft. above sea level and accessible by car. Fishing in Øvre (Upper) Elsvatn means walking approx. 1 hour. There are also other waters in the area that can be reached by road and/or paths. Red char dominates the lower-lying lakes, trout the higher ones. Stocks are somewhat uneven, size will vary from a couple of ounces to

several pounds, but the quality is always good. Season: End of July to end of August.
Centre: Hattfjelldal.
Fishing permits: The Vefsen ticket is valid to most of the Hattfjelldal waters. Available locally.

NARVIK

In the mountains surrounding Narvik trout fishing may be enjoyed in several lakes.

NARVIK area (C 5). Travel by plane from Oslo to Bardufoss in 2 hours and then 2 hours by bus to Narvik. Or go by train from Trondheim to Fauske in 11 hours followed by 6 hours on the bus to Narvik. Road distance from Trondheim 575 miles. Maps: Narvik and Skjomen.
Fishing is offered in the Jerjangsfjell, Beisfjord, Rombaksbotn, Haugfjell and Sildvik areas. The Herjangsfjell and Beisfjord areas are approached by road, the Sildvik and Haugfjell areas by rail. But from rail or road one must be prepared to walk some distance to the waters which are situated from 300 to 2,000 ft. above sea level. Stocks are reasonable in most lakes and trout will weigh from 5 to 10 ounces. Season from beginning of July end of Aug.
Centres: Narvik and Bjerkvik.
Fishing permits: The Narvik Hunting and Angling Association's ticket (inexpensive) covers all areas. Available in Narvik (ask at the Tourist Office).

RANA

The water courses in the Rana district have been severely affected by hydro-electric developments, but there are still many waters where fair sport may be expected.

MO — UMBUKTA area (C 7). Travel by train from Trondheim to Mo in 8 hours and then by bus 1 hour to Umbukta. Road distance from Trondheim to Mo is 314 miles. Map: Umbugten.
Highway 79 Mo — Umbukta runs through the area. Some waters are found along this road and the road to Akersvatn, others are reached on foot. All lakes are situated between 1,300 and 2,000 ft. above sea level. The main waters are: Grunnvatn (1 hour's walk from Akersvatn) stocked with trout weighing approx. 1 pound, Fiskeløsvatn (1 hour's walk from Akersvatn) stocked with red char scaling 8 ounces, Tverrvatn (on Highway 79) containing red char around 10 ounces, Akersvatn holds red char and trout — average weight 10 ounces, Umskarvatn (on Highway 79) contains both red char and trout weighing approx. 8 ounces, Umbukta (on Highway 79) holds trout — average

weight 10 ounces, Lille Rauvatn (on the Akersvatn — Kjennsvatn road) holds some 1-pound red char, Kaldvatn (on the Brennåsen — Kaldvatn county road) has trout — average weight 10 ounces, Rauvatn (on Highway 79) is stocked with 10-ounce red char. There are bigger fish in all lakes, but the lakes along the roads have been heavily fished. Fishing in more distant lakes off the road is better. The waters can be fished from June to the end of Aug., but Aug. is the best month. The season is closed from Sept. 10 to June 1. There is also trout fishing in the Rana river above the Kobbfoss falls. Here trout are said to average 1 pound, max. size 6 pounds, and fishing can be enjoyed in July — Aug. Closed season: Sept. 9 — Jan. 1.
Centres: Mo i Rana and Umbukta (not listed).
Fishing permits: The Rana Fishing Administration's ticket (inexpensive) is available from sports shops, Rana Tourist Office, Meyergården Hotel and Fishing Administration's Office (O.T. Olsensgt. 2), all situated in Mo i Rana.

SORTLAND

A number of waters in the Vesterålen islands can be fished from the village of Sortland.

SORTLAND area (B 5). Travel by boat from Bodø to Sortland in 12 hours or by bus from Narvik in 8 hours. Road distance from Narvik is 121 miles and 1 ferry. Map: Kvæfjord.
The waters are widely scattered, but Sortland is the best base for all of them.
The Blokken water course on Hinnøy island is reached by ferry (to Djupfjord) and road. The lower lakes are just a few ft. above sea level, the higher lakes lie som 1,500 ft. higher and are only accessible on foot. The whole water course holds plenty of red char and trout. Red char are too numerous and the quality has deteriorated. In the upper lakes big trout can be caught. The Djupfjord water course, reached by ferry from Sortland, includes several lakes, most of them situated in the mountains and far from the road. Most of these waters are stocked with good trout. We shall mention two more waters on Hinnøy, lake Osdalsvatn and Reinsnesvatn (130 ft.) both within easy reach by ferry and road from Sortland. Both have runs of salmon and seatrout, and in both lakes red char threaten to become too numerous, whereas trout are of better quality. Season: July and Aug. On the island of Langøy we recommend the following lakes: Blåhammervatn (only 1/2 mile from the nearest road) which has been cultivated by the local angling association, and is now well supplied with trout and red char.

Lake Middagsvatn in the same water course is also worth trying. Harshalsvatn (reached by road) has a fair stock of red char and runs of salmon and sea trout. Kovvatn (2 miles from the nearest road) is well stocked with 10-ounce trout. Lake Lamarkvatn in the same area (260 ft.) holds trout and red char (big fish). Lake Storvatn (45 ft.) is reached by car. Red char are quite numerous and fairly big in this water where also salmon and sea trout occur. Season: July and August.

Centre: Sortland.

Fishing permits: Tickets to Blokken and Djupfjord water courses are available in Blokken and Djupfjord. Fishing cards are also sold locally to Osdalsvatn whereas permission must be asked to fish Reinsnesvatn. Tickets to all Langøya lakes mentioned above, except Lamarkvatn where permission must be asked, are sold by sports shops in Sortland.

STEIGEN

Nordland may be off your beaten path, but Steigen is even off the beaten paths of Nordland. Yet, there is plenty of exciting fishing on this beautiful peninsula.

STEIGEN area (B 6). Travel: See Bodø. From Bodø you can either go by boat to Steigen direct or by bus and ferry via Røsvik in 5 — 6 hours. Distance by road from Fauske to Røsvik is 19 miles and the ferry to Nordfold on Steigen takes 1 1/2 hours. Map: Steigen and Nordfold.

The first of the two Holmvågvatna lakes lies only 600 yards from the road and 260 ft. above sea level. The second lake lies 2 miles from the road and 650 ft. above sea level. Both lakes are stocked with fine trout. Lake Laksåvatn (80 ft.) is reached by road and holds sea trout and red char of good quality. Salmon only occur occasionally. Lake Nonsvatn (10 ft.) is situated 2 miles from the nearest road and holds sea trout and char of very good quality, both trout and char will average 2 pound. Lake Rundvatn (13 ft.) is a sea trout and migratory char water with trout around 2 pounds and 1-pound char. Lake Storvatn (177 ft.) is reached by boat from Alvnes to Lille Balkjosen. Both trout and char are numerous. Salmon and sea trout enter the lake from the Storvasselv river. The biggest fished killed (with a spinner) weighed 33 pounds. Lake Åsjordvatn (107 ft.) is reached on foot from the Botn — Helnesund road. This forest lake is stocked with fine trout and red char. Fishing in all Steigen waters is best in Aug. — Sept. before the season is closed.

Centre: Nordfold (listed) and Helnessund (not listed).

Fishing permits: Tickets to Storvatnet are available from Statens Skogforvaltning (Forestry Board), Fauske. Permission to fish the other waters must acquired from the local farmers.

TROMS

The county of Troms with its big island, inland forests and mountain plateaus offers a varied picture to the visitors and great possibilities to energetic anglers. Some of the classical waters of Troms have been regulated and turned to hydro-electric power. Others have been too heavily fished. But in this vast and sparsely populated wilderness there will always be fishing for those who are willing to live an outdoor life. If the mountain moors are not the answer to your fisherman's prayer, try the islands. The lakes and rivers there are not often fished.

BARDU

This is one of the areas which have been affected by hydro-electrical developments. Trout do not take too kindly to damming, but red char seem to thrive and in North Norway the char is a sporting fish.

ALTEVATN area (C 4). Travel by plane to Bardufoss from Oslo in 2 hours or by bus from Narvik in 2 1/2 hours. Road distance from Narvik 55 miles (Trondheim — Narvik 575 miles). Map: Altevatn or 1532 II(Altevatn), 1623 III(Julusvarri), 1631 IV(Leinavatna) and 1531 I(Gævdnjajarvi).

There is a local road from Bardu (Setermoen) to the west end of lake Altevatn (1,580 ft.), a distance of 24 miles. The rest of the area is roadless and access to a boat (outboard) is almost a condition for successful angling. Apart from lake Altevatn the biggest lakes in the area are Gævdnjajavrre (1,772 ft.) and lake Leinavatn (1,670 ft.). There is also lake Lagojavrre (2,734 ft.) and the rivers Gamasjokka and Gævdnjajokka. These lakes must be said to be very well stocked with fine red char, average weight 2 pounds with chances of 8-pounders. There are not many trout in these lakes now, but what remain are big fish. Trout is much more numerous in the rivers and both the Gamasjokka and the Gævdnjajokka are very popular rivers. Season: July and August.

Centres: Bardu and Bardufoss. No centres nearer to the waters, but there are some huts on lake Altevatn that may be rented.

Fishing permits: Available form Altevatn Kafé, Hoffman Kiosk and the Bus Station Kiosk in Bardu. In Tromsø they are sold by Andresens Vaabenforretning, Storgt. 53 and in Narvik by Arvid Arnholdt, Kongensgt. 32.

GRATANGEN AND SALANGEN

In the mountains and fjords north of Narvik there are a few good trout water.

GRATANGEN area (C 4). Travel: See Bardu above. Gratangen lies 45 miles south of Bardufoss and 32 miles north of Narvik. Maps: Narvik and Salangen.

Access to fishing in some smaller lakes having a good stock of trout (Sortvatn) and red char (Rauvatn). To Sortvatn one hour on foot, to Rauvatn 30 mins. by car and one hour on foot. Fishing also in lake Reisavatn (774 ft.) close to E 6. These are popular waters with some trout and red char. Season: July — September.

Centre: Gratangen.

Fishing permits: Tickets to the Gratangen waters available at Gratangen Tourist Station.

SALANGEN area (C 4). Travel: See Bardu above. Sjøvegan lies 34 miles south of Bardufoss and 58 miles north of Narvik. Map: Salangen.

The Masterbakkvatna lakes (1,820 ft.), one hour on foot from Tverset farm, hold fine red char weighing up to 4 pounds. In the Plassvatna lakes (1,476 ft.) trout are numerous, fish up to 8 pounds have been caught. The lakes are reached on foot in approx. 1 hour from Skjelnesplassen farm. Also fishing in the Sagelv river, good trout fishing in the upper reaches. The Spansdalselv river holds a fair amount of trout above the Kirkhaugfossen waterfall. Highway 84 runs along part of the Sagelv and Highway 84 and E 6 cover most of the Spansdalselv. The Salangen mountain lakes should be fished in July — Sept.,the rivers in June — July.

Centres: Lapphaugen (not listed) and Sjøvegan.

Fishing permits: Fishing is free in the Masterbakkvatna, tickets to Plassvatna are sold locally. Permission to fish the Sagelv and the Spansdalselv (above Fossbakken) must be acquired from the farmers. Tickets are sold to the Spansdalselv below Fossbakken.

HARSTAD AND KVÆFJORD

The town of Harstad and Kvæfjord, the neighbouring parish, together make up quite a fishing district.

HARSTAD area (B 5). Travel by boat from Trondheim in 43 hours, by plane from Bodø in 1 hour or by bus from Narvik in 3 hours. Road distance from Narvik is 78 miles, from Trondheim 572 miles and 2 ferries. Map: Harstad.

Lake Grunnvatn (328 ft.) in Harstad Folkepark by the Youth Hostel holds plenty of 1-pound trout. Other lakes within the town area are Gausvikvatn (148 ft.) with plenty of 1/2-pound trout, Haukebøsvatn (252 ft.) well stocked with red char and trout (average trout will scale 10—12 ounces, the red char are numerous and smaller). Kasfjordvatn (10 ft.) where red char are too numerous and Melvikvatn (200 ft.) which is moderately stocked with trout. Melvikvatn lies 1 mile from the nearest road, the other lakes are reached by car. Other Harstad lakes will be recommended by the Tourist Office on request. Season: July and Aug. Closed season: Sept. 1 — Dec. 31.

Centre: Harstad.

Fishing permits: Tickets are available from sports shops in Harstad and local farmers at reasonable prices.

KVÆFJORD area (B 5). Travel: See Harstad. Kvæfjord village lies 12 miles west of Harstad. Map: Kvæfjord.

The Mellå water course with its seven lakes and several tarns used be a sportsman's dream. It has been too heavily fished lately, but experienced anglers will certainly find good sport. The lakes are situated from 1,115 ft. to 2,260 ft. above sea level and contain trout and red char. Trout dominate the lower waters, red char are more numerous in the upper lakes. Trout are said to be easily scared. The lakes are numbered, not named, and from the Mellå farm First Lake is reached in approx. one hour on foot. Other Kvæfjord lakes reported to hold fair stocks of trout are Bremnesvatn (692 ft. — 3/4 hour on foot), Salvatn (600 ft. — 3/4 hour on foot), Torskvatn (820 ft.) and Vebbestadvatn (1,279 ft. — 1 1/2 hours on foot). Season: July and Aug, is probably best for all the Kvæfjord waters. Closed season: Sept. 1 — Dec. 31.

Centre: Harstad.

Fishing permits: Fishing has been free up to now on State ground parts of the Mellå water course and in lake Vebbestadvatn. Permission to fish the other lakes must be acquired from the owners.

KVÆNANGEN

Fishing on the mountain plateau, which merges with the Finnmarksvidda 1,500 —2,000 ft. above sea level, and in a few rivers near the head of the Kvænangsfjord.

KVÆNANGSBOTN area (C 3). Travel by plane to Alta in 3 hours from Oslo and then 3 hours by bus to Kvænangsbotn, or by bus from Narvik in 1 1/2 days. Road distance from Narvik is 236 miles. Maps: 1734 I(Kvænangen) and 1734 II(Kvænangsbotn). From Kvænangsbotn a construction road leads to the mountain plateau and provides

access to some of the lakes. The majority of the lakes are reached on foot. Lakes like Badajavrre, Baddervatn, Ballanjavrre, Brattvatna, Cuiokkajavrre and Tverrvatn are stocked with red char, average weight 2 pounds with fair chances of bigger fish. Gærbevatn, Larsvatn, Njarbesjavrre and Fiskevatn are typical trout lakes where trout will average 12 ounces and fish up to 6 pounds may be killed. Fishing is best in July and Aug. The Badajokka river is worth trying, especially the upper reaches where there are some fine pools. Red char are numerous, average weight 1 pound, also some small trout of inferior quality. The middle parts of the Kvænangselv river holds red char (the first 5 km of the river is salmon water) of fine quality and between the two lower waterfalls the Nordbotnelv is a good trout river with specimens up to 6 pounds. Above the second waterfall this river holds red char, average weight 1/2 pound, of good quality. River fishing is best from the middle of July to the middle of Aug. in this area.
Centres: Kvænangsfjell and Burfjord.
Fishing permits: The waters belong to the State, but some of them have been leased to a local angling club which should be contacted before fishing. Tickets are sold to the Nordbotnelv.

SENJA WITH BERG, LENVIK. TORSKEN AND TRANØY

Senja — Norway's second biggest island — offers fishing in beautiful surroundings and in many areas.

BERG area (B 4). Travel by plane to Bardufoss from Oslo in 2 hours and go by bus to Finnsnes in 1 hour. Another hour or so on the bus will take you to Berg, Torsken, Lenvik or Tranøy. You can also go by boat from Trondheim to Finnsnes in 48 hours or by bus from Narvik in 3 hours. Road distance from Narvik to Finnsnes is 106 miles. Map: Hekkingen.
In this area one should perhaps try the lakes Nedre Svanvatn (443 ft.) and Steinvatn (440 ft.) in the Svanelv water course. They are not far from Highway 86 (less than one mile) and are said to be well stocked with 1/2-pound trout and red char. Season: July — Aug. There are also fine char in lake Øvre Hesvatn situated in the mountains between Bergsbotn and Mefjordbotn. Season: August.
Centre: Finnsnes.
Fishing permits: Tickets to Steinvatn and Hestvatn are available at Berg. Tickets to Svanvatn can be bought in the kiosk at Svanelvplass.

LENVIK area (B 4). Travel: See Berg above. Map: Hekkingen.
In this area we would recommend fishing in the Mefjordbotnvatna lakes situated approx. 2 miles from the road at Stønnesbotn. There are plenty of trout in these lakes, somewhat small in size but of good quality. Season: July — August.
Centre: Finnsnes
Fishing permits: Fishing is probably free in these lakes.

TORSKEN area (B 4). Travel: See Berg above. Maps: Torsken and Tranøy. Lake Bumannsvatn, Giskevatn, Lille Ostervatn, Selfjordvatn and others are situated 600 to 1,200 ft. above sea level and are reached on foot in 1—2 hours from Highway 86. These lakes have been cultivated for years by the local angling club and are reported to be well stocked with fine trout, average weight nearly 2 pounds.
Season: August.
Centre: Gryllefjord (not listed).
Fishing permits: Available from Gryllefjord Jeger- og Fiskeforrening to Bumannsvatn and Lille Ostervatn. Fishing has been free up to now in Seljordvatn, probably also in Giskevatn.

TRANØY area (B 4). Travel: See Berg above. Maps: Bjarkøy and Tranøy.
Åvatn and Rødsandvatn have runs of sea trout and migratory char in July and Aug., average weight 1 pound, also non-migratory trout and red char in lake Rødsandvatn (63 ft.). Salmon (2—12 pounds), sea trout (1 pound) and migratory char (12 ounces) occur in lake Tennevatn (75 ft.) in the same months.
Centre: No accomodation locally, nearest hotel in Finnsnes.
Fishing permits: Tickets are sold to lake Tennevatn. Permission must be acquired from the farmers to fish in Rødsandvatn and Åvatn.

SKÅNLAND

This parish between Harstad and Narvik has a couple of reliable waters.

ANNAMO area (B 5). Travel: See Narvik. Annamo lies some 40 miles north of Narvik. Map: Narvik.
Fishing in the lakes Skoddebergvatn (325 ft.) and Saltvatn (72 ft.) on Highway 825 and in lake Revvatn (705 ft.) approx. 1 1/2 hour's walk from the road. In Skoddebergvatn there are plenty of small red char (inferior quality), lake Saltvatn holds both red char (numerous) and trout of better quickly and size. Lake Revvatn is well stocked with trout of good size and quality, weighing up to 4 pounds.

Boats may be hired. Fishing is best in July and Aug. Closed season: Sept. 15 to Oct. 30.
Centres: Narvik, Bjerkvik and Holmevatn (not listed in «Hotels in Norway»).
Fishing permits: Tickets to these lakes are sold locally.

TENNEVIK area (C 4). Travel: See Narvik and Harstad. Tennevik lies approx. 22 miles south of Harstad and 67 miles west of Narvik. Map: Ofoten.
Lake Saltvatn (130 ft.) in the Tennevik water course is reached by car. It is reported to hold plenty of 1/2-pound trout of very good quality. Trout are not as numerous in the other lakes of this water course, where fishing is best in July and Aug. Closed season: Sept. 15 — Oct. 31.
Centre: Harstad.
Fishing permits: Tickets are sold by the supervisor of the water course.

FINNMARK
In area the county of Finnmark is bigger than Denmark. It is sprinkled with lakes, small and big, and criss-crossed by rivers. Possibilities for anglers are greater than anywhere else in Northern Europe, and some of the best waters are found far out in the wildeness. The Finnmark mountain plateau is a gently undulating country situated 1,200—1,600 ft. above sea level with only a few steep mountain formations. The vegetation is open birch forest, brushwood and stunted bushes (which may be thick and difficult to traverse), or heather and turf. Walking is, on the whole, easy everywhere except where brushwood, soft marshes and rivers hamper progress. Distances are considerable and human habitations are few and far between. Only three roads traverse the area: Alta—Kautokeino—Finland, Lakselv—Karasjok—Finland and the Karasjok—Kautokeino road. Off the roads you can travel on foot or by river boat only. Anglers on the plateau must carry their own equipment and provisions. Warm clothes and good footwear are essential, and so is mosquito repellant. Visitors who are not accomplished map-readers should not venture into the wilderness. There are a few mountain lodges in the roadless parts of the plateau where one can spend the night (in your own sleeping bag), get meals or prepare your own food. Some of the mountain lodges are convenient bases for anglers. On the mountain plateau fish that have come from the east — pike, perch, gwyniad, grayling and burbot — are numerous in most lakes. Gwyniad is probably the most important fish (from an edible point of view) on the plateau, and it can be caught on the fly which is not the case in most other areas in Norway. Grayling is a very sporting

fish and pike occur in most water courses and can become very big. Red char again are more abundant than trout, and fully equal to trout in quality and the sport it offers. In the more mountainous areas towards the coast and on the great peninsulas the «invasion from the east» has not been that extensive, and most water courses are stocked with only trout and red char.
All angling on State ground in Finnmark — and that is practically speaking everything — is administered by Finnmark Jordsalgskontor in Vadsø for the Directorate of Hunting and Fishing. Since Feb. 24 1978 there are new regulations in force. Their main content is: Rod - and handline fishing is available to Norwegians in all not - leased waters, when the general fishing duty has been paid. In waters that have been leased, and they include most of the salmon rivers and some lakes, local tickets must be bought. For foreigners fishing is more restricted. Rod fishing is permitted in all leased waters, but in un-leased waters only in a 3-mile (5 km) zone on both sides of the highroads (riksveier). Where those zones are running into lakes, the whole lake may be fished. There is only one ticket covering all Finnmark, below referred to as the "Finnmark ticket". Day tickets, 3-day tickets and week tickets are available at reasonable prices. The total catch of trout and red char that a foreigner may take with him is limited to 10 lbs. Boats brought in from abroad are not allowed. Foreigners may seek permission to fish outside the zones from Finnmark Jordsalgskontor, Vadsø. Such permissions will only be granted in special cases. Because of the zone limits some of the waters described below are out of bounds for residents of other countries. In order to buy a Finnmark ticket foreigners must produce a certificate showing that their gear has been disinfected. This can be done by district "vets" and in some petrol stations. The Finnmark ticket is available from post offices all over Finnmark.

ALTA
Alta is known to anglers the world over for its salmon river, but there are many other promising waters in this district.

ALTA area (C 3). Travel by plane from Oslo to Alta in 3 hours, or by boat to Hammerfest from Trondheim in 64 hours and bus to Alta in 3 1/2 hours. Road distance from Narvik is 317 miles, from Trondheim 892 miles. Maps: 1834 I (Alta) and 1934 IV (Gargia).
Doulbbajavrre, Martinvatn, Rattalananjavrre and Suoppatjavrre are situated on the mountain plateau, approx 1,500 ft. above sea level and some 15 to 20 miles east of Elvebakken.

98

It is a long walk, but in the area one is assured of good trout fishing, which is best in June and July.
Centre: Nearest centre is Alta.
Fishing permits: Available from camping sites, petrol station in Alta and shopkeeper Arne Halvorsen, Tverrelvdalen (from where the shortest route leads to the area).

JOATKAJAVRRE area (C 3). Travel: See Alta. The mountain lodge is reached in 1/2 hour by taxi plane (by special permission) from Alta or in 7—9 hours on foot from Tverrelvdalen. Map: or 1934 I (Cåkkerassa) and 1934 IV (Gargia).
Fishing in Øvrevatn, Nedrevatn, Midtrevatn, Storvatn and other lakes situated 1,300 to 1,800 ft. above sea level. These lakes are stocked with trout, red char, grayling and gwyniad, average weight 1 pound, max. size (trout) 8 pounds. There is also good red char fishing in the first 500 yards of the Joatkaelv. 5 mins. to 1 hour's walk to the waters. Best season June—July.
Centre: Joatkajavrre mountain lodge (not listed).
Fishing permits: The Finnmark ticket. Permission to fish the private waters of the lodge must be paid for separately.

GARGIA area (C 3). Travel: See Alta. Gargia lies 15 miles south of Alta, 1/2 hour by bus. Map: 1934 IV (Gargia).
Fishing in the Orrosjavrek lakes 600 to 1,600 ft. above sea level and 15 mins. to 2 hour's walk from the lodge. Red char, grayling and gwyniad. Red char will scale 1/2 pound, max. size 4 pounds. Best season: June—July.
Centre: Gargia mountain lodge (see Alta in «Hotels in Norway»).
Fishing permits: The Finnmark ticket. Permission to fish the private waters of the lodge must be paid for separately.

KARASJOK
Karasjok is an enormous parish and the fishing areas are scattered. Some of the areas can be reached by car, others may be approached by river boat or on foot.
KARASJOK area (D 3). Travel by plane from Oslo to Lakselv in 4 hours and then by bus to Karasjok in 2 hours. Or go by boat to Hammerfest from Trondheim in 64 hours and spend 5 hours on the bus to Karasjok. Distance by road from Narvik is 425 miles, from Trondheim 1,000 miles. Map: Karasjok or 2033 I (Karasjok) and 2033 IV (Jiesjåkka).
Fishing in several lakes and rivers situated 800 to 1,500 ft. above sea level and reached in 30 mins. to 3 hours on foot from the nearest road. Bitijavrre (1,014 ft.) 5 miles north of

the village offers good char fishing in June. Gorzzejokka river, 6 miles south of Iskuras (road from Karasjok) holds trout, grayling, gwyniad and pike as well as salmon, and is a very popular river. Gæimejokka, which joins the Karasjokka at Assebakte (road from Karasjok), is another sporting river, well stocked with trout above the waterfall. Below the waterfall there are also small salmon, grayling and pike. Fishing is best in July and Aug. Lake Tverrvatn (921 ft.) is reached on foot from the road at Halddenjargga, holds pike (numerous), perch and some fine trout.
Centre: Karasjok.
Fishing permits: The Finnmark ticket and (in the salmon waters) the Tana salmon ticket available from Karasjok Police Station (Lensmannskontor).

JERGGUL area (D 3). Travel: See Karasjok. From Karasjok along Highroad 92 to Jerggul (approx. 16 miles). Maps: 2033 IV (Jiesjåkka) and 1933 I (Suosjavri).
Fishing in the Jiesjokka and several lakes and rivers 1,000—1,400 ft. above sea level, reached in from 5 mins. to 1 hour from the mountain lodge. Apart from salmon the Jiesjokka holds grayling, gwyniad, trout, burbot and a few red char. There are not many salmon in the river. Season: June—August.
Centre: Jerggul mountain lodge.
Fishing permits: The Finnmark ticket. The salmon ticket must be bought from the Karasjok Police Station.

MOLLISJOK area (D 3). Travel: See Alta. Taxi plane (by special permission) from there to Mollisjok in 3/4 hour. Maps: 1934 II (Jiesjavri) and 1933 I (Suosjavri).
Fishing in lake Jiesjavrre (1,279 ft.), the biggest water on the Finnmark plateau and richly stocked with grayling, red char, trout, pike and burbot. Grayling and red char are numerous, and there are very fine trout, 20-pounders having been caught. There is also fishing in the Jiesjokka river and many lakes on the Finnmark plateau.
Centre: Mollisjok mountain lodge (not listed).
Fishing permits: The Finnmark ticket. The Jiesjokka is covered by the Tana salmon ticket, see Karasjok.

RAVNA area (D 3). Travel: See Karasjok. The mountain lodge is reached on foot in 4—5 hours from Assebakte. Maps: 2034 III (Stiipanavzi) and 2034 IV (Jiesjåkka).
Fishing in Sadijavrre, Ravddojavrek, Gæimejavrre, Roussajavrre, Røyrvatn, Maillejavrre and several other lakes, situated from 15 mins. to 3 hour's walk from the lodge. These lakes are well stocked with 1-pound trout, fish up to 8 pounds have been caught. In

Sadijavrre, where pike abound, trout up to 10 pounds have been caught. Good trout fishing in the Sadejokka river close to the lodge. Boats in some of the lakes may be hired from the lodge. Season: June—August.
Centre: Ravnastua mountain lodge (not listed).
Fishing permit: The Finnmark ticket.

SOUSJAVRRE area (D 3). Travel: See Karasjok. The mountain lodge lies on Highway 92 some 36 miles west of Karasjok village. Map: 1933 I (Suosjavri).
Fishing in lakes and rivers in the area, 1,150 to 1,500 ft. above sea level and reached in 1 hour on foot from the lodge. Trout in these waters are said to weigh around 2 pounds, max. size 9 pounds, and red char 1 pound, max. size 4 1/2 pounds. Season: June—July.
Centre: Suosjavrre mountain lodge.
Fishing permit: The Finnmark ticket.

KAUTOKEINO
This is the biggest parish in Norway and the most sparsely populated. Nobody has bothered to count the fishing waters.

KAUTOKEINO area (D 3). Travel: See Alta. Kautokeino lies on Highway 93—81 miles south of Alta or 3 hours by bus. Map: Kautokeino.
Around the village of Kautokeino fishing may be enjoyed in several waters situated 900 to 1,300 ft. above sea level and reached on foot in 30 mins. to 3 hours. In these waters are red char up to 2 pounds, trout up to 4 pounds, gwyniad up to 4 pounds, grayling up to 2 pounds, perch up to 1 pound and pike up to 20 pounds. Fishing is from June to September.
Centre: Kautokeino.
Fishing permit: The Finnmark ticket.

AIDDEJAVRRE area (D 3). Travel: See Alta. Aiddejavrre mountain lodge is situated on Highway 93 some 20 miles south of Kautokeino and 100 miles south of Alta. Maps: Agjet and Lavvooaivve.
Aiddejavrre offers fishing in the lakes Calbmejavrre and Luovosjavrre and several other waters situated between 1,150 and 1,300 ft. above sea level and reached on foot in 10 mins. to 1 hour. The lakes are well stocked with red char, gwyniad, grayling, perch and pike. Char, grayling and perch may weigh as much as 2 pounds, gwyniad 4 pounds and 20-pound pike have been killed. Season: June—August.
Centre: Aiddejavrre mountain lodge (not listed).
Fishing permit: The Finnmark ticket.

MASI—BIGGELUOBBAL area (D 3). Travel: See Alta. Masi lies 43 miles, Biggeluobbal 41 miles south of Alta. Map: Masi.
Try Biggejavrre (1,256 ft.) two miles from Biggeluobbal, Saivva (1,385 ft.) three miles away or other lakes in the area. You will probably find that they are well stocked with high quality red char, average weight 1—2 pounds with fish up to 4 pounds. Lake Biggejavrre holds gwyniad and pike as well. For river fishing Masijokka with fine pools and glides might be the answer. Plenty of red char, average weight from 1/2 to 1 pound with fish up to 4 pounds. Season: July.
Centre: Masi.
Fishing permit: The Finnmark ticket.

SICCAJAVRRE area (D 3). Travel: See Kautokeino. The lodge is situated 6 miles from Highway 93 east of Aiddejavrre. Map: Lavvooiavve.
This area offers fishing in lake Bajasjavrre and other waters situated from 1,300 to 1,600 ft. above sea level and from 10 mins. to 1 hour's walk from the lodge. The lakes contain red char, gwyniad, grayling, perch and pike — the usual Kautokeino "mixture " — and fishing can be enjoyed from June to the beginning of September.
Centre: Siccajavrre mountain lodge (not listed).
Fishing permit: The Finnmark ticket.

SUOLOVUOBME area (C 3). Travel: See Alta. The lodge is situated on Highway 93—31 miles south of Alta. Map: 1934 II (Suoluvuobmi).
This area offers fishing in a great number of lakes situated 1,300 to 1,600 ft. above sea level and reached on foot in 1/2—2 hours from the lodge. The lakes close to the lodge have been heavily fished and better results may be expected if one walks a few hours, for instance to lakes like Coalbmejavrre (good stock of red char), Guollehisjavrre (moderately stocked), Gæssenjavrre (well stocked) or Salgganjavrre (moderately stocked). All these lakes hold red char weighing from 1 to 6 pounds. July is the best season.
Centre: Suolovuobme (Solovomi).
Fishing permit: The Finnmark ticket. Permission to fish the private waters of the lodge must be paid for separately.

KVALSUND
Most of the lakes are found on the Finnmark mountain plateau south of Skaidi.

SKAIDI area (C 2). Travel by plane to Alta in 3 1/2 hours and then by bus to Skaidi in 2 hours. Or by boat from Trondheim to

Hammerfest in 64 hours and bus to Skaidi in 2 hours. Road distance from Narvik 370 miles, from Trondheim 944 miles. Maps: Komagfjord and Stabbursdalen or 1935 II (Stabbursdalen).

Here are a few lakes that ought to yield fair sport: Bollevatna (approx. 1,600 ft.) 3 hours walk from Aisaroive bridge on Highway 6, Doggejavvre (950 ft.) 45 mins. walk from Highway 6 and Skaidejavrre (1,063 ft.). There are plenty of 1-pound red char (fish up to 8 pounds have been killed) in the Bollevatna lakes, Doggejavrre is well stocked with 8-ounce red char and Skaidejavrre is a really good lake, stocked with trout (average weight 4 pounds) and red char. The Gukkesgurajokka tributary to the Repparfjordelv rises in the Gukkesgurajavrre (1,222 ft.) which holds plenty of red char, average weight 10 ounces. Njagetjavrre (866 ft.) 1 1/2 hours on foot from Highway 6 on Sennaland is well stocked with trout and red char, average weight 1 pound, trout up to 10 pounds. Fishing in the above mentioned waters is probably best in July—August.
Centre: Skaidi.
Fishing permit: The Finnmark ticket, available at the Skaidi hotels.

LEBESBY

Lebesby is the parish on both sides of the Laksefjord, and Ifjord is a hamlet on Highway 6 almost at the head of the fjord.

IFJORD area (D 2). Travel by plane to Lakselv in 4 hours from Oslo and then 3 hours by bus to Ifjord. Or go by boat to Hammerfest from Trondheim in 64 hours and spend 7 hours on the bus to Ifjord. Distance by road from Narvik is 500 miles, from Trondheim 1,076 miles. Map: Lebesby. Fishing in numerous lakes on the Ifjord mountain plateau 1,000 to 1,700 ft. above sea level and from 15 mins. to 2 hours' walk from the nearest road. The waters in this area are reported to be partly overpopulated with trout and red char, yet average weight is given as high 2 pounds and max. size 12 pounds. Trout fishing is said to be best in the latter half of June and in July.
Centre: Ifjord (see Lebesby).
Fishing permits: The Finnmark ticket should be available at the lodge.

NORDKAPP

The Magerøy island on which North Cape is situated is a truly arctic island where Lapps have their summer pastures and reindeer roam almost everywhere. On such an island, and the nearest mainland, nobody should be surprised to find a few lakes stocked with trout.

NORDKAPP area (C 2). Travel by plane to Lakselv in 4 hours from Oslo and then by bus and ferry to Honningsvåg in 4 hours. Or go by boat from Trondheim to Honningsvåg in 72 hours. Road distance from Narvik is 417 miles and 1 ferry from Trondheim 992 miles and 3 ferries. Maps: Nordkapp and Honningsvåg.

Duksfjordvatn and Kaldfjordvatna lakes 1/2 mile to 3 miles from Highway 95 and situated 160 to 500 ft. above sea level hold a moderate amount of trout. Lake Opnan (go by motor boat from Skarsvåg or Kamøyvær) lies almost level with the sea. Moderately stocked with red char, migratory char enter this water in July—Aug. Lake Kjæftavatn (98 ft.) is reached from the North Cape Road, moderate stock of red char (up to 4 pounds) and some trout. Lake Næringsvatn approx. 50 ft. above sea level is moderately stocked with 1-pound trout. Lake Storskogvatn (80 ft.) holds both trout and red char weighing up to 2 pounds, and lake Svartvatn (approx. 100 ft.) holds plenty 10-ounce trout, fish up to 4 pounds. Næringsvatn, Storskogvatn and Svartvatn are all in the Gjesvær area. The Nordkapp waters may be fished in July, but Aug. is the best season.
Centre: Honningsvåg.
Fishing permits: The Finnmark ticket.

PORSANGER

This parish on the Porsangerfjord have a few lakes that can be fished from the highways and many more in the roadless wilderness.

LAKSELV area (D 2). Travel by plane to Lakselv in 4 hours from Oslo. Or go by boat from Trondheim to Hammerfest in 64 hours and spend 4 hours on the bus to Lakselv. Road distance from Narvik is 426 miles and 1 ferry, from Trondheim 1,000 miles and 4 ferries. Maps: Stabbursdalen and Skoganvarre or 1935 II (Stabbursdalen), 2035 III (Lakselv), 2034 I (Halkavarri) and 2034 IV (Skoganvarre).

Lake Gaggajavrre (318 ft.) reached by local road from Highway 96 south of Skoganvarre is well stocked with 10-ounce red char, burbot and pike. Loustejokka between lake Gaggajavrre and the confluence with Steinelva is a good trout river, fish between 1 and 2 pounds (6-pounders have been killed), also moderate stocks of red char and some pike. In the Lakselv water course lake Nedrevatn (213 ft.) holds too many red char (inferior quality), but the grayling stock is good. Lake Øvrevatn (230 ft.) is stocked with perch and grayling. Both these lakes, situated on Highway 96, belong to the Lakselv salmon water. The Vuolajokka tributary is also part of the salmon water. It is moderately stocked with trout and red char, average weight 1 pound and fish up to 8 pounds, and is considered an excellent grayling river. Grayling will scale 1 1/2 pound in this water. The Stabbursdalen National Park and the upper reaches of the Stabburselv river offer very good trout fishing, fish will scale 2—4 pounds with specimens up to 13 pounds. Season for the Porsanger waters: July—August.

Centre: Lakselv.

Fishing permit: The Finnmark ticket.

SØR-VARANGER

There is plenty of fishing in this border region, both south, east and west of the mining town of Kirkenes. Some of the best waters are far from any roads, and a taxi plane (by special permission) from Kirkenes might be the solution to a busy fisherman's problems.

KIRKENES area (D/E 2). Travel by plane to Kirkenes from Oslo in 4 to 5 hours, or by boat from Trondheim in 78 hours. Road distance from Narvik is 649 miles, from Trondheim 1,220 miles and 2 ferries. Maps: Garsjøen, Neiden, Jarfjorden, Svanvik and Krokfjell.

Lake Fiskevatn (243 ft.) and the Holmvatn lakes (460 ft.), situated respectively 14 miles south and 14 miles west of Kirkenes, are red char waters with some trout. In the Pasvik area the lakes in the Husmoelv water course some 300 ft. above the sea level are reported to be well stocked with trout and red char and so are the Spurvvatna lakes (400 ft.) still further south in the valley. The Husmovatna lies 6 miles and the other waters mentioned above approx. 3 miles from the nearest road. In the Jarfjord district east of Kirkenes the lakes in Karpelv water course are fairly well stocked with trout and red char and the same applies to the Kobbholmvatna (545 ft.). The Kobbholmvatna are situated on the Grense Jakobselv road, whereas fishing the Karpelv lakes is a strenuous business. Lake Brannvatn (692 ft.) in the Munkfjord area, 4 miles from the road, is well stocked with red char, some trout. The Braselv river enters the Munkfjord far from any road, a few salmon, sea trout and more migratory char run up the river, whereas the lakes in the area are well stocked with trout and red char. Lake Gallokjavrre (480 ft.), 15 miles west of Highway 6 between Neiden and Bugøyfjord, has been heavily fished by "taxiplaners" but there is still plenty of red char (not so many trout) in the water. The Klokkerelv river flows partly along Highway 6 towards Bugøyfjord, a few salmon and sea trout occur in the river, but trout and red char are said to be numerous in the lakes, for instance Galzzajavrek 2 miles from the road. Garsjøen (710 ft.) and Guol-

lebastemjavrre are not only difficult to pronounce but also difficult to reach, except by taxi plane frome Kirkenes. Trout and red char abound in both lakes. Vuostemusjavrek (643 ft.) lies 6 miles from Highway 6 at Bygøyfjord and is probably just as good. The Korsdalselv enters the Munkfjord at the head of the fjord. There is a forest road from Highway 6 leading 1 1/2 miles up the valley, but there is still a walk of several miles to reach such lakes as Oaggomjavrek and Steinholmvatn where plenty of red char and some trout may be caught. Sobbarjavrre, Hibojavrre and Justemokka some 20 miles west of Neiden involve very long walks (or short flights). Especially Justemokka and the small lakes above Hibojavrre are fine trout and red char waters. Season (all Kirkenes waters): July—August.

Centres: Kirkenes and Neiden.

Fishing permits: The Finnmark ticket. Fiskevatn are sold by Sør-Varanger Jeger- og Fiskerforening.

TANA

Tana literally means the "Big River". This is the biggest and most important salmon river in Norway, even if anglers may get more in other Norwegian rivers. The mountains and moors on both banks of the Tana afford interesting and varied fishing. Those who are prepared to walk, and run the risk that the weather may affect flyfishing greatly, may enjoy some of the best trout and red char fishing in Norway.

TANA—POLMAK area (D 2). Travel by plane to Kirkenes in 4 to 5 hours from Oslo, or by boat from Trondheim in 78 hours, and take the bus to Tana—Polmak in 4—5 hours. Distance by road from Narvik is 565 miles, from Trondheim 1,136 miles. Maps: Polmak, Vestertana and Tana.

In the Polmak district the lakes Akkajavrre (820 ft.) Gæssejavrre (820 ft.), Skoarrojavrre (278 ft.) and Soavveljavrre (650 ft.) are worth trying. They all contain trout and red char of good quality, average weight around 1 pound with fish up to 8 pounds. With the exception of Skogarrojavrre, which lies only 2 miles from Highway 92 at Hillagurra, the other waters are situated from 12 to 19 miles from the nearest road. The Buktelv—Luoftejokka (local road along the Buktelv from Luoftjok) is reputed to be a good trout river, and the Gæssejokka (12 miles from Highway 6 at Maskjok) offers both grayling and trout fishing. There is also the Laksjokka which, some 3 miles from Highway 92 at Fossholm, turns into a fine sporting river with long glides interrupted by small rapids. The river holds both salmon and trout, the latter only above the Lavsjokkfoss. The Klokkevatn lakes near Highway 890 (path from Skugge) have numerous trout and red char. 5-pound trout have been caught in these lakes. Season (all waters): July—August.

Centres: Skipagurra (listed), Rustefjelbma and Polmak (not listed in «Hotels in Norway»).

Fishing permit: The Finnmark ticket covers most of the waters.

LEVAJOK area (D 2). Travel: See Tana. Levajok lies on the Tana and Highway 92 some 60 miles from Tana bridge: Maps: Laksefjordvidda and Rastigaissa or 2135 II (Ullugaissa) and 2134 I (Viddaoiave).

This area comprises some 25 lakes and several rivers situated from 1,300 to 2,500 ft. above sea level and reached on foot in 1/2 hour to 6 hours from the mountain lodge or by taxi plane in 15 mins. to 1/2 hour. The waters hold trout, red char, grayling, gwyniad, pike and perch. Trout and red char from 10 ounces to 2 pounds, max. size trout 6 pounds and red char 10 pounds. Try for instance the Borsejokka river and its tributaries for trout, the lakes Gumppijavrre and Ullokjavrre for red char. The upper reaches of the Levajokka holds plenty of trout, rather small in size. Season: July and August.

Centre: Levajok mountain lodge.

Fishing permits: The Finnmark ticket. In salmon waters the Tana salmon ticket is required.

In the sea as well as in the narrows and tidal currents anglers will find unlimited possibilities and reap rich rewards, as for example this happy fisherman at the Saltstraumen eddy east of Bodø. When the current is strong, Saltstraumen is positively «boiling» with fish Especially saithe abound and keep the angler busy all the time.

Photo: Hans Schmidt Luchs.

Stick to sea-fishing in Norway and you will never go hungry. The locals will tell you where to fish. Follow their advice, and cod and saithe will soon be queuing up for your spinner, as here in Øksfjord on the coast of Finnmark.

Photo: Tufte.

Every year in July and Aug. three big fishing festivals, or sea angling competitions, take place in Norway: in Stavanger, Haugesund and Harstad. Hundreds of competitors come to these events and literally tons of fish are hauled from the sea, among them fine cod such as this specimen killed during the Harstad festival.

Photo: Johan Berge.

SEA FISHING

Facilities for sea fishing in Norway are almost unlimited, since the country has a coastline so extensive that there would be room enough for every sports fisherman in the world, if they all decided to turn up at once! One of the most attractive features of the Norwegian coast, from the angler's point of view, is that countless creeks, fjord, and bays break the shoreline, penetrating far inland. In good weather, when the sea is calm, fishing can be enjoyed far out in the skerries, near the open sea. When the sea is rough, the sportsman can enjoy his fishing in the shelter of numerous skerries, islands, and holms, and even in the fjords themselves. Another typical feature of the Norwegian coastline is that it shelves steeply into the sea: the shoals and shallows so typical of other European countries are non-existent in Norway: this means that cod, one of the most important deepwater fishes, is to be found close inshore practically all the year round. The cod is a glutton, and keen to take your bait. Often he will run to well over three foot in length, weighing 20, 30, or even 40 pounds. The usual weight is somewhere betweeen 2 and 10 pounds. So it is advisable to use a strong line if you are going to fish for big cod from the rocks, where the cod is in his element foraging for minute crabs and other crustaceans among swaying fronds of seaweed. When angling for cod, reel in you line slowly and take care that the bait or spinner remains close to the bottom. Better than a spinner with 3 hooks is often a one-hook spinner (fasten your line so that the hook points upwards). Then you can reel it through the seaweed without getting hooked, and cods will take it just as eagerly.

The best time for large cod is spring and autumn. In midsummer, when the coastal waters warm up, the fish generally swim deeper, and may have to be caught from a boat. At other times cod is fished from shore, using an ordinary spinner.

In the northern parts of Norway the water never gets really warm, even in summer, and here you can be sure of good fishing even in midsummer. Remember that the place to catch your fish is along the bottom, in areas where seaweed and other marine plants grow.

Another saltwater fish that stands high in the esteem of the angler is the saithe (Norw. "sei") or coalfish. In appearance and temperament he is not unlike the salmon: he is a very game fighter, and will provide splendid sport, particularly the husky fully-grown fish on their way out to the open sea. Many a line has been snapped by one of these sporting fish before the angler has had time to realise that his spinner had been taken.

The coalfish is a typical summer fish: in Western Norway and further up the coast, shoals often gather in narrow sounds, and on such occasions it is no exaggeration to say that you can catch a fish with every cast. The average size of saithe ranges from half a pound to 2 pounds. This applies to fish taken on a spinner from land. If you use a boat a little further offshore, the chances of getting larger fish, often more than 2 pounds, will increase.

We have said a few words about cod and saithe. There are, of course, many other species: halibut, flounder, turbot, wolffish, pollack, wrasse, ling, cusk, dogfish, mackerel and needlefish, to mention the more popular. The dogfish, for instance, is of great importance to the competitors in the fishing festivals, because it often makes up the bulk of their catch. Mostly spinners are used, but especially off Jæren flies are also used for bait.

To the many angling for wrasse in the skerries of the Oslo fjord and the South Coast, a bamboo rod and crabs for bait, has a special attraction. The wrasse is a strong fish, and as you don't use a reel, it will be a short and hefty battle when a big one takes your bait.

Casting with spinners is the most exciting form of sea fishing, and below we point out some tidal currents where rod fishing from the shore is especially rewarding. But the majority of holiday-makers in Norway stick to bottom fishing with baits or trolling from a boat. Trolling is very popular during the mackerel season along the South Coast and coalfish is caught that way in West and North Norway during the summer. Baits used are rubber worms and small spoons (mackerel spoons). Spoon hook fishing with a vertical line ("pilkefiske" in Norwegian) is an old and trusted method and apt to yield results at almost any time of the year. There are several types of spoons hooks to choose between. Cod along the Norwegian coast will take to most of them, provided you know where the fish are. The local population will tell you where to take your boat. Keep it there, or let it drifts slowly. To find the right kind of gear for coastal fishing is not difficult. Generally speaking the line should not be less than 0.40, often much stronger, and the weight of the sink must increase with the depths. When using a hand-line for cod, whiting, haddock or flounder mussels are probably the best bait. Mussels are found everywhere, but it takes some practice to make them stick to the hook. Raw prawns are favoured by many anglers. Anyhow, one may safely say that angling in coastal waters in Norway can be enjoyed without expensive equipment and that you are almost invariably rewarded with a good catch.

TIDAL CURRENTS

In several places in Norway there are tidal currents in narrow sounds or fjords where the sea water may run at from 4 or 10 knots. Some of these currents or eddies are known for their extremely good fishing, and from a visitor's point of view the combination of strong current and plenty of fish is particularly exciting. In these currents saithe are more numerous than other fish. The only limit on your bag is what you can use yourself. The locals are not likely to be interested in your catch. In the following pages we have listed some of these curretns — by counties — with references to the nearest centres.

VESTFOLD/BUSKERUD

SVELVIKSTRØMMEN (D12). Popular current in the Drammensfjord at Svelvik 14 miles south of Drammen. Casting with spinners from the shore and boat fishing. Quite a few sea trout are hooked in Svelvikstrømmen.
Centres: Svelvik, Drammen and Oslo.

MØRE AND ROMSDAL

VEVANGSTRØMMEN (B10). Fine fishing spot close to Highway 663, 30 miles north of Molde, where cod, saithe, pollack and sometimes haddock may be caught.
Centres: Eide (not listed) and Molde.

RAKVÅGSTRAUMEN (B10) on the Otrøy island west of Molde, reached by road and ferry in approx. 1 hour. Swift fjord current with cod, saithe, pollack and sometimes even small salmon and sea trout.
Centre: Nearest is Molde.

SØR-TRØNDELAG

STORSTRAUMEN AND VETTA-STRAUMEN (B9) are both found close to Highway 714 on the island of Hitra west of the entrance to the Trondheimsfjord. Both currents hold plenty of fish with saithe as the dominant species during the summer months. Boats for thire at Strømsvik Camping.
Centre: Ansnes, see Hitra in «Hotels in Norway».

NORD-TRØNDELAG

SKARNSUNDET (C9) between Vangshylla and Kjerringvik on Highway 755, 22 miles south of Steinkjer, is a popular fishing spot. Saithe fishing during the summer may yield good results, especially from a boat.
Centres: Jektvollen (not listed) and Steinkjer.

TRONGSUNDET (C9). If one continues some 15 miles on the county road from Kjerringvik one ends up at Trongsundet where more fishing may be enjoyed.

FOLDEREIDSTRAUMEN (C 8), where Highway 17 goes on a bridge across the Inner Foldfjord, offers exciting saithe fishing. 60 miles north of Namsos.
Centre: Foldereid.

KORSNESSTRAUMEN (B8) near Highway 770 in Kolvereid is probably the best known of the Nord-Trøndelag currents. Cod, saithe, pollack and halibut. Boats can be hired locally. Kolvereid lies 85 miles north of Namsos.
Centre: Kolvereid.

STRAUMEN (B 8) at the entrance to Sørsalten, on Highway 770 south of Ottersøy, is a well known fishing spot. Ottersøy lies 90 miles north of Namsos.
Centre: Rørvik.

NORDLAND

KOLLSTRAUMEN (B 8) is a strong tidal current close to Highway 17 just 7 miles north of Foldereid (see above). There are plenty of fish in the eddy and good spots for casting from the shore.
Centre: Foldereid.

STRAUMEN (B7), 20 miles from Mo i Rana (branch off from Highway 805 at Jamtjord), offers good sport. Boats are said to be available locally.
Centre: Mo i Rana.

SALTSTRAUMEN (B 6) is the most famous of all Norwegian currents and the most visited. Max. speed is 10 knots and it carries more water than the mightiest Norwegian rivers. There are cod, pollack, haddock, halibut and other fish to be hooked in the eddies, but first and foremost the Saltstraumen saithe which take to almost any bait a fisherman might use. Saltstraumen lies on Highway 813 only 20 miles east of Bodø.
Centres: Saltstraumen and Bodø.

RØDTANGSTRAUMEN (B 5) is all yours if you branch off from E 6 at Innhavet between Fauske and Narvik. Only a couple of miles along a county road and you can really start fishing. Innhavet lies 80 miles south of Narvik.
Centre: Innhavet.

KANSTADSTRAUMEN (B 5). If you are bound for the Lofoten isles, where you will no doubt enjoy terrific sea fishing, we recom-

mend that you try this eddy 75 miles west of Narvik (or just a few miles north of Lødingen). Saithe and cod abound in Kanstadstraumen and boats can be hired from Åsestua Café.
Centre: Lødingen.

TROMS
ÅRSTEINSTRAUMEN (C 4) in the Gratangen lies only 4 miles from Storfossen on E 6. Storfossen again is 30 miles north of Narvik and there is a local road to the current where cod, saithe and other fish will rise quickly to your bait.
Centre: Gratangen.

GROVFJORDSTRAUMEN (B 5) in Grovfjord at the junction of highroads 825 and 829, approx. 37 miles from Harstad and 48 miles from Narvik. Angling from land or from the bridge across the current. Mostly sea-fish but trout is occasionally killed.
Centres: Narvik, Bjerkvik, Bogen, Evenes and Harstad.

STRAUMEN IN SØRREISA (N 4). If you branch off E 6 at Fossbakken (40 miles north of Narvik) and follow Highway 84 some 20 miles to Sørreisa you can enjoy exciting fishing in the local eddy. This time not only sea fish is involved, but salmon and sea trout as well. Therefore you must acquire permission to fish from the landowners.
Centre: Sørreisa.

ROSSFJORDSTRAUMEN (B 4). Continue north on Highway 86 to Finnfjordbotn and follow 856 to Rossfjordstraumen, which lies only 20 miles from Finnsnes. Then you can start "harvesting" — cod, saithe, haddock, pollack and even catch a salmon, sea trout or halibut. If you ask Steinar Nordås, Rossfjordstraumen he will take you out in his boat, but you can always cast from the shore.
Centre: Finnsnes.

STRAUMEN (B4). We have not quite exhausted the possibilities of Highway 86. If you continue from Finnsnes and drive across the island of Senja to Straumsnes (25 miles only) there is Straumen going at 7 knots and brimful of cod and saithe.
Centre: Finnsnes.

STRAUMFJORD (C). But there are more currents in Troms. This one you come across on Highway 6, 12 miles north of Nordreisa (Storslett). You will find sturdy Finns and resolute Swedes, and perhaps a few Norwegians, on the shore but there is enough saithe for all motorists who care to stop.
Centre: Straumfjord (not listed) and Sørkjosen.

SØRSTRAUMEN (C 3). In case you missed Straumfjord, Troms offers you Sørstraumen, a very strong tidal current in the narrows of the Kvænangen fjord, on Highway 6 between Lyngen and Alta. Most excellent fishing for saithe and cod.
Centres: Kvænangsfjell or Burfjord.

RYSTRAUMEN (B 4) is more heavily fished than any other Troms current, but the sound (where Rystraumen runs at 6 knots) is inexhaustible. Rystraumen is reached on Highway 862. It lies only 20 miles south of Tromsø town.
Centre: Tromsø.

FINNMARK
LANGFJORDSTRAUMEN (E 2). 9 miles before E 6/Highway 6 comes to rest at Kirkenes it crosses the Langfjord. Underneath the bridge runs the Langfjordstraumen where good fishing may be enjoyed.
Centre: Kirkenes.

STRAUMEN (D 1), the 'Current', lies 25 miles south of Berlevåg, approx. 1/2 hour's walk from Highway 890. Once you are there, fabulous fishing is guaranteed. But be careful, the swells of the Artic Sea are not to be disregarded.
Centre: Berlevåg.

ORGANISED TRIPS IN FISHING SMACKS
Touists offices up and dawn the coast arrange fishing trips during the summer season. Visitors are transported in fishing smacks, and equipment may be rented on board. On these trips the question of actually catching fish never arises: these are 'guaranteed' trips, where every participant is bound to pull in fish, generally in considerable quantities. These tours often include a picnic, where fish caught at sea can be prepared, barbecue-fashion, over an open fire. These open-air parties, which include entertainment of various kinds, are popular with a great many tourists who are not necessarily hardbitten anglers, but enjoy a fishing trip in the land of the long, bright summer nights.
Here are some centres which offer organised fishing trips to visitors. Apply to the tourist offices in:

Bergen	Narvik
Bodø	Oslo
Brønnøysund	Sandefjord
Hammerfest	Stavanger
Haugesund	Tromsø
Honningsvåg	Trondheim
Molde	Ålesund
Namsos	

DEEP-SEA FISHING AND FISHING FESTIVALS

For the last 15 to 20 years fishing festivals have been arranged in Norway and gained great popularity. Hundreds of partakers both from Norway and abroad attend and tons of fish are hauled from the sea during these events, where individual competitors may catch several hundred pounds of fish.

THE INTERNATIONAL FISHING FESTIVAL IN STAVANGER/TANANGER has been arranged since 1960. This festival has the approval of EFSA (European Federation of Sea Anglers) and follows its regulations. The competiton lasts 3 days and usually takes place in the second week of August.

NORTH SEA FESTIVAL AT HAUGESUND was first arranged in 1968. Rod fishing from boats only. 300—400 competitors from many countries attend and prizes worth more than kr. 10 000 are rewarded. This event usually takes place the last week-end in July.

HARSTAD INTERNATIONAL FISHING FESTIVAL comprises both boat and shore fishing. Rod fishing from boats according to EFSA regulations in the second week of July, starting on a Wednesday with a get-together party. Competitions on Thursday and Friday. Non-competitive angling on Saturday, and distribution of prizes at the 'Sea Anglers' Party' in the evening.

Details and programs for the above-mentioned festivals are available from the tourist offices of Stavanger, Haugesund and Harstad.

FRESHWATER AND MIGRATORY FISH IN NORWAY

The Latin namnes have been translated into (Am)erican, (E)nglish, (N)orwegian, (S)wedish and (D)anish. Official Norwegian names are italicized.

ABRAMIS BRAMA — bream (E) — brasme, brasen, brasp (N) — braxen (S) — brasen (D) — found in south-east Norway from river Lågen (Larvik) to Elverum, weight up to 6 pounds, fine food.

ACERINA CERNUA — ruffe, pope (E) — hork, steinbit, bergnebbe, steinpurke, sugge, garsgjøs, gorgylte, hørke, rysil, skrukle, ruskle, gjørrgjøs (N) — gärs (S) — hork (D) — found mainly in Glomma, Mjøsa and Drammenselva, seldom over 20 cm long.

ACIPENSER STURIO — Atlantic sturgeon (Am) — sturgeon (E) — stør (N) — stør (S) — stør (D) — found all along the coast, up to 4—5 metres long, but does not spawn in Norwegian waters.

ANGUILLA ANGUILLA — European eel (Am) — eel (E) — ål (N) — ål (S) — aal (D) — found all along the Norwegian coast. Glass Eel (glassål) (Leptocepthalus larvae) wanders up rivers and brooks in spring, where they thrive as Yellow Eel (gulål) for several years, when they migrate as Blank Eel (blankål), spawning in the Sargasso Sea, as does the American Eel (Anguilla rostrata), but whereas the transformation to Glass Eel takes only 1 year in respect of the American eel, the European eel takes 3—4 years.

ASPIUS ASPIUS — carp (E) — asp, blåspol, blåmann (N) — asp (S) — asp (D) — in Norway found only in the Glomma waterway, particularly in lake Øyeren, weight up to 12 pounds, found in shoals in spring, otherwise individually only.

BLICCA BJOERKNA — white bream (E) — flire, flisebrasme, sørv (N) — blicka, bjørkna (S) — flire (D) — found in Norway only in Østfold county, length up to 30—35 cm, poor food.

CARASSIUS CARASSIUS — not in USA — crucian carp (E) — karuss (N) — ruda (S) — karuds (D) — introduced into Norway by Catholic monks, found in ponds almost anywhere in SE Norway, seldom in lakes and rivers, small sized but can attain weight of up to 7 pounds, poor food.

COREGONUS ALBULA — not in USA — vendace (E) — lagesild, vemme, høstsik, stinte (N) — sikløja (S) — heltling (D) — found in Norway in large shoals in lake Mjøsa and lake Storsjø and other lakes near Sweden, also in lake Tyrifjord, average length 15 to 23 cm, max length 33 cm, usually caught in nets throughout summer, annual catch in lake Mjøsa around 150 000 pounds.

COREGONUS LAVARETUS — European whitefish (Am) — gwyniad (E) — sik, risling, skadd (N) — sik (S) — helt (D) — found in most lakes in eastern and southern Norway, weight up to 12 pounds, caught mainly in fall and winter.

COTTUS POECILOPUS — not in USA — steinulke, ulke, ferskvannsulke, steinsmett, steinbit, steinsut, klumplake (N) — bergsimpa (S) — finnestribet ferskvandsulk (D) — found in lakes and rivers in south-east Norway, particularly in river Glomma, length up to 9 cm.

CYPRINUS CARPIO — carp (E) — karpe (N) — karp (S) — karpe (D) — found in Norway only in ponds near Kragerø on South Coast and near Bergen on West Coast.

ESOX LUCIUS — northern pike (Am) — pike (E) — gjedde (N) — gädda (S) — gedde (D) — found in lakes all over Norway, can attain a weight of up to 40 pounds, fished throughout the year, mainly with spoons and nets, but also on handline.

LEUCISCUS CEPHALUS — chub (E) — *stam,* årbuk, buk, stamme, rødfjæring, skal (N) — farna (S) — døbel (D) — found in lower regions of rivers Tista, Glomma and Drammenselva, length up to 60 cm.

LEUCISCUS IDUS — not in USA — *vederbuk,* buk, id, idmort, årbuk, hersling, hisling, raufjæring (N) — id (S) — rimte (D) — found in south-east Norway, weight up to 6 pounds, length up to 60 cm.

LEUCISCUS LEUCISCUS — not in USA — dace (E) — *gullbust,* haslung, hersling, hisling, træl, slom (N) — stäm (S) — strømskall (D) — found sporadically in south-east Norway, length up to 30 cm.

LOTA LOTA — burbot (E) — *lake,* låkå, ålkøys (N) — lake (S) — knude (D) — the one and only freshwater fish which belongs to the codfish species. Weight up to 14 pounds or more. In Norway found in many districts. Good food, caught with handline or fixed traps. In winter also 'clubbed' under blank ice in shallow lakes.

LUCIOPERCA LUCIOPERCA — pike-perch (E) — *gjørs* (N) — gøs (S) — sandart (D) — found in south-east Norway, mainly in lakes Vansjø, Øyeren and Femsjø, caught in nets and fixed traps, also on handline.

ONCORHYNCHUS GORBUSCHA — pink salmon (Am) — humpback salmon (E) — *pukkellaks* (N) (D). Found in Norway since 1960 in rivers and lakes, also along coast, but it is still unknown whether it has spawned in Norwegian rivers.

OSMERUS EPERLANUS — European smelt (Am) — smelt (E) — *krøkle,* nors, slom, blågjel, kot (N) — nors (S) — smelt (D) — found in large numbers in lake Mjøsa also in other lakes and rivers in east Norway, length up to 26 cm, but rarely more than 15 cm, used mainly as bait.

PERCA FLUVIATILIS — European perch (Am) — perch (E) — *åbor,* abbor, tryte, skjebbe (N) — Aborre (S) — aborre (D) — found in eastern Norway, in South Coast lakes and rivers, never on West Coast, sporadically in Trøndelag, Nordland and Troms, frequently in Finnmark. Small average weight, but can attain length of 60 cm and weight of 3 pounds under favourable conditions.

PHOXINUS PHOXINUS — bait minnow (Am) — minnow (E) — *ørekyt,* gåloye, gorkime, gorkyte, pøyt, kue, simen, åkyte, årkyte, aurkyte, blindsild, gorsild, gorøye, gørleie (N) — kvidd or elritsa (S) — elritse (D) — found all over Norway, up to 15 cm long, mainly used as bait.

RUTILUS RUTILUS — roach (E) — *mort,* flassrøye, raufjæring, syril, sørrenne (N) — mört (S) — skalle (D) — found in most rivers and lakes in SE-Norway, length up to 40 cm, used mainly as bait.

SALMO IRIDEUS — rainbow trout (E) — *regnbueaure,* regnbueørret (N) — regnbågsforell (S) — regnbueørred (D) — recently transplanted from USA into Norway, where private rivers are now being stocked with rainbow trout.

SALMO SALAR — Atlantic Salmon (Am) — salmon (E) — *laks* (N) — lax (S) — laks (D) — in Norway it migrates from river to ocean when 10 to 15 cm long, returns after 1 to 4 years, large salmon returning April to July, small salmon (called tert, svele, svidde, leksing) returning from end of June onwards.

SALMO TRUTTA — brown trout (Am) — trout (E) — *aure,* ørret (N) — laxøring (S) — ørred (D).

SALMO TRUTTA forma furio — *bekkaure,* bekkørret (N() — bäckøring (S) — bækørred (D).

SALMO TRUTTA forma lacustris — brown trout (Am) — *ferskvannsaure,* ferskvannsørret, krede, kjøe (N) — innsjøøring (S) — søørred (D).

SALMO TRUTTA forma trutta — sea trout (E) — *sjøaure,* sjøørret, blege, butung, byting, sjølbanke, sjøbysting, strending, kludd, isdøling (N) — havsøring (S) — havørred (D).

SALVELINUS ALPINUS — alpine trout (Am) — red char (E) — *røye,* røyr, rør, ferskvannsrøye, sjørøye, bleike, gautefisk, gib, kolmunn, røe, stilk, vassrør (N) — røding (S) — fjeldørred (D) — there are two varities in Norway: (1) Storrøye (forma salvelinus), and (2) Fjellrøye (forma alpinus). In most of southern Norway it occurs as an entirely freshwater fish, but in Trøndelag and northwards to Finnmark it migrates between fresh and salt water. Also found in Spitsbergen, where it is called spitsberglaks. Average weight in Norway when 7—8 years old, about a pound, max 24 pounds.

SALVELINUS FONTINALIS — char or brook trout (Am) — brook trout (E) — *bekkrøye* , amerikansk aure (N) — bäckröding (S) — kildeørred (D) — introudced into Norway from USA in 1876, but with success only in Telemark.

SCARDINIUS ERYTHROPHTHALAMUS — not in USA — rudd (E) — *sørv,* sørve, syril, flosmort, raufjæring, planken (N) — sarv (S) — rudskalle (D) — similar species as roach and found in Norway in same areas as roach, westwards to Kragerø.

THYMALLUS THYMALLUS — grayling (E) — *harr,* horr, børting, hørr (N) — harr (S) — stalling (D) — found in rivers and lakes all over Norway except in southwest and western Norway, max weight 6 pounds, caught with spoons and flies, also netted.

TINCA TINCA — golden tench (Am) — tench (E) — *suter,* sut, sutar, sudre (N) —

sutare (S) — suder (D) — found in Norway only near Arendal and Kragerø on the South Coast, introuduced by German or Dutch mine workers in the beginning of the 19th Century.

INDEX

The suffixes elv (river), vatn (lake), sjø (water) and lågen (river) have been omitted in most names.